Toward an
Ecological Society

Toward an Ecological Society

by Murray Bookchin

BLACK ROSE BOOKS   Montréal

BLACK ROSE BOOKS No. J 57
Hardcover — ISBN: 0-919618-99-5
Paperback — ISBN: 0-919618-98-7

Canadian Cataloguing in Publication Data

Bookchin, Murray, 1921-
    Toward an ecological society
Bibliography: p.
ISBN 0-919618-99-5 (bound). — ISBN 0-919618-98-7 (pbk.)
1. Human ecology. I. Title.
HM206.B66   304.2   C81-090025-4

Cover Design: Point Studio, Dan O'Leary based on details of
Diane Shatz's drawing "Visions of Ecotopia", courtesy RAIN
magazine

BLACK ROSE BOOKS LTD.
3981 St-Laurent Boulevard,
Montréal H2W 1Y5, Québec, Canada

Printed and bound in Québec

For
Debbie,
my daughter

Contents

Introduction

These essays have been collated for a special purpose: to recover the very *idea* of a radical critique of social life.

At the outset it should be clear that this is no abstract or insignificant task. Perhaps at no time in modern history has radical thought been in such grave peril of losing its very identity as a consistent critique of the existing social order and a coherent project for social reconstruction. Unless we are prepared to retreat to the sectarian politics of a by-gone era, it must be bluntly asserted *that hardly any authentic revolutionary opposition exists in North America and Europe.* Worse, the mere notion of what a revolutionary opposition consists of has itself become blurred and diluted to the point of sheer opaqueness. If the ghosts of Gerrard Winstanley, Jacques Danton, Gracchus Babeuf, Mikhail Bakunin, Louise Michel — yes, even Marx, Luxemburg, and Lenin — occasionally haunt us, they have become so spectral and inchoate that we can no longer see or hear them, even as voices of social conscience.

What we now call "radical" is an odious mockery of three centuries of revolutionary opposition, social agitation, intellectual enlightenment, and popular insurgency. Radical politics in our time has come to mean the numbing quietude of the polling booth, the deadening platitudes of petition campaigns, car-bumper sloganeering, the contradictory rhetoric of manipulative politicians, the spectator sports of public rallies, and finally, the knee-bent, humble pleas for small reforms — in short, the mere shadows of the direct action, embattled commitment, insurgent conflicts, and social idealism that marked every revolutionary project in history. Not that petitions, slogans, rallies, and the tedious work of public education have no place in these projects. But we do not have to hypostasize adventuristic escapades to recognize the loss of a balanced revolutionary stance, one that has enough sense of time and place to evoke the appropriate means to achieve appropriate goals. My point is that the very *goals* of contemporary radicalism have all the features of a middle-aged bourgeois opportunism — of "trade-offs" for small gains, of respectability for "mass" but meaningless constituencies, of a degenerative retreat into the politics of the "lesser evil" that itself generates a world of narrowing choices, finally of a sclerotic ossification of social ideas, organizational habits, and utopistic visions.

What is most terrifying about present-day "radicalism" is that the piercing cry for "audacity" — «*L'audace! L'audace! encore l'audace!*» — that Danton voiced in 1793 on the hightide of the French Revolution would simply be *puzzling* to self-styled radicals who demurely carry attaché cases of memoranda and grant requests into their conference rooms, suitcases of their books into their lecture halls, and bull horns to their rallies. The era of the "managerial radical" (to use Andrew Kopkind's damning phrase) has pushed radicalism itself into the shadows of history. What we encounter today is the universal bureaucratization and technocratization of radicalism as such — not merely in the triumph of organizational bureaucracies and centralized leaderships but in the very outlook, vision, and ideas of its most articulate acolytes. The "managerial radical" is the practitioner of organizational technique, of efficient manipulation, of mass mobilization *as goals in themselves*. Technique has become the substitute for social idealism.

Radical theory, in turn, fares even worse as the ideology for this historic turn in radical politics. Where socialism and even anarchism have not been reduced to dogmatic echoes of the last century, they have become disciplines within the academy, where they serve to garnish "managerial radicalism" with theoretical exotica. Much that now passes for "radical" theory are either footnotes to the history of ideas or intellectual obscurantism that supports the pragmatic obscurantism of the political marketplace. The term "marketplace" should not be taken as a metaphor. The colonization of society by a bourgeois sensibility — a result of the colonization of society by the market — is now complete. For the market has absorbed not only every aspect of production, consumption, community life, and family ties into the buyer-seller nexus; it has permeated the opposition to capitalism with bourgeois cunning, compromise, and careerism. It has done this by restating the very meaning of opposition to conform with the system's own parameters of critique and discourse.

In any case it is not "anti-intellectual" or "anti-theoretical" to slap academic snobbery in the face by demanding that radical theory at least provide *some* guide to radical practice. But it is surely tedious punditry to so completely divorce theory from practice that it ceases to have anything but professional relevance to intellectual careerists — the academy's counterpart of the political careerists in today's "radical" movements.

If my remarks seem overly contentious, it is because I am deeply concerned with the integrity of new, inherently radical issues that have emerged in recent years — issues that potentially at least have more far-reaching emancipatory implications than the radical ones of the past. I refer to ecology, feminism, and community control — a group of problems that reaches beyond the largely economistic conflicts of the movements of the last generation. These new problems raise expansive notions of freedom and an emancipatory moral sensibility, not merely of justice and material exploitation. What is at stake, today, particularly in the movements and tendencies that have formed around ecology, feminism, and community control is the extent to which they can be fully actualized as liberatory forces.

These movements and tendencies are now faced with a crisis that threatens to warp their emancipatory logic into aborted, subservient, and conventional ideologies of the status quo. Their destiny may well be determined by our ability to unearth that emancipatory logic, to reveal its revolutionary content, and to explore the new meaning it can give to the word "freedom." Should we fail in this momentous endeavour, the colonization of society by a deeply sedimented bourgeois sensibility will be complete — perhaps so complete that it is doubtful if a revolutionary opposition will emerge again in the present century.

The traditional locus of modern radicalism — the workers movement — is dead. My essays on socialism and Marxism in this book elucidate in detail the inherent limits and mystified premises on which it rested historically. The ecology, feminist, and community movements that have emerged in the 1970s have demonstrably shattered the silence that socialism has left in its wake. They are vital, rebellious, and richly promising, but the conflicts that face these new movements have been grossly miscast. The central conflict confronting the ecology, feminist, and community movements is not merely with those who wish to despoil the environment or those who foster sexism or those who oppose community control. The despoilers, sexists, and municipal bureaucrats wear their identities on their sleeves. They can be singled out, disputed, and removed from their positions of authority. The central conflict confronting the ecology, feminist, and community movements lies *within* the movements themselves. Here, the problem they face is the need to discover the sweeping implications of the issues they raise : the achievement of a totally new, non-hierarchical society in which the domination of nature by man, of woman by man, and of society by the state is completely abolished — technologically, institutionally, culturally, and in the very rationality and sensibilities of the individual.

The socialist movement never raised these issues clearly in the century that it flourished between 1840 and 1940. Its primary concerns were economic and turned on the abolition of wage labour and capital, of economic classes and material exploitation. That these concerns remain with us to this day need hardly be emphasized and their resolution must be achieved if freedom is to have any substantive meaning. But there can be a decidedly classless, even a non-exploitative society in the *economic* sense that still preserves hierarchical rule and domination in the *social* sense — whether they take the form of the patriarchal family, domination by age and ethnic groups, bureaucratic institutions, ideological manipulation, or a pyramidal division of labour. The successive layers of the hierarchical pyramid may confer no material privileges whatever on those who command and no material renunciation by those who obey; indeed, the ideological tradition of domination that associates "order" with hierarchy, the psychic privileges that confer prestige on status, the historical inertia that carries the traditional forms and sensibilities of the past into the present and future — all of these may preserve hierarchy even after classes have been abolished. Yet classless or not, society would be riddled by domination and, with domination, a general condition of command and obedience, of unfreedom and humiliation, and perhaps most decisively, an abortion of each individual's potentiality for consciousness, reason, selfhood, creativity, and the right to assert full control over her or his daily life.*

The ecology, feminist, and community movements implicitly challenge this warped destiny. Ecology raises the issue that the very notion of man's domination of nature stems from man's domination of man. Feminism reaches even further and reveals that the domination of man by man actually originates in the domination of woman by man. Community movements implicitly assert that in order to replace social domination by self-management, a new type of civic self — the free, self-governing citizen — must be restored and gathered into new institutional forms such as popular assemblies to challenge the all-pervasive state apparatus. Followed through to their logical conclusion, all of these movements challenge not only class formations but hierarchies, not only material exploitation but domination in every form. Although hierarchical structures reach into the most intimate aspects of social and personal life, the supraclass problems they raise nowhere falls within the limited orbit of the socialist and labour movements. Hence, if we are to complete the logic of the ecology, feminist, and community movements, we must extend our very notion of freedom beyond any concept we have held of this notion in the past.

---

* It remains supremely ironical that, in the history of elitism and vanguardism that runs through millenia of social theory, hierarchy did not confer material privileges on the rulers of ideal societies but austerity and renunciation of the material world. Plato's "guardians" are notably denied the sensuous pleasures of life. Their training is demanding, their responsibilities awesome, their needs severely restricted, their possessions communal and limited. The Church was to make the same austere demands on the clerical elite in society, however much these were honored in the breach. Even in modern times the early Bolsheviks were expected to live harsh, self-abnegating lives — more confining and materially impoverished than their proletarian followers. The ideal of hiearchy was based on a concept of service, not on privilege. That such a notion remained an ideal does not alter the extra-material goals it raised and the surprising extent to which these goals were retained throughout its history.

But will these new movements be permitted to follow the logic of their premises, to complete them in a consistent and coherent fashion?

It is around this crucial issue that we encounter two major obstacles: the attempt by socialists to reduce these expansive concepts of freedom to economistic categories and the attempt by the "managerial radicals" to compromise them. Of the two, the socialist view tends to be the most deceptive. Slogans like "pollution is profitable," "wages for housewives," and "fight the slumlords" involve a subtle denaturing of the more sweeping revolutionary demands for an ecological society, the abolition of domination, and the restoration of community control. The real "slime of history," to reinterpret Sartre's phrase, is the muck of the past that is flung upon the present to re-sculpture it into forms that accord with an archaic vision of social reality. A "socialist" ecology, a "socialist" feminism, and a "socialist" community movement — with its red flags, clenched fists, and sectarian verbiage — are not only contradictions in terms; they infest the newly formed, living movements of the future with the maggots of cadavers from the past and must be opposed unrelentingly.

A special onus must be borne by ideologists who perpetuate the infestation and even conceal it with theoretical cosmetics. One thinks, here, of the Andre Gorzs and Herbert Marcuses who not only worship at the mausoleum of socialism but promote it as a viable habitat for the living. What uniquely distinguishes their ideological obscurantism from that of the socialist sectarians is their repeated attempts to reformulate *both* sides of the issue: the old socialist categories and the new libertarian ones. The result that inevitably follows is that the logic of each is warped and its inherent opposition to the other is blurred. Marcuse, by wedding Freud to Marx and anarchism to socialism in the sixties, muddled the meaning of all the partners in these forced alliances. What emerged from works like *Eros and Civilization* and *One-Dimensional Man* was a mass of half-truths and gross inconsistencies. Characteristically, in Marcuse's latest works, it was Marx who triumphed over Freud, socialism that triumphed over anarchism — and Eurocommunism that triumphed over everything.

What is at least theoretical probing in Marcuse is facilely reduced to pop culture in Gorz — with even more telling practical consequences. His *Strategy for Labour,* by miscasting students and intellectuals as a "new proletariat," deflected the growing insight of sixties' radicals from *cultural* movements into classical economistic ones, thereby producing massive confusion in the American student movement of the time. More than any single journalistic work, this book brought Marxism into the Students for a Democratic Society, producing the ideological chaos that eventually destroyed it.

Much the same danger now faces the ecology movement if Gorz's treatment of the subject exercises any appreciable influence. His recent *Ecology and Freedom* (retitled *Ecology* as *Politics*) is essentially the *New Strategy for Labour* writ in ecological verbiage. It perpetuates all the incompatibilities of a mythic "libertarian socialism" that sprinkles anarchist concepts of decentralized organization with Social Democratic concepts of mass political parties and, more offensively, "radical ecology" with the opportunistic politics of conventional environmentalism. Thus Jerry Brown, governor of California, sits side-by-side with Ho Chi Minh, Fritz Schumacher, and Buddha as evidence of "*les neo-anarchistes*" in the American ecology movement. Imperturbably, Gorz degrades each new concept raised by ecological theory and the practice of authentically radical tendencies in the ecological movement into his own current variant of Marxian socialism.

Neither Marx nor ecology emerge untainted from this crude eclecticism. Clarity of thought, coherence of views, and, above all, the full logic of one's radical premises are blunted by an ideological dilettantism that leaves every concept unfinished, every personality miscast, and every practice compromised — be it direct action or electoral action, decentralization or centralization, a Jerry Brown or a Ho Chi Minh. The melding of all these contradictory views becomes insufferable not because ecology is distorted into Marxism, for the evidence of distortion would be clear on first inspection to any knowledgeable reader. Rather, it lies in the fact that one can recognize neither Marxism *nor* ecology and the problems they raise because *both* are equally distorted in order to reconcile utterly alien premises that lead to completely conflicting conclusions. We must either choose between ecology, with its naturalism, its anarchistic logic of decentralization, its emphasis on humanly scaled alternate technologies, and its non-hierarchical institutions, or socialism, with its typically Marxian anti-naturalism, its political logic of centralization, its emphasis on high technology, and its bureaucratic institutions. Gorz gives us neither alternative in the name of both and perpetuates a confusion that has already produced an internal crisis in every American and European ecology movement.

I have singled out Gorz primarily because of his recent interest in ecological issues. What I have said about his hybridization of ideas could apply equally to Juliet Mitchell's treatment of feminist issues or David Harvey's treatment of urban community issues. These names, in fact, are mere metaphors for a large number of socialist ideologists who have made eclecticism fashionable as a substitute for probing theoretical exploration. The issues that divide ecology, feminist, and community movements are basically similar. Feminism is reduced to a matter of class oppression, community issues to a matter of economic oppression. Beyond these categories—certainly true as far as they go—the intellectual horizon of the socialist eclectics tends to become opaque. Broader problems of freedom, hierarchy, domination, citizenship, and self-activity seem misty, ineffable, at times even "incomprehensible," beside the "nuts-and-bolts" issues of political economy. Orchestrated by an all-pervasive tendency toward economic reductionism, *homo collectivicus* is consistently reduced to *homo economicus* and Brecht's notorious maxim, "Feed the face, then give the moral," becomes a strategy for political immorality and socialist apologetics. As I have tried to show in my essays on Marx, this may be "hard" sociology, based on the "material facts of life," but it is bourgeois to the core.

No less disquieting than the socialists who have been tracking the ecology, feminist, and community movements are the technocrats from within who have been trying to degrade them for opportunistic ends. Here, ignorance is fetishized over knowledge and action over theory in the name of acquiring large constituencies, practical results, and, of course, personal power. If the Gorzs, Mitchells, and Harveys distort the premises and logic of the issues that concern them, the "managerial radical" ignores them when possible or conceals them when necessary. Technique tends to take the place of principles; journalism, the place of education; spectacles, the place of serious action; floating constituencies that can be mobilized and demobilized, the place of lasting organizations; elites, the place of grass-roots and autonomous movements. This is the stock-in-trade of the social engineer, not the committed idealist. It is self-serving and sterile, when it is not simply odious and treacherous.

What makes it possible for this new class of managers to appear radical? Partly, it is the result of a lack of theoretical insight by their own followers. The "managerial radical" capitalizes on a chronic American syndrome: the pragmatic hypostasization of action, of quick results and immediate success. Fast food is not the only attribute of the American spirit; its ideological counterpart is fast politics, indeed, fast radicalism. The sixties were plagued by feverish turns in ideological fads and cultural fashions that swept through the New Left and the counterculture with dazzling rapidity. Movements leap-frogged over entire eras of historical experience and theoretical development with an arrogant indifference for the labours of the past, abandoning anarchism for Marxism, machismo militancy for feminism, communal living for privatism, sexual promiscuity for monogamy, rock music for disco, only to revert again to new libertarian fads, sado-masochism, singles' bars, punk rock in criss-crossing patterns that more closely resemble the scrawl of an infant than the decipherable messages of maturing individuals. That young men and women can write marketable, often salacious "biographies" at the age of thirty or less is not surprising; there is detail aplenty to entertain the reader — but nothing of significance to communicate.

What counts is the extent to which appearance can so easily replace reality in the American mind. Rebellion, too, can become mere theater when it lacks the substance of knowledge, theory, and wisdom. Indeed, the myth that "doing" is more important than "thinking," that "constructive action" is more important than rational critique — these are actually mystified forms of theory, critique, and rationalism. The traditional American maxim that "philosophy is bunk" has always been a philosophical judgement in its own right, a statement of empirical philosophy as against speculative, of sensuous knowledge as against intellectual. The gruff attack upon theory and reason does not annul intellectual activity. "Common sense" is merely "sense" that is common, that is, untutored, uninformed, and riddled by acquired biases. It merely replaces the presuppositions of self-conscious wisdom by the presuppositions of unconscious prejudice. In either case, presuppositions are always being made and thereby involve theory, philosophy, and mentality in one form or another.

The "managerial radical" capitalizes upon this anti-theoretical syndrome, particularly on its myth of fast success. Immediacy of reward, a psychologically formative technique, fosters the infantile demand for immediate gratification and the infantilism of the manager's constituency. Radicalism thus ceases to be a body of theory and informed practice; it becomes the fastest route to the most immediate goals. The notion that basic social change may require the labours and dedication of a lifetime — a notion so basic to revolutionary idealism — has no place in this technocratic constellation. Radicalism thus becomes methodology rather than morality, fast success rather than patient struggle, a series of manic responses rather than lasting commitment. A superficial "extremism," which the "managerial radical" often orchestrates with the hidden cooperation of the very authorities she or he professes to oppose, turns out to be merely another device to bring an alienated constituency into complicity with its own oppressors.

The ecology movement, even more than the feminist and community movements, thrives in this highly charged, often contrived ambience of opposition. "Anti-nuke" groups and alliances rise and fall at a metabolic rate that excludes serious reflection on their methods and goals. To "Stop Nukes" has far-reaching social implications that go beyond the problems of adequate energy resources and radioactive pollution. The demand poses such questions as *how* should we try to "Stop Nukes" — by direct action or political action? How should we *organize* to "Stop Nukes" — by decentralized forms of autonomous affinity groups or national mobilizations and perhaps centralized parties? What will *replace* nukes — huge high technology solar installations managed by conventional power utilities or simple, often hand-crafted popular technologies that can be constructed and managed by a moderate-sized community? These questions alone, not to speak of innumerable issues that range around notions of the communal ownership and management of society's resources, non-hierarchical structures of social organization, and changes in human sensibility, reach far beyond the more limited issue of nuclear power. "No Nukes" is not enough — at least if we wish to remove the deep-seated social forces that produced nuclear power in the first place.

"Managerial radicalism" fosters a preoccupation with method rather than an exploration of goals. It is noteworthy that surprisingly few leaders of the anti-nuke movement have tried to educate their followers (assuming they are themselves informed) as to the implications of a serious opposition to nuclear power. They have provided no theoretical transition from the construction and operation of nuclear power plants to the social forces that promote them. The goal tends to remain fixed: "No Nukes!" Their principal concerns have been with the "strategies" and "tactics" that will achieve this end: a mobilization of docile constituencies that can be assembled and conveniently disassembled at nuclear reactor sites, in demonstrations, and more recently, at polling booths.

"Managerial radicalism" exhibits no real concern over the nature of these constituencies or their qualities as educated, socially committed, and active personalities. "Mass actions" outweigh *self*-action; numbers outweigh ideals; quantity outweighs quality. The concept of direct action, a concept that was meant to develop active personalities who as individuals and individuated communities *could take the social realm directly into their own hands* — an authentic *public* guided by ethical considerations rather than legislative edicts — is odiously degraded into a mere matter of "tactics" rather than self-activity, self-development, and self-management. Affinity groups, an anarchist notion of organization that was meant to provide the intimate, human-scaled, decentralized forms to foster the new selves and sensibilities for a truly free society, are seen merely as "task forces" that quickly assemble and disperse to perform very limited and concrete actions. "Managerial radicalism," in short, is primarily concerned with managing rather than radicalizing. And in the process of cultivating the manipulation of its mass following, it grossly denatures every libertarian concept of our times, often at a historic cost that yields a repellent careerism within its self-appointed elite and cynicism within its naive following.

The essays, articles, and papers that comprise this volume have been selected precisely for their critical thrust in the hope that we may yet recast the ecological, community, and theoretical issues of our time in a revolutionary direction. My omission of discussions on feminism and the feminist movement is merely a personal recognition that the best critiques and reconstructive notions in this area have already come from women, as indeed the best scholarship in anthropology and social theory. The works which follow were written entirely during the seventies and, almost without exception, are free of the proclivities of socialists and "managerial radicals" to follow trendy issues. If certain concepts and terms in this book now seem familiar, it is often because they were picked up later by elements in the Left who found one or another sizable constituency to exploit for their own dogmatic ends. Thus these writings can justifiably claim to "lead" intellectually: certainly, they do not follow—nor do they adapt new problems to shopworn causes.

That my writings in ecology urbanism, and technics have not always been celebrated by my colleagues on the Left can, in my view, be attributed to one reason: my commitment to anarchism. I hold this commitment with pride, for if nothing else it has been an invisible moral boundary that has kept me from oozing over to neo-Marxism, academicism, and ultimately reformism. I have not tried to mix contradictions and incompatibilities in order to gain the approval of my peers. A revolutionary ethical opposition has seemed to me to be a much better destiny than the social acceptance of those eminently practical "radicals" who basicaly despise the "masses" and in time grow to despise themselves. Hence the reader will find no convenient "uncertainties," no recipies for "success," no shifts of focus to suit a new "lesser evil" around which to embrace an even worse evil in the long run.

A second observation I would like to make is that this collection does not stand in any contradiction to my earlier sixties collection of essays, *Post-Scarcity Anarchism*. On the contrary, it largely elaborates problems in the first volume within the changing context of the seventies. The counterculture, in my view, is not "dead"; it was aborted by many factors and, if anything, awaits a richer, more perceptive, and more *conscious* development. The ideals it raised of communal living, openness of relations, love, sexual freedom, sensuousness of dress and manner are the abiding goals of utopian thought at its best. To dismiss the sixties as a "phase" is to dismiss utopianism as a "dream" — to deny the relevance of a Charles Fourier and a William Morris to our times — and to restrict the concept of a revolutionary movement to an apparatus, denying its significance as a culture. Such rejections of goals and traditions would be nothing less than an acquiesence to the status quo. What is remarkable about the sixties counterculture is not that it has been aborted; this could have been anticipated in the absence of a theoretical armamentarium suitable to its needs. What is remarkable is that the counterculture of the sixties emerged at all in the face of a middle-aged, smug, and middle-class environment or that it survived in different ways despite the hucksters who preyed upon it, be they the media-oriented canaille who became its "spokesmen" and clowns and the leeches of the dogmatic Left who parasitized it.

Post-Scarcity Anarchism tried to explain the emergence of this astonishing cultural phenomenon — so alien to the adults of the Eisenhower era — and to offer it a perspective. That my essays advanced ecological, technological, organizational, and theoretical perspectives that are still viable today attests to the relevance of the book as a whole.

The term "post-scarcity," however, has encountered curious difficulties that require some discussion. "Scarcity" is not a mystical or absolute condition, a floating sense of "need" that is autonomous in its own right. It is a relative term whose meaning has changed with the emergence of new needs and wants. Marshall Sahlins has emphasized that technically primitive hunting bands lack the modern body of needs that center around sophisticated energy sources, dwellings, vehicles, entertainment, and the steady diet of food that Euro-Americans take for granted. Their "tool kit" is, in fact, so utterly primitive and their needs so limited that they lack a sense of "scarcity" that riddles our own comparatively opulent society. In this sense, they are seemingly "post-scarcity" communities or, to be more accurate, "non-scarcity" communities.

This line of reasoning is often convincing enough to suggest that a modern society based on "voluntary simplicity" — to use a new trendy term — might also become a "post-scarcity" society if it imposed "limits to growth" and "voluntary limits" on needs. Indeed, the implication of Sahlins's views have been used with telling effect to demand a more austere, labour-intensive, relatively self-sufficient society — presumably one whose needs were in fact so limited that our seeming energy problems and raw materials shortages would be removed. Anthropology has been placed again in the service of the status quo — not to remove material want but to validate it.

What this line of reasoning ignores is the considerable losses a drastic reduction of needs would create — losses in intellectual, cultural, and psychological complexity and ultimately a wealth of selfhood and personality. However much a hunting band may be in equipoise with its primitive tool-kit and its limited needs, it remains primitive and limited nevertheless. Even if one assumes that the "noble savage" is not a myth, it is a condition of "savagery" as well as nobility — one that is rooted in the limitations of the blood tie rather than citizenship, tribal parochialism rather than *humanitas,* a sexual division of labour rather than a professional one, revenge rather than justice, in short custom rather than reason and biological inflexibility instead of social malleability. It lies within human potentialities to be more than a "noble savage," a product of natural history alone. To leave humanity's latent capacity for actualizing the fullness of reason, creativity, freedom, personality and a sophisticated culture only partially or one-sidedly fulfilled is to deny the rich dialectic of the human condition in its full state of realization and even of nature as life rendered self-conscious.

Hence even were a "non-scarcity" society to exist, humanity would still suffer the same privation of form and development that exists in a "scarcity" society. "Post-scarcity" does not denote an affluence that would stifle the fulfillment of the human condition; indeed, an abundance of needs that can be fulfilled is more likely to perpetuate unfreedom than the "non-scarcity" condition of a hunting band. "Post-scarcity" denotes a free society that can *reject* false, dehumanizing needs *precisely because it can be substantially free of need itself.* It can decide to adopt a simpler way of material life because there is enough available for everyone to accept or reject. That it can even make such a decision reflects a high degree of social freedom in itself, a new system of social relations and values that renders libertarian social judgements possible. Gauged merely by our current agricultural and industrial output, North Americans and Europeans clearly have the *material* means for making such a judgement; gauged by our *social relations*, on the other hand, we lack the freedom, values, and sensibility to do so. Hence our affluent society—all myths of depleted or shrinking resources notwithstanding to the contrary—is as gripped by scarcity as our medieval ancestors centuries earlier. A "post-scarcity" society, in effect, would have to be a libertarian communist society that possessed enough material resources to limit growth and needs as a matter of choice, not as a matter of need—for if its limits were determined by needs that emerge from scarcity, it would still be limited by need and scarcity whether resources were in short supply or not. The *need* to diminish need would materially provide the basis, if not the cause, of hierarchy and domination based on privilege.

Marx hypostasized the problem of needs as the "realm of necessity," a concept that reaches back to Aristotle, and thereby absolutized it in a way that obscured the historical formation of needs. How needs are formed—this, in contrast to the acceptance of needs as they exist—represents a complex problem which I shall not attempt to explore here. It suffices to point out that the formation of the "realm of necessity," with the harsh split between the "realm of necessity" and the "realm of freedom," is not a natural fact that has always been with our species or must always exist with it into the future. The "realm of necessity" is a distinctly historical phenomenon. In my view it emerged when primitive communities ceased to view nature as a co-existent phenomenon to be accepted or revered and, to use Marx's simplistic metaphors, had to "wrestle with nature" as an "other" ultimately to be "dominated." Once early humanity's mutual reciprocity with the natural world dissolved into antagonism and its oneness into duality, the process of recovering a new level of reciprocity and oneness doubtless includes the scars of millenia-long struggles to master the "forces" of nature. I share the Hegelian view that humanity had to be expelled from the Garden of Eden to attain the fullness of its humanness. But I emphatically deny that this exile necessarily taints utopia with the blood and toil of history; that the "realm of necessity" must always be the "basis" or precondition for the "realm of freedom." It remains Fourier's lasting contribution that the "realm of necessity" *can* be colonized by the "realm of freedom," the realm of toil by the realm of work, the realm of technics by the realm of play, fantasy, and imagination.

In any case, the "realm of necessity" can never be viewed as a *passive* "basis"; it must always infiltrate and malform the "realm of freedom" until Fourier's ideal becomes a conscious reality. Marx's tragic fate can be resolved into the fact that, integral to his entire theoretical edifice, he colonizes the "realm of freedom" by the "realm of necessity as its basis." The full weight of this theoretical approach, with its consequent reduction of social relations to economic relations, of creative to "unalienated labour," of society to "associated producers," of individuality to embodied "needs," and of freedom to the "shortening of the working day" has yet to be grasped in all its regressive content.

The opening essays in this compilation are united by the emphasis I place on the synthesizing role of ecology — a term I sharply distinguish in my very first essay from "environmentalism." I claim that, having divided humanity from nature many millennia ago, we must now return to a new unity between the social and the natural that preserves the gains achieved by social and natural history. Thus the *real* history of humanity (which Marx contrasted to the irrational "prehistory" prior to a communistic future) must be wedded to natural history. Perhaps these are no longer the brave words they seemed to be when I advanced them sixteen years ago in "Ecology and Revolutionary Thought," but their implications have not been fully developed by the so-called "radical" movement today. The separation of humanity from nature, its sweeping social trajectory into a history that produced a rich wealth of mind, personality, technical insight, culture, and self-reflective thought, marks the potential for mind in nature itself, the latent spirit in substance that comes to consciousness in a humanity that melds with the natural world. The time has come to integrate an ecological natural philosophy with an ecological social philosophy based on freedom and consciousness, a goal that has haunted western philosophy from the pre-Socratics onward.

Doubtless, the practical implications of this goal are paramount. If we are to survive ecological catastrophe, we must decentralize, restore bioregional forms of production and food cultivation, diversify our technologies, scale them to human dimensions, and establish face-to-face forms of democracy. On this score, I agree with innumerable environmentalists such as Barry Commoner who argue, perhaps a bit belatedly, for decentralization and "appropriate" technologies on grounds of pragmatism and efficiency. But my concerns go much further. I am occupied with the value of alternate technologies not only because they are more efficient and rest on renewable resources; I am even more concerned with their capacity to restore humanity's contact with soil, plant and animal life, sun and wind, in short, with fostering a new sensibility toward the biosphere. I am equally concerned with the individual's capacity to understand the operations of these new technologies so that personality itself can be enriched by a new sense of self-assurance and autonomy over the material aspects of life. Hence my emphasis on simpler forms — more "passive" forms, to use the vernacular of alternate technology — of solar collectors, wind machines, organic gardens and the like. By the same token, I am occupied with decentralization not only because it renders these technologies more feasible and more adaptable to the bio-regions in which they are employed; I am even more concerned with decentralization as a means of restoring power to local communities and to the individual, to give genuine meaning to the libertarian vision of freedom as a system of direct democracy. Small, in my view, is not merely "beautiful"; it is also ecological, humanistic, and above all, emancipatory.

Thus, the ages-old desideratum of the "good life" converges in ecology (as I would define the term) with the thrust of historical development. The French students of 1968 inscribed the slogan "Be practical, do the impossible" on the walls of Paris; to this slogan, I have added, "If we do not do the impossible, we will be faced with the unthinkable." Utopia, which was once a mere dream in the preindustrial world, increasingly became a possibility with the development of modern technology. Today, I would insist it has become a necessity — that is, if we are to survive the ravages of a totally irrational society that threatens to undermine the fundaments of life on this planet.

But above all, my emphasis on achieving a new totality between humanity and nature is part of a larger endeavour to transcend all the divisions on which hierarchy has been reared for centuries — the division between the "realm of necessity" and the "realm of freedom," between work and play, town and country, mind and body, between the sexes, age groups, ethnic groups and nationalities. Hence, the holistic outlook that pervades this book, a distinctly ecological, indeed, dialectical outlook, leads to an examination of community problems in their urban form, to Marxism, and to the problems of self-management. That I have compiled my articles not only on ecology and the ecology movement, but on city planning, the urban future, Marxism, should be seen as a meaningful and logical sequence. The modern urban crisis largely reflects the divisions that capitalism has produced between society and nature. "Scientific socialism," in turn, reflects these divisions ideologically in Marx's own dualism between "necessity" and "freedom." My essays on spontaneity and organization essentially deal with ecological "politics" within the revolutionary paradigms and organizational issues formulated by the past century of radical practice.

Finally, this book as a whole is guided by its emphasis on hierarchy and domination as the authentic "social question" of human development, — this as distinguished from the economistic question of class and the exploitation of labour. The irreducible "problem areas" of society lie not only in the conflict between wage labour and capital in the factory; they lie in the conflicts between age-groups and sexes within the family, hierarchical modes of instruction in the schools, the bureaucratic usurpation of power within the city, and ethnic divisions within society. Ultimately, they stem from a hierarchical sensibility of command and obedience that begins with the family and merely reaches its most visible social form in the factory, bureaucracy and military. I cannot emphasize too strongly that these problems emerged long before capitalism. Bourgeois society ironically concealed these problems for centuries by giving them an economistic form. Marx was to fall victim to this historic subterfuge by ignoring the subsurface modes of obedience and command that lie in the family, school, bureaucracy, and age structure, or more precisely, by identifying the "social problem" with class relations at the expense of a searching investigation into the hierarchical relations that produced class forms in the first place. Indeed, Marxism may well be the ideology of capitalism *par excellence* precisely because the essentials of its critique have focused on capitalist production without challenging the underlying cultural sensibilities that sustain it. My insistence that every revolutionary movement must be a cultural one as well as a social one is not simply the product of an exaggerated aversion for mass culture; it has deeper roots in my conviction that the revolutionary project remains incomplete if it fails to reach into the problems of hierarchy and domination as such — in short, if it fails to seek the substitution of an ecological sensibility for a hierarchical one.

Accordingly, this book is marked by a host of contrasts that ordinarily remain unstated or blurred in the radical and environmental literature I have encountered. It contrasts ecology with environmentalism, hierarchy with class, domination with exploitation, a people's technology with an "appropriate" technology, self-management with "economic democracy," cultural movements with economistic parties, direct democracy with representative democracy, utopia with futurism. I have not tried to develop all of these contrasts in these introductory remarks. The reader must turn to the book for a clearer elucidation of them. Let me merely voice one caveat. I nowhere claim that a hierarchical analysis of society involves a denial of a class analysis and its significance. Obviously the former includes the latter. I am certain that this caveat will be magnificently ignored by socialists and syndicalist-oriented libertarians alike. Let it merely be stated so that the reader has been alerted to "criticisms" that more often involves bias rather than analysis.

To return to my opening remarks, this book is primarily intended to give voice to a revolutionary idea of social change, particularly in terms of the problems that have emerged with the decline of the traditional workers' movement. Owing to the growing sense of powerlessness that freezes us into adaptive strategies for survival, an all-pervasive pragmatic mentality now invades our thinking. We live in a society of "trade-offs" which are rooted in a pseudo-ethics of "benefits versus risks." An "ethics" of "trade-offs" involves a choice between lesser evils that increasingly carries us to the brink of the worst evils conceivable. Such, in fact, was the destiny of the German Left, which chose right-wing Social Democrats rather than conservative center parties, only to be faced with reactionaries who opposed fascists, finally to choose a Hindenburg against a Hitler who then proceeded to make Hitler chancellor of the Reich. Our modern "ethics" of "trade-offs" and lesser evils, an "ethics" rooted in adaptation, pragmatism, and careerism stands in historic contrast to the ethics of pre-capitalist society. Even to such conservative thinkers as Plato and Aristotle, politics — a realm that could never be disassociated from ethics — denoted the achievement of virtue in the form of justice and the good life. Hence, authentic politics stood opposed to evil and called for its complete negation by the good. There are no "trade-offs" in Plato's *Republic* or in Aristotle's *Politics*. The ultimate goals of these works are to assure the success of virtue over evil, of reason over superstition and custom.

Modern politics, by contrast, has decisively separated itself from this tradition. Not only have we disassociated politics from ethics, dealing with the former strictly as a pragmatic body of techniques and the latter as a corpus of relativistic values based on personal taste and opinions; we have even turned the pragmatic techniques of politics into a choice between lesser evils, of "trade-offs," that thereby replace virtue by evil as the essence of political norms.*

Politics has now become a world of evil rather than virtue, of injustice rather than justice, a world that is mediated by "lesser" versus "greater" transgressions of "the good," "the right," and "the just." We no longer speak of what is "right" or "good" or "just" *as such* but what is less or more evil in terms of the "benefits" we derive, or more properly, the privations and dangers to which we are exposed. Only the general ignorance of culture that is slowly gathering like a darkening cloud over the present society has made it difficult for social theorists to understand the decisive nature of this shift in the historical norms of humanity. This shift is utterly subversive of any significant reconstruction of the body politic as an agent for achieving the historic goal of the good life, not merely as a practical ideal but as an ethical and spiritual one.

To reverse this denormatization of politics by a leprous series of "trade-offs," to provide an ethical holism rooted in the objective values that emerge from ecology and anarchism, is fundamental to this book. For this objective to be lost to the reader is to ignore the very meaning of the essays in this compilation. It is on this classical ethics that all else rests in the pages that follow.

August 1979

---

* Even so intractable a bourgeois as Bentham based his ethics on a definition of good, however philistine and quantitative its norms. The transmutation of the utilitarian credo of good as the greatest happiness for the greatest number into the modern credo of "benefits versus risks" marks a degradation even in the sphere of bourgeois morality that has no precedent in the cultural history of western sociey.

The Power
to Destroy,
The Power
to Create

The power of this society to destroy has reached a scale unprecedented in the history of humanity — and this power is being used, almost systematically, to work an insensate havoc upon the entire world of life and its material bases.

In nearly every region, air is being befouled, waterways polluted, soil washed away, the land desiccated, and wildlife destroyed. Coastal areas and even the depths of the sea are not immune to widespread pollution. More significantly in the long run, basic biological cycles such as the carbon cycle and nitrogen cycle, upon which all living things (including humans) depend for the maintenance and renewal of life, are being distorted to the point of irreversible damage. The proliferation of nuclear reactors in the United States and throughout the world — some 1000 by the year 2000 if the powers-that-be have their way — have exposed countless millions of people to some of the most carcinogenic and mutagenic agents known to life. The terrifying menace to the very integrity of life may be with us for hundreds of thousands of years. To these radioactive wastes we should add long-lived pesticides, lead residues, and thousands of toxic or potentially toxic chemicals in food, water, and air; the expansion of cities into vast urban belts, with dense concentrations of populations comparable in size to entire nations; the rising din of background noise; the stresses created by congestion, mass living, and mass manipulation; the immense accumulations of garbage, refuse, sewage, and industrial wastes; the congestion of highways and city streets with vehicular traffic; the profligate destruction of precious raw materials; the scarring of the earth by real estate speculators, mining and lumbering barons, and highway construction bureaucrats. This ecological list of lethal insults to the biosphere has wreaked a degree of damage in a single generation that exceeds the damage inflicted by thousands of years of human habitation on this planet. If this tempo of destruction is borne in mind, it is terrifying to speculate about what lies ahead in the generation to come.

The essence of the ecological crisis in our time is that this society — more than any other in the past — is literally undoing the work of organic evolution. It is a truism to say that humanity is part of the fabric of life. It is perhaps more important at this late stage to emphasize that humanity depends critically upon the complexity and variety of life, that human well-being and survival rest upon a long evolution of organisms into increasingly complex and interdependent forms. The development of life into a complex web, the elaboration of primal animals and plants into highly varied forms, has been the precondition for the evolution and survival of humanity and nature.

THE ROOTS OF THE ECOLOGICAL CRISIS

If the past generation has witnessed a despoilation of the planet that exceeds all the damage inflicted by earlier generations, little more that a generation may remain before the destruction of the environment becomes irreversible. For this reason, we must look at the *roots* of the ecological crisis with ruthless honesty. Time is running out and the remaining decades of the twentieth century may well be the last opportunity we will have to restore the balance between humanity and nature.

Do the roots of the ecological crisis lie in the development of technology? Technology has become a convenient target for bypassing the deep-seated social conditions that make machines and technical processes harmful.

How convenient it is to forget that technology has served not only to subvert the environment but also to improve it. The Neolithic Revolution which produced the most harmonious period between nature and post-paleolithic humanity was above all a technological revolution. It was this period that brought to humanity the arts of agriculture, weaving, pottery, the domestication of animals, the discovery of the wheel, and many other key advances. True there are techniques and technological attitudes that are entirely destructive of the balance between humanity and nature. Our responsibilities are to separate the promise of technology — its creative potential — from the capacity of technology to destroy. Indeed, there is no such word as "Technology" that presides over all social conditions and relations; there are different technologies and attitudes toward technology, some of which are indispensable to restoring the balance, others of which have contributed profoundly to its destruction. What humanity needs is not a wholesale discarding of advanced technologies, but a sifting, indeed a further development of technology along ecological principles that will contribute to a new harmonization of society and the natural world.

Do the roots of the ecological crisis lie in population growth? This thesis is the most disquieting, and in many ways the most sinister, to be advanced by ecology action movements in the United States. Here, an effect called "population growth," juggled around on the basis of superficial statistics and projections, is turned into a *cause*. A problem of secondary proportions at the present time is given primacy, thus obscuring the fundamental reasons for the ecological crisis. True, if present economic, political and social conditions prevail, humanity will in time overpopulate the planet and by sheer weight of numbers turn into a pest in its own global habitat. There is something obscene, however, about the fact that an effect, "population growth," is being given primacy in the ecological crisis by a nation which has little more than seven percent of the world's population, wastefully devours more than fifty percent of the world's resources, and is currently engaged in the depopulation of an Oriental people that has lived for centuries in sensitive balance with its environment.

We must pause to look more carefully into the population problem, touted so widely by the white races of North America and Europe — races that have wantonly exploited the peoples of Asia, Africa, Latin America, and the South Pacific. The exploited have delicately advised their exploiters that, what they need are not contraceptive devices, armed "liberators," and Prof. Paul R. Ehrlich to resolve their population problems; rather, what they need is a fair return on the immense resources that were plundered from their lands by North America and Europe. To balance these accounts is more of a pressing need at the present time than to balance birth rates and death rates. The peoples of Asia, Africa, Latin America, and the South Pacific can justly point out that their American "advisors" have shown the world how to despoil a virgin continent in less than a century and have added the words "built-in obsolescence" to the vocabulary of humanity. This much is clear: when large labour reserves were needed during the Industrial Revolution of the early nineteenth century to man factories and depress wages, population growth was greeted enthusiastically by the new industrial bourgeoisie. And the growth of population occurred despite the fact that, owing to long working hours and grossly overcrowded cities, tuberculosis, cholera, and other diseases were pandemic in Europe and the United States. If birth rates exceeded death rates at this time, it was not because advances in medical care and sanitation had produced any dramatic decline in human mortality; rather, the excess of birth rates over death rates can be explained by the destruction of pre-industrial family farms, village institutions, mutual aid, and stable, traditional patterns of life at the hands of capitalist "enterprise." The decline in social morale ushered in by the horrors of the factory system, the degradation of traditional agrarian peoples into grossly exploited proletarians and urban dwellers, produced a concommitantly irresponsible attitude toward the family and the begetting of children. Sexuality became a refuge from a life of toil on the same order as the consumption of cheap gin; the new proletariat reproduced children, many of whom were never destined to survive into adulthood, as mindlessly as it drifted into alcoholism. Much the same process occurred when the villages of Asia, Africa, and Latin America were sacrificed on the holy altar of imperialism.

Today, the bourgeoisie "sees" things differently. The roseate years of "free enterprise" and "free labour" are waning before an era of monopoly, cartels, state-controlled economies, institutionalized forms of labour mobilization (trade unions), and automatic or cybernetic machinery. Large reserves of unemployed labour are no longer needed to meet the needs of capital expansion, and wages are largely negotiated rather than left to the free play of the labour market. From a need, idle labour reserves have now turned into a threat to the stability of a managed bourgeois economy. The logic of this new "perspective" found its most terrifying expression in German fascism. To the Nazis, Europe was already "overpopulated" in the thirties and the "population problem" was "solved" in the gas chambers of Auschwitz. The same logic is implicit in many of the neo-Malthusian arguments that masquerade as ecology today. Let there be no mistake about this conclusion.

Sooner or later the mindless proliferation of human beings will have to be arrested, but population control will either be initiated by "social controls" (authoritarian or racist methods and eventually by systematic genocide) or by a libertarian, ecologically oriented society (a society that develops a new balance with nature out of a reverence for life). Modern society stands before these mutually exclusive alternatives and a choice must be made without dissimulation. Ecology action is fundamentally social action. Either we will go directly to the social roots of the ecological crisis or we will be deceived into an era of totalitarianism.

Finally, do the roots of the ecological crisis lie in the mindless consumption of goods by Americans and by peoples of European origin generally? Here a half-truth is used to create a whole lie. Like the "population issue," "affluence" and the inability of a "grow-or-die" economy to impose limits to growth is used to anchor the ecological problem in the ordinary and powerless peoples of the world. A notion of "original sin" is created that deflects the causes of the ecological problem to the bedroom, where people reproduce, or to the dinner table, where they eat, or to the vehicles, home furnishings and clothing that in large part have become indispensable to ordinary living—indeed, mere survival of the average person as seen in the context of the present society.

Can we blame working people for using cars when the logistics of American society were deliberately structured by General Motors and the energy industry around highways? Can we blame middle-class people for purchasing suburban homes when cities were permitted to deteriorate and real-estate hucksters merchandised an "American Dream" of subdivisions, ranch-type dwellings, and a two-car garage? Can we blame blacks, Hispanic peoples, and other minority groups for reaching out to own television sets, appliances, and clothing when all the basic material means of life were denied to them for generations?

The all-engulfing inflation engineered by the energy industry, multinational corporations, banks, and agribusiness has already made a mockery of the meaning of "limits to growth" and "voluntary simplicity." The savings accounts, earnings, and credit of working, middle-class and minority peoples have already reached *their* "limits" and "simplicity" of living is no longer a choice — it has become a necessity. What has grown in size and complexity beyond all decency have been the incredible profits, the interlocking directorates and the corporate structure in the United States and throughout the world. Viewed in terms of this structure, we can no longer speak of "limits to growth," "voluntary simplicty," and "conservation," but rather in terms of unlimited expansion, unlimited accumulation of capital and wealth, and unlimited waste of raw materials for useless, even toxic, commodities and of a formidable, ever-growing arsenal of weaponry.

If we are to find the roots of the present ecological crisis, we must turn not to technics, demographics, growth, and a diseased affluence alone; we must turn to the underlying institutional, moral, and spiritual changes in human society that produced hierarchy and domination — not only in bourgeois, feudal and ancient society, nor in class societies generally, but at the very dawn of civilization.

ECOLOGY AND SOCIETY

The basic conception that humanity must dominate and exploit nature stems from the domination and exploitation of man by man. Indeed, this conception goes back earlier to a time when men began to dominate and exploit women in the patriarchal family. From that point onward, human beings were increasingly regarded as mere resources, as objects instead of subjects. The hierarchies, classes, propertied forms, and statist institutions that emerged with social domination were carried over conceptually into humanity's relationship with nature. Nature too became increasingly regarded as a mere resource, an object, a raw material to be exploited as ruthlessly as slaves on a latifundium. This "worldview" permeated not only the official culture of hierarchical society; it became the way in which slaves, serfs, industrial workers and women of all social classes began to view themselves. As embodied in the "work ethic," in a morality based on denial and renunciation, in a mode of behaviour based on the sublimination of erotic desires, and in other worldly outlooks (be they European or Asian), the slaves, serfs, workers, and female half of humanity were taught to police themselves, to fashion their own chains, to close the doors on their own prison cells.

If the "worldview" of hierarchical society is beginning to wane today, this is mainly because the enormous productivity of modern technology has opened a new vision: the possibility of material abundance, an end to scarcity, and an era of free time (so-called "leisure time") with minimal toil.

By "material abundance" we do not mean the wasteful, mindless "affluence" based on false needs, the subtle coercion of advertising, and the substitution of mere objects — commodities — for genuine human relations, self-reflection, and self-development. We refer to a sufficiency in food, shelter, clothing and basic comforts of life with a minimum of toil that will permit everyone in society — not a specialized elite — to directly manage social affairs.

Society is becoming permeated by a tension between "what is" and "what-could-be," a tension exacerbated by the irrational, inhuman exploitation and destruction of the earth and its inhabitants. The greatest impediment that obstructs a resolution of this tension is the extent to which hierarchical society still fashions our outlook and actions. It is easier to take refuge in critiques of technology and population growth; to deal with an archaic, destructive social system on its own terms and within its own framework. Almost from birth, we have been socialized by the family, religious institutions, schools, and by the work process itself into accepting hierarchy, renunciation, and state systems as the premises on which all thinking must rest. Without shedding these premises, all discussions of ecological balance must remain palliative and self-defeating.

By virtue of its unique cultural baggage, modern society — our profit-oriented bourgeois society — tends to exacerbate humanity's conflict with nature in a more critical fashion than pre-industrial societies of the past. In bourgeois society, humans are not only turned into objects; they are turned into commodities; into objects explicitly designed for sale on the market place. Competition between human beings, qua commodities, becomes an end in itself, together with the production of utterly useless goods. Quality is turned into quantity individual culture into mass culture, personal communication into mass communication. The natural environment is turned into a gigantic factory, the city into an immense market place; everything from a Redwood forest to a woman's body has "a price." Everything is reduced to dollars-and-cents, be it a hallowed cathedral or individual honour. Technology ceases to be an extension of humanity; humanity becomes an extension of technology. The machine does not expand the power of the worker; the worker expands the power of the machine, indeed, she or he becomes a mere part of the machine.

It is surprising, then, that this exploitative, degrading, quantified society pits humanity against itself and against nature on a more awesome scale than any other in the past?

Yes, we need change, but change so fundamental and far-reaching that even the concept of revolution and freedom must be expanded beyond all earlier horizons. No longer is it enough to speak of new techniques for conserving and fostering the natural environment; we must deal with the earth communally, as a human collectivity, without those trammels of private property that have distorted humanity's vision of life and nature since the break-up of tribal society. We must eliminate not only bourgeois hierarchy, but hierarchy as such; not only the patriarchal family, but *all* modes of sexual and parental domination; not only the bourgeois class and propertied system, but *all* social classes and property. Humanity must come into possession of itself, individually and collectively, so that all human beings attain control of their everyday lives. Our cities must be decentralized into communities, or ecocommunities, exquisitely and artfully tailored to the carrying capacity of the ecosystems in which they are located. Our technologies must be readapted and advanced into ecotechnologies, exquisitely and artfully adapted to make use of local energy sources and materials, with minimal or no pollution of the environment. We must recover a new sense of our needs — needs that foster a healthful life and express our individual proclivities, not "needs" dictated by the mass media. We must restore the human scale in our environment and in our social relations, replacing mediated by direct personal relations in the management of society. Finally, all modes of domination — social or personal — must be banished from our conceptions of ourselves, our communities, and nature. The administration of humans must be replaced by the administration of things. The revolution we seek must encompass not only political institutions and economic relations, but consciousness, life style, erotic desires, and our interpretation of the meaning of life.

What is in the balance, here, is the age-long spirit and systems of domination and repression that have not only pitted human against human, but humanity against nature. The conflict between humanity and nature is an extension of the conflict between human and human. Unless the ecology movement encompasses the problem of domination in all its aspects, it will contribute *nothing* toward eliminating the root causes of the ecological crisis of our time. If the ecology movement stops at mere reforms in pollution and conservation control — at mere "environmentalism" — without dealing radically with the need for an expanded concept of revolution, it will merely serve as a safety valve for the existing system of natural and human exploitation.

GOALS

In some respects the ecology movement today is waging a delaying action against the rampant destruction of the environment. In other respects its most conscious elements are involved in a creative movement to totally revolutionize the social relations of humans to each other and of humanity to nature.

Although they closely interpenetrate, the two efforts should be distinguished from each other. Ecology Action East* supports every effort to conserve the environment: to eliminate nuclear power plants and weapons, to preserve clean air and water, to limit the use of pesticides and food additives, to reduce vehicular traffic in streets and on highways, to make cities more wholesome physically, to prevent radioactive wastes from seeping into the

---

* This organisation no longer exists and this revised essay is dated 1979.

environment, to guard and expand wilderness areas and domains for wildlife, to defend animal species from human depredation.

But Ecology Action East does not deceive itself that such delaying actions constitute a definitive solution to the fundamental conflict that exists between the present social order and the natural world. Nor can such delaying actions arrest the overwhelming momentum of the existing society for destruction.

This social order plays games with us. It grants long-delayed, piecemeal and woefully inadequate reforms to deflect our energies and attention from larger acts of destruction. In a sense, we are "offered" a patch of Redwood forest in exchange for the Cascades, a nuclear power site in exchange for a neutron bomb. Viewed in a larger perspective, this attempt to reduce ecology to a barter relationship does not rescue anything; it is a cheap *modus operandi* for trading away the greater part of the planet for a few islands of wilderness, for pocket parks in a devastated world of concrete. It is the sick strategy of "benefits-versus-risks" of "trade-offs" that has reduced ethics to the pursuit of "lesser evils" rather than greater good.

Ecology Action East has two primary aims: one is to increase in the revolutionary movement the awareness that the most destructive and pressing consequences of our alienating, exploitative society is the ecological crisis, and that any truly revolutionary society must be built upon ecological precepts; the other is to create, in the minds of the millions of Americans who are concerned with the destruction of our environment, the consciousness that the principles of ecology, carried to their logical end, demand radical changes in our society and our way of looking at the world.

Ecology Action East takes its stand with the life-style revolution that, at its best, seeks an expanded consciousness of experience and human freedom. We seek the liberation of women, of children, of gay people, of black people and colonial peoples, and of working people in all occupations as part of a growing social struggle against the age-old traditions and institutions of domination — traditions and institutions that have so destructively shaped humanity's attitude toward the natural world. We support libertarian communities and struggles for freedom wherever they arise; we take our stand with every effort to promote the spontaneous self-development of the young; we oppose every attempt to repress human sexuality, to deny humanity the eroticization of experience in all its forms. We join in all endeavours to foster a joyous artfulness in life and work: the promotion of crafts and quality production, the design of new ecocommunities and ecotechnologies, the right to experience on a daily basis the beauty of the natural world, the open, unmediated, sensuous pleasure that humans can give to each other, the growing reverence for the world of life.

In short, we hope for a revolution which will produce politically independent communities whose boundaries and populations will be defined by a new ecological consciousness; communities whose inhabitants will determine for themselves within the framework of this new consciousness the nature and level of their technologies, the forms taken by their social structures, world views, life styles, expressive arts, and all the other aspects of their daily lives.

But we do not delude ourselves that this life-oriented world can be fully developed or even partially achieved in a death-oriented society. American society, as it is constituted today, is riddled with racism and sits astride the entire world, not only as a consumer of its wealth and resources, but as an obstacle to all attempts at self-determination at home and abroad. Its inherent aims are production for the sake of production, the preservation of hierarchy and toil on a world scale, mass manipulation and control by centralized, state institutions. This kind of society is unalterably counterposed to a life-oriented world. If the ecology movement does not direct its main efforts toward a revolution in all areas of life — social as well as natural, political as well as personal, economic as well as cultural — then the movement will gradually become a safety valve of the established order.

It is our hope that groups like our own will spring up throughout the country, organized like ourselves on a humanistic, libertarian basis, engaged in mutual action and a spirit of cooperation based on mutual aid. It is our hope that they will try to foster a new ecological attitude not only toward nature but also toward humans: a conception of spontaneous, variegated relations within groups and between groups, within society and between individuals.

We hope that ecology groups will eschew all appeals to the "heads of government" and to international or national state institutions, the very criminals and political bodies that have materially contributed to the ecological crisis of our time. We believe the appeals must be made to the people and to their capacity for *direct action* that can get them to take control of their own lives and destinies. For only in this way can a society emerge without hierarchy and domination, a society in which each individual is the master of his of her own fate.

The great splits which divided human from human, humanity from nature, individual from society, town from country, mental from physical activity, reason from emotion, and generation from generation must now be transcended. The fulfillment of the age-old quest for survival and material security in a world of scarcity was once regarded as the precondition for freedom and a fully human life. To live we had to survive. As Brecht put it: "First feed the face, then give the moral."

The situation has now begun to change. The ecological crisis of our time has increasingly reversed this traditional maxim. Today, if we are to survive, we must begin to live. Our solutions must be commensurable with the scope of the problem, or else nature will take a terrifying revenge on humanity.

EDUCATION AND ORGANIZATION

Today, all ecological movements stand at a crossroad. They are faced with basically conflicting alternatives of policy and process — whether to work within the existing institutions or to use direct action, whether to form centralistic, bureaucratic, and conventional forms of organization or affinity groups. These problems have reached their most acute form in the great anti-nuke alliances like Clamshell, Shad, Abalone, Catfish, to cite only a few. And it is the destiny of these alliances that now concerns us most profoundly.

THE MEANING OF DIRECT ACTION AND
AFFINITY GROUPS

At their inception, the marvelous genius of the anti-nuke alliances is that they intuitively sensed the need to break away from the "system", that they began to function outside it and *directly* enter into social life, pushing aside the prevailing institutions, its bureaucrats, "experts," and leaders, and thereby pave the way for *extra-legal, moral,* and *personal* action. To a large extent, to be sure, they adopted direct action because earlier attempts to stop nuclear power plants by operating within the "system" had failed. Endless months or years of litigation, hearings, the adoption of local ordinances, petition and letter-writing campaigns to congressmen and the like — all, had essentially failed to stop the construction of nukes. Clamshell, the earliest of the great regional alliances, was literally born from the futility of trying to prevent the construction of the Seabrook nuke by "working within the system." Its very *identity* as an alliance was literally defined by the need to directly occupy the Seabrook site, to invoke moral principles over statutory laws. For any of the alliances to ever surrender their commitment to direct action for "working within the system" is to destroy their personality as socially innovative movements. It is to dissolve back into the hopeless morass of "mass organizations" that seek respectability rather than change.

What is even more important about direct action is that it forms a decisive step toward recovering the personal power over social life that the centralized, over-bearing bureaucracies have usurped from the people. By action *directly*, we not only gain a sense that we can control the course of social events again; we recover a new sense of selfhood and personality without which a truly free society, based on self-activity and self-management, is utterly impossible. We often speak of self-management and self-activity as our ideals for a future society without recognizing often enough that it is not only the "management" and "activity" that has to be democratized; it is also the "self" of each individual — as a unique, creative, and competent being — that has to be fully developed. Mass society, the real basis for hierarchy, domination, command and obedience, like class society, is the spawning ground for a society of homogenized spectators whose lives are guided by elites, "stars," and "vanguards," be they in the bureaucratic society of the United States or the totalitarian societies of the socialist world. A truly free society does not deny selfhood but rather supports it, liberates it, and actualizes it in the belief that everyone is competent to manage society, not merely an "elect" of experts and self-styled men of genius. Direct action is merely the free town meeting writ large. It is the means whereby each individual awakens to the hidden powers within herself and himself, to a new sense of self-confidence and self-competence; it is the means whereby individuals take control of society directly, without "representatives" who tend to usurp not only the power but the very personality of a passive, spectatorial "electorate" who live in the shadows of an "elect." Direct action, in short, is not a "tactic" that can be adopted or discarded in terms of its "effectiveness" or "popularity"; it is a moral principle, an ideal, indeed, a sensibility. It should imbue every aspect of our lives and behaviour and outlook.

Similarly, the affinity group — a term devised by the Spanish Anarchists (FAI) in the 1920's — is not merely a "task force" that can be flippantly collected and disbanded for short-lived occupations. It is a permanent, intimate, decentralized *community* of a dozen or so sisters and brothers, a family or commune as it were, who are drawn together not only by common actions and goals, but by a need to develop new libertarian social relations between themselves, to mutually educate each other, share each others' problems, and develop new, non-sexist, non-hierarchical ties as well as activities. The affinity group should form the real cellular tissue from which the alliance evolves, the very protoplasm that turns it into an organic being. In contrast to the party-type of organization, with its centralized, bureaucratic skeleton to which all parts of the structure are mechanically appended in a system of command and obedience, the affinity group is linked together by proliferation and combination in its authentic locality as a truly ecological entity. It always remains part of its local community, sensitive to its needs and unique requirements, yet it can coordinate locally and regionally into clusters and coordinating committees whose *delegates* (as distinguished from "representatives") can always be recalled, rotated, and strictly mandated to reflect the views of the various groups in every detail. Thus, within the affinity groups structure of an alliance, power actually diminishes rather than increases at each ascending level of coordination, this in sharp contrast to party-type or "league" — type or chapter-type of organization so rooted in the existing systems of "representation" and politics. Thus, the affinity group, like direct action, is not merely an organizational device, a "task force," a "tool" for implementing nuke occupations; it too is based on a moral principle, an ideal, and a sensibility that goes beyond the issue of nuclear power to that of spiritual power, new, humanly scaled, decentralized, ecological forms of human association as well as human action.

BETWEEN TWO CHOICES

With the Three-Mile-Island meltdown this year and even earlier, in the summer of 1978, when the Seabrook occupation was arbitrarily turned into a star-studded "legal" festival by the Clamshell leadership, there has been growing evidence in many alliances of attempts to convert the anti-nuke movement as a whole into a political and media event. It is doubtful if many of the self-styled "founders" of Clamshell clearly understood the idea that direct action and affinity groups were more than mere "tactics" and "task forces." Doubtless the terms sounded attractive — so they were widely used. By the same token, many of the Clamshell "founders" viewed "No Nukes!" as an effective rallying point for mass, media-oriented actions, for large spectacles in which people with basically conflicting social views could "unite" whether they believed in "free enterprise" or no property, for huge audiences before which they could display their oratorical talents and abilities. To go beyond "No Nukes!" — even as an educational responsibility — was taboo. At various alliance conferences and congresses, even at local clusters in which Coordinating Committee "regional travellers" (so reminiscent of the old SDS "regional travellers" of the sixties) surfaced, thoughtful anti-nuke activists were urged to keep the anti-nuke issue "clear." They were called upon to limit their educational activities to the growing public interest in nuclear reactors, not to develop a richer, more searching public consciousness of the social roots of nuclear power. In trying to find a low common denominator that would "mobilize" virtually everyone, the new "anti-nuke establishment" really educated no one. It was Three-Mile-Island that did much of the education, and often public understanding of the issue goes no further than problems of technology rather than problems of society. Respectability was stressed over principles, popularity over dissidence, mass mobilizations in Washington and Battery Park over occupations, and more insidiously, politics over direct action.

Yes, the fact is that there is now an "anti-nuclear establishment" that resembles in many structural, manipulatory, tactical, and perhaps even financial respects the very nuclear establishment it professes to oppose. It is not a very holy alliance, this career-oriented, star-studded, and politically ambitious establishment that often stands in harsh opposition or contradiction to the libertarian principles of major alliances like Clamshell, Shad, Abalone, and Catfish. Its elite membership has been recruited in some cases from the self-styled "founders" of the libertarian alliances themselves. Others, like Tom Hayden, the Cockburn-Ridgeway axis, PIRG luminaries, and Barry Commoner openly shunned the alliances or their equivalent — Hayden and Cockburn-Ridgeway, by denouncing all environmental groups at one time or another as white, middle-class, self-indulgent movements; Commoner, by disdainfully refusing to even take cognizance of Clamshell's requests for verbal support of its 1977 Seabrook occupation, that is, until the occupation received massive press reportage. Today, this new flower in the anti-nuke bouquet is the prize orator of recent anti-nuke rallies and, according to some reports, a potential presidential candidate for the recently concocted "Citizen's Party." The Tom and Jerry side-show from California, as the Washington rally revealed, seems to have a distinct political odour of its own.

Finally, MUSE and similar "fund-raising" groups, reportedly orchestrated in part by Messrs. Sam Lovejoy and Harvey Wasserman, have added the tint of grass-roots activism to what is a jet-set organization. The drift toward mass constituencies, personal careerism, political power, party-type structures, bureaucratic manipulation — in short, toward "effective" means for operating within the system with the excuse that the anti-nuke movement can use the system against itself — is now unmistakable. The huge crowd that assembled at Battery Park to hear the anti-nuke establishment and its rock stars were passive people, often depersonalized and homogenized like any television audience. This may have well been the case for many people who attended the Washington mobilization. The anti-nuclear establishment has brought to what was once a consistently populist and libertarian movement an alien taste for politics, high-finance (where possible), mass followings, public "spokesmen," and institutional recognition.

The danger of this elitist alliance to the non-hierarchical alliances that have emerged throughout the United States is a grave one. Were the anti-nuclear establishment easily defined with a clear identity of its own, it could easily be resisted. But this establishment emerges in our very midst — as one of us. By dissolving many real and far-reaching differences that should be explored and resolved with the simplistic slogan, "No Nukes!"; by staking out claims as "stars" with media-appeal, or "power brokers" with financial appeal, or "legislators" with political appeal, or "scientists" with technical appeal or "just plain folks" who helped found the alliances, the anti-nuclear establisment incubates in our midst like pathogenic spores that periodically break out in acute illnesses. To speak bluntly, it cultivates our worst vices. It appeals to our desire for "effectiveness" and our hope of achieving "mass support" without revealing the immoral, in fact, demoralizing implications of the methods it employs. It conceals the fact that its methods are borrowed from the very social structures, indeed, the very advertising agencies, that reduce people to "masses," media-orchestrated spectators, "groupies" of the "stars" who seem larger than life because their appetites for power are often larger than their egos.

We have emphasized the problems created by the anti-nuclear establishment not from any desire for divisiveness or any sense of personal malice. There is a deeper sense of tragedy that runs through my remarks rather than anger. A few members of this establishment are doubtless naive; others are frankly opportunists whose careers and ambitions by far outweigh their commitment to a humanistic, ecological society. My emphasis stems basically from a need not only to acknowledge that serious differences exist within the anti-nuclear movement and should not be concealed by specious demands for "unity"; my main concern is that we recover and advance *our own identity* in the years that lie ahead — our commitment to direct action, to affinity groups, decentralization, regionalism, and libertarian forms of coordination.

The future of the anti-nuke movement, particularly of its great alliances, depends not only upon what we reject but what we *accept* — and the *reasons* why we accept certain principles, organizational forms, and methods. If we limit ourselves to "No Nukes! is enough," we will remain simplistic, naive, and tragically innocent whom careerists can cynically and shrewdly manipulate. If we see direct action and affinity groups merely as "tactics" or "task forces," we will foreclose any real contact with those millions of restive Americans who are looking for an alternative to a system that denies them any power over their lives. If our alternate energy fairs extol solar or wind energy as such without warning people that huge, space-age solar collectors and wind mills are on the drawing boards of power utilities and multi-national corporations, we will help the powers-that-be meter the sun and the wind in much the same way that Con Edison meters electrical energy. We should educate people not simply into an alternate, "appropriate" (for what?), or "soft" technology. We should raise the vision of a *people*'s technology — the passive, simple, decentralized solar, wind, and food-producing technologies that the individual can understand, control, maintain, and even build.

By the same token, to call for "decentralization" and to plead for "voluntary simplicity" are completely meaningless if their functions are simply logistical or conservation-oriented. We can easily have a "decentralized" society that is little more than a huge suburbia, managed by the same political bureaucrats, fed by the same agribusiness plantations and shopping malls, policed by the same Kojaks, united by the same corporate directors, interlaced by the same highways, and sedated by the same mass-media that manages our existing centralized society. To demand "decentralization" without self-management in which every person freely participates in decision-making processes in every aspect of life and all the material means of life are communally owned, produced, and shared according to need is pure obscurantism. To delude Americans into the belief that a mere change in design necessarily yields a real change in social life and spiritual sensibility is sheer hypocrisy. To leave questions like "who owns what" and "who runs what" unanswered while celebrating the virtues or beauties of "smallness" verges on demagoguery. Decentralization and human scale, yes!—but in a society whose property, produce, and environment are shared communally and managed in a non-hierarchical manner.

To call for "voluntary simplicity," yes!—but only when the means of life are really simple and available to all. Gloria Vanderbilt jeans and fringed suede jackets do not "voluntary simplicity" make. The Stanford Research Institute's plea for "voluntary simplicity" and "limits to growth" as the fastest growth industry on the commercial horizon parallels Exxon's and Mobil's claims to energy conservation. That a multi-million dollar "think-tank" for big business advances "voluntary simplicity" as a new growth industry for future capital investment; that agribusiness may well turn to organic food cultivation to meet the growing market for "natural foods"; that the Club of Rome can advance a gospel of "limits to growth" reveal how utterly superficial these demands can become when they do not challenge the basic corporate, property, bureaucratic, and profit-oriented social structure at its most fundamental level of ownership and control.

The most effective steps we can take at our congresses and conferences to assure a meaningful future for the anti-nuke movement is to unrelentingly foster the development of affinity groups as the bases of our alliances and direct action as the bases of our activities. Direct action does not merely mean nuclear site occupations; it means learning how to manage every aspect of our lives from producing to organizing, from educating to printing. The New England town meetings, during their more revolutionary periods around the 1760's, were near-models of direct action as carried into the social world. So, too, for direct action—of which our affinity groups and congresses can be models no less than Seabrook or Shoreham or Rocky Flats. Direct action, however, decidedly does not mean reducing oneself to a passive spectator of a "star's" performance, whether it be at a speakers rostrum, a rock band's stage, or on the portico of the State House in Sacramento or the White House in Washington.

On the other hand, if we are afraid to remain in a minority by speaking out openly and honestly — even at the risk of being "ineffective" or insolvent for a time — we deserve the fate that awaits us — respectability at the price of surrender, "influence" at the price of demoralization, power at the price of cynicism, "success" at the expense of corruption. The choice lies in either direction and there is no "in-between" terrain on which to compromise. In any case, for once, the choice we make will be the future we will create.

Revised:
November, 1979

Toward an
Ecological Society

The problem of environmental degradation seems to be falling into a curious focus. Despite massive public support for environmentalist measures — as witness the positive public response in recent state referendums on such issues — we are being warned about a backlash against "extremists" who are raising "radical" demands for arresting environmental degradation. Much of this "backlash" seems to be generated by industry and by the White House, where Mr. Nixon complacently assures us that "America is well on the way to winning the war against environmental degradation; well on the way to making our peace with nature". This rhetoric is suspiciously familiar; presumably we are beginning to see the "light" at the end of the environmental tunnel. In any case, advertising compaigns by the petroleum, automobile, lumber, and chemical industries are urging Americans to be more "reasonable" about environmental improvements, to "sensibly" balance "benefits" against "losses", to scale down norms for cleaner air and water that have already been adopted by the Environmental Protection Administration, to show "patience" and "understanding" for the ostensibly formidable technical problems that confront our friendly neighborhood industrial oligopolies and utilities.

I will not try, here, to discuss the scandalous distortions that enter into propaganda of this kind. Many of you are already familiar with the recent study by a committee of the National Academy of Sciences that accuses the automobile industry of concentrating (in the words of a New York Times report) on the "most expensive, least satisfactory means" of meeting the 1975 Federal exhaust emission standards. As to the pious rhetoric from the White House, Mr. Nixon's efforts to make "peace" with nature seem to be several cuts below his efforts to produce peace in Indonesia. As the Times opines editorially, Mr. Nixon's statement "is totally at variance with the facts... The air over the nation's cities is getting only marginally cleaner, if at all. Every major river system in the country is badly polluted. Great portions of the Atlantic Ocean are in danger of becoming a dead sea. Plastics, detergents, chemicals and metals are putting an insupportable burden on the biosphere. The land itself is being eroded, blighted, poisoned, raped."

Far from adhering to the claim that many environmentalist demands are too "radical", I would argue that they are not radical enough. Confronted by a society that is not only polluting the planet on a scale unprecedented in history, but undermining its most fundamental biogeochemical cycles, I would argue that environmentalists have not posed the strategic problems of establishing a new and lasting equilibrium with nature. Is it enough to stop a nuclear plant here or a highway there? Have we somehow missed the essential fact that environmental degradation stems from much deeper sources than the blunders or ill-intentions of industry and government? That to sermonize endlessly about the possibility of environmental apocalypse — whether as a result of pollution, industrial expansion, or population growth — inadvertently drops a veil over a more fundamental crisis in the human condition, one that is not exclusively technological or ethical but profoundly social? Rather than deal again with the scale of our environmental crisis, or engage in the easy denunciation that "pollution is profitable", or argue that some abstract "we" is responsible for producing too many children or a given industry for producing too many commodities, I would like to ask if the environmental crisis does not have its roots in the very constitution of society as we know it today, if the changes that are needed to create a new equilibrium between the natural world and the social do not require a fundamental, indeed revolutionary, reconstitution of society along ecological lines.

I would like to emphasize the words "ecological lines". In trying to deal with the problems of an ecological society, the term "environmentalism" fails us. "Environmentalism" tends increasingly to reflect an instrumentalist sensibility in which nature is viewed merely as a passive habitat, an agglomeration of external objects and forces, that must be made more serviceable for human use irrespective of what these uses may be. "Environmentalism", in effect, deals with "natural resources", "urban resources", even "human resources". Mr. Nixon, I would suppose, is an "environmentalist" of sorts insofar as the "peace" he would establish with nature consists of acquiring the "know-how" for plundering the natural world with minimal disruption of the habitat. "Environmentalism" does not bring into question the underlying notion of the present society that man must dominate nature; rather, it seeks to facilitate that domination by developing techniques for diminishing the hazards caused by domination. The very notion of domination itself is not brought into question.

Ecology, I would claim, advances a broader conception of nature and of humanity's relationship with the natural world. To my thinking, it sees the balance and integrity of the biosphere as an end in itself. Natural diversity is to be cultivated not only because the more diversified the components that make up an ecosystem, the more stable the ecosystem, but diversity is desirable for its own sake, a value to be cherished as part of a spiritized notion of the living universe. Ecologists have already pointed out that the more simplified an ecosystem — as in arctic and desert biomes or in monocultural forms of food cultivation — the more fragile the ecosystem and more prone it is to instability, pest infestations, and possible catastrophes. The typically holistic concept of "unity in diversity", so common in the more reflective ecological writings, could be taken from Hegel's works, an intellectual convergence that I do not regard as accidental and that deserves serious exploration by contemporary neo-Hegelians. Ecology, furthermore, advances the view that humanity must show a conscious respect for the spontaneity of the natural world, a world that is much too complex and variegated to be reduced to simple Galilean physico-mechanical properties. Some systems ecologists notwithstanding, I would hold with Charles Elton's view that "The world's future has to be managed, but this management would not be like a game of chess... (but) more like steering a boat". The natural world must be allowed the considerable leeway of a spontaneous development — informed, to be sure, by human consciousness and management as nature rendered self-conscious and self-active — to unfold and actualize its wealth of potentialities. Finally, ecology recognizes no hierarchy on the level of the ecosystem. There are no "kings of the beasts" and no "lowly ants". These notions are the projections of our own social attitudes and relationships on the natural world. Virtually all that lives as part of the floral and faunal variety of an ecosystem plays its coequal role in maintaining the balance and integrity of the whole.

These concepts, brought together in a totality that could be expressed as unity in diversity, spontaneity, and complementarity, comprise not only a judgement that derives from an "artful science" or "scientific art" (as I have described ecology elsewhere); they also constitute an overall sensibility that we are slowly recovering from a distant archaic world and placing it in a new social context. The notion that man is destined to dominate nature stems from the domination of man by man — and perhaps even earlier, by the domination of woman by man and the domination of the young by the old. The hierarchical mentality that arranges experience itself — in all its forms — along hierarchically pyramidal lines is a mode of perception and conceptualization into which we have been socialized by hierarchical society. This mentality tends to be tenuous or completely absent in non-hierarchical communities. So-called "primitive" societies that are based on a simple sexual division of labour, that lack states and hierarchical institutions, do not experience reality as we do through a filter that categorizes phenomena in terms of "superior" and "inferior" or "above" and "below". In the absence of inequality, these truly organic communities do not even have a word for equality. As Dorothy Lee observes in her superb discussion of the "primitive" mind, "equality exists in the very nature of things, as a byproduct of the democratic structure of the culture itself, not as a principle to be applied. In such societies, there is no attempt to achieve the goal of equality, and in fact there is no concept of equality. Often, there is no linguistic mechanism whatever for comparison. What we find is an absolute respect for man, for all individuals irrespective of age and sex".

The absence of coercive and domineering values in these cultures is perhaps best illustrated by the syntax of the Wintu Indians of California, a people Lee apparently studied at first hand. Terms commonly expressive of coercion in modern languages, she notes, are so arranged by the Wintu that they denote cooperative behavior. A Wintu mother, for example, does not "take" her baby into the shade; she "goes" with it into the shade. A chief does not "rule" his people; he "stands" with them. In any case, he is never more than their advisor and lacks coercive power to enforce his views. The Wintu "never say, and in fact they cannot say, as we do, 'I have a sister', or a 'son', or 'husband'" Lee observes. *"To live with* is the usual way in which they express what we call possession, and they use this term for everything they respect, so that a man will be said to live with his bow and arrows".

"To live with" — the phrase implies not only a deep sense of mutual respect and a high valuation of individual voluntarism; it also implies a profound sense of oneness between the individual and the group. The sense of unity within the group, in turn, extends by projection to the relationship of the community with the natural world. Psychologically, people in organic communities must believe that they exercise a greater influence on natural forces than is afforded by their relatively simple technology, an illusion they acquire by group rituals and magical procedures. Elaborate as these rituals and procedures may be, however, humanity's sense of dependence on the natural world, indeed, on its immediate environment, never entirely disappears. If this sense of dependence may generate abject fear or an equally abject reverence, there is also a point in the development of organic society where it may generate a sense of symbiosis, more properly, of mutualistic interdependence and cooperation, that tends to transcend raw feelings of terror and awe. Here, humans not only propitiate powerful forces or try to manipulate them; their ceremonials help (as they see it) in a creative sense: to multiply food animals, to bring changes in season and weather, to promote the fertility of crops. The organic community always has a natural dimension to it, but now the community is conceived to be part of the balance of nature — a forest community or a soil community — in short, a truly ecological community or *eco-community* peculiar to its ecosystem, with an active sense of participation in the overall environment and the cycles of nature.

This outlook becomes evident enough when we turn to accounts of ceremonials among peoples in organic communities. Many ceremonials and rituals are characterized not only by social functions, such as initiation rites, but also by ecological functions. Among the Hopi, for example, the major agricultural ceremonies have the role of summoning forth the cycles of the cosmic order, of actualizing the solstices and the different stages in the growth of maize from germination to maturation. Although the order of the solstices and the stages in the growth of maize are known to be predetermined, human ceremonial involvement is integrally part of that predetermination. In contrast to stricly magical procedures, Hopi ceremonies assign a participatory rather than a manipulatory function to humans. People play a mutualistic role in natural cycles: they facilitate the workings of the cosmic order. Their ceremonies are part of a complex web of life which extends from the germination of maize to the arrival of the solstices. "Every aspect of nature, plants and rocks and animals, colors and cardinal directions and numbers and sex distinctions, the dead and the living, all have a cooperative share in the maintenance of the universal order", Lee observes. "Eventually, the effort of each individual, human or not, goes into this huge whole. And here, too, it is every aspect of a person which counts. The entire being of the Hopi individual affects the balance of nature; and as each individual develops his inner potential, so he enhances his participation, so does the entire universe become invigorated".

It is not difficult to see that this harmonized view of nature follows from the harmonized relations within the early human community. Just as medieval theology structured the Christian heaven on feudal lines, so people of all ages have projected their social structure onto the natural world. To the Algonkians of the Norht American forests, the beaver lived in clans and lodges of their own, wisely cooperating to promote the well-being of the community. Animals, too, had their "magic", their totem ancestors, and were invigorated by the Manitou, whose spirit nourished the entire cosmos. Accordingly, animals had to be conciliated or else they might refuse to provide humans with skins and meat. The cooperative spirit that formed a precondition for the survival of the organic community thus entered completely into the outlook of preliterate people toward nature and the interplay between the natural world and the social.

The break-up of these unified organic communities, based on a sexual division of labour and kinship ties, into hierarchical and finally class societies gradually subverted the unity of society with the natural world. The division of clans and tribes into gerontocracies in which the old began to dominate the young; the emergence of the patriarchal family in which women were brought into universal subjugation to men; still further, the crystallization of hierarchies based on social status into economic classes based on systematic material exploitation; the emergence of the city, followed by the increasing supremacy of town over country and territorial over kinship ties; and finally, the emergence of the state, of a professional military, bureaucratic, and political apparatus exercising coercive supremacy over the remaining vestiges of community life — all of these divisions and contradictions that eventually fragmented and pulverized the archaic world yielded a resocialization of the human experimental apparatus along hierarchical lines. This resocialization served not only to divide the community internally, but brought dominated classes into complicity with their own domination, women into complicity with their own servitude. Indeed, the very psyche of the individual was divided against itself by establishing the supremacy of mind over body, of hierarchical rationality over sensuous experience. To the degree that the human subject became the object of social and finally self-manipulation according to hierarchical norms, so nature became objectified, despiritized, and reduced to a metaphysical entity in many respects no less contrived conceptually by a physico-mechanical notion of external reality than the animistic notions that prevailed in archaic society. Time does not permit me to deal in any detail with the erosion of archaic humanity's relationship with the natural world. But perhaps a few observations are appropriate. The heritage of the past enters cumulatively into the present as lurking problems which our own era has never resolved. I refer not only to the trammels of bourgeois society, which bind us with compelling immediacy, but also those formed by millenia of hierarchical society that bind the family in patriarchy, age groups in gerontocracies, and the psyche in the contorted postures of renunciation and self-abasement.

Even before the emergence of bourgeois society, Hellenistic rationalism validates the status of women as virtual chattels and Hebrew morality places in Abraham's hands the power to kill

Isaac. The reduction of humans to objects, whether as slaves, woman, or children, finds its precise parallel in Noah's power to name the beasts and dominate them, to place the world of life in the servitude of man. Thus from the two mainstreams of western civilization, Hellenism and Judaism, the Promethean powers of the male are collected into an ideology of repressive rationality and hierarchical morality. Woman "became the embodiment of the biological function, the image of nature", observe Horkheimer and Adorno, "the subjugation of which constituted that civilization's title to fame. For millenia men dreamed of acquiring absolute mastery over nature, of converting the cosmos into one immense hunting-ground. It was to this that the idea of man was geared in a male-dominated society. This was the significance of reason, his proudest boast. Woman was weaker and smaller. Between her and man there was a difference she could not bridge — a difference imposed by nature, the most humiliating that can exist in a male-dominated society. Where the mastery of nature is the true goal, biological inferiority remains a glaring stigma, the weakness imprinted by nature as a key stimulus to aggression". It is not accidental that Horkheimer and Adorno group these remarks under the title of "Man and Animals", for they provide a basic insight not only into man's relationship with woman, but man's relationship in hierarchical society with the natural world as a whole.

The notion of justice, as distinguished from the ideal of freedom, collects all of these values into a rule of equivalence that denies the entire content of archaic equality. In organic society, all human beings have a right to the means of life, irrespective of what they contribute to the social fund of labour. Paul Radin calls this the rule of the "irreductible minimum". Archaic equality, here, recognizes the fact of inequality — the dependence of the weak upon the strong, of the infirm upon the healthy, of the young and old upon the mature. True freedom, in effect, is an equality of unequals that does not deny the right to life of those whose powers are failing or less developed than others. Ironically, in this materially undeveloped economy, humanity acknowledges the right of all to the scarce means of life even more emphatically — and in the spirit of tribal mutualism that makes all kin responsible for each other, more generously — than in a materially developing economy that yields growing surpluses and a concomitant scramble for privileges.

But this true freedom of an equality of unequals is degraded on its own terms. As material surpluses increase, they create the very social classes that glean from the labour of the many the privileges of the few. The gift which once symbolized an alliance between men akin to the blood tie is slowly turned into a means of barter and finally into a commodity, the germ of the modern bourgeois bargain. Justice emerges from the corpse of freedom to guard the exchange relationship — whether of goods or morality — as the exact principle of equality in all things. Now the weak are "equal" to the strong, the poor to the wealthy, the infirm to the healthy in all ways but their weakness, poverty, and infirmity. In essence, justice replaces freedom's norm of an equality of unequals with an inequality of equals. As Horkheimer and Adorno observe: "Before, the fetishes were subject to the law of equivalence. Now equivalence itself has become a fetish. The blindfold over Justitia's eyes does not only mean that there should be no assault upon justice, but that justice does not originate in freedom".

Bourgeois society merely brings the rule of equivalence to its logical and historic extreme. All men are equal as buyers and sellers — all are sovereign egos on the free market place. The corporate ties that once united humanity into bands, clans, tribes, the fraternity of the polis, and the vocational community of the guild, are totally dissolved. Monadic man replaces collective man; the exchange relationship replaces the kinship, fraternal, or vocational ties of the past. What unites humanity in the bourgeois market place is competition: the universal antagonism of each against all. Graduated to the level of competing capitals, of grasping and warring bourgeois enterprises, the market place dictates the ruthless maxim: "Grow or die" — he who does not expand his capital and devour his competitor will be devoured. In this constellation of ever-regressive asocial relationships, where even personality itself is reduced to an exchangeable object, society is ruled by production for the sake of production. Equivalence asserts itself as exchange value; through the mediation of money, every artistic work, indeed every moral qualm, is degraded to an exchangeable quantum. Gold or its paper symbol makes it possible to exchange the most treasured cathedral for so many match sticks. The manufacturer of shoe laces can transmute his wares into a Rembrandt painting, beggaring the talents of the most powerful alchemist.

In this quantitative domain of equivalences, where society is ruled by production for the sake of production and growth is the only antidote to death, the natural world is reduced to natural resources— the domain of wanton exploitation *par excellence.* Capitalism not only validates precapitalist notions of the domination of nature by man; it turns the plunder of nature into society's law of life. To quibble with this kind of system about its values, to try to frighten it with visions about the consequences of growth is to quarrel with its very metabolism. One might more easily persuade a green plant to desist from photosynthesis than to ask the bourgeois economy to desist from capital accumulation. There is no one to talk to. Accumulation is determined not by the good or bad intentions of the individual bourgeois, but by the commodity relationship itself, by what Marx so aptly called the cellular unit of the bourgeois economy. It is not the perversity of the bourgeois that creates production for the sake of production, but the very market nexus over which he presides and to which he succumbs. To appeal to his human interests over his economic ones is to ignore the brute fact that his very authority is a function of his material being. He can only deny his economic interests by denying his own social reality, indeed, by denying that very authority which victimizes his humanity. It requires a grotesque self-deception, or worse, an act of ideological social deception, to foster the belief that this society can undo its very law of life in response to ethical arguments or intellectual persuasion.

Yet the even harsher fact must be faced that this system has to be undone and replaced by a society that will restore the balance between human society and nature —an ecological society that must first begin by removing the blindfold from Justitia's eyes and replacing the inequality of equals by the equality of unequals. In other writings, I have called such an ecological society anarcho-communism; in my forthcoming book it is described as "eco-topia". You are welcome to call it what you will. But my remarks up to now will mean nothing if we fail to recognize that the attempt to dominate nature stems from the domination of human by human; that to harmonize our relationship with the natural world presupposes the harmonization of the social world. Beyond the bare bones of a scientific discipline, natural ecology will have no meaning for us if we do not develop a social ecology that will be relevant to our time.

The alternatives we face in a society ruled by production for the sake of production are very stark indeed. More so than any society in the past, modern capitalism has brought the development of technical forces to their highest point, to a point, in fact, where we could finally eliminate toil as the basic condition of life for the great majority of humanity and abolish the ages-old curse of material scarcity and insecurity as the underlying feature of society. We live today on the threshold of a post-scarcity society in which the equality of unequals need no longer be the primordial rule of a small group of collective kin, but the universal condition of humanity as a whole, of the individual whose social affiliations are determined by free choice and personal affinities rather than the archaic blood oath. The Promethean personality, the patriarchical family, private property, repressive reason, the territorial city, and the state have done their historic work in ruthlessly mobilizing the labour of humanity, developing the productive forces, and transforming the world. Today, they are totally irrational as institutions and modes of consciousness — the so-called "necessary evils" in Bakunin's words that have turned into absolute evils. The ecological crisis of our time is testimony to the fact that the means of production developed by hierarchical society and particularly by capitalism have become too powerful to exist as means of domination.

On the other hand, if the present society persists indefinitely to do its work, the ecological problems we face are even more formidable than those which we gather under the rubric of "pollution". A society based on production for the sake of production is inherently anti-ecological and its consequences are a devoured natural world, one whose organic complexity has been degraded by technology into the inorganic stuff that flows from the end of the assembly line; literally, the simple matter that formed the metaphysical presuppositions of classical physics. As the cities continue to grow cancerously over the land, as complex materials are turned into simple materials, as diversity disappears in the maw of a synthetic environment composed of glass, bricks, mortar, metals, and machines, the complex food chains on which we depend for the health of our soil, for the integrity of our oceans and atmosphere, and for the physiological viability of our beings will become ever more simple. Literally, the system in its endless devouring of nature will reduce the entire biosphere to the fragile simplicity of our desert and arctic biomes. We will be reversing the process of organic evolution which has differentiated flora and fauna into increasingly complex forms and relationships, thereby creating a simpler and less stable world of life. The consequences of this appalling regression are predictable enough in the long run — the biosphere will become so fragile that it will eventually collapse from the standpoint of human survival needs and remove the organic preconditions for human life. That this will eventuate from a society based on production for the sake of production is, in my view, merely a matter of time, although when it will occur is impossible to predict.

We must create an ecological society — not merely because such a society is desirable but because it is direly necessary. We must begin to live in order to survive. Such a society involves a fundamental reversal of all the trends that mark the historic development of capitalist technology and bourgeois society — the minute specialization of machines and labour, the concentration of resources and people in gigantic industrial enterprises and urban entities, the stratification and bureaucratization of life, the divorce of town from country, the objectification of nature and human beings. In my view, this sweeping reversal means that we must begin to decentralize our cities and establish entirely new ecocommunities that are artistically molded to the ecosystems in which they are located. I am arguing, here, that decentralization means not the wanton scattering of population over the country-side in small isolated households or countercultural communes, vital as the latter may be, but rather that we must retain the urban tradition in the Hellenic meaning of the term, as a city which is comprehensible and manageable to those who inhabit it, a new polis if you will scaled to human dimension which, in Aristotle's famous dictum, can be comprehended by everyone in a single view.

Such an ecocommunity, I will argue, would heal the split between town and country, indeed, between mind and body by fusing intellectual with physical work, industry with agriculture in a rotation or diversification of vocational tasks. An ecocommunity would be supported by a new kind of technology — or ecotechnology — one composed of flexible, versatile machinery whose productive applications would emphasize durability and quality, not built-in obsolesence, and insensate quantitative output of shoddy goods, and a rapid circulation of expendable commodities. Let me emphasize, here, that I am not advocating that we abandon technology and return to paleolithic food-gathering. Quite to the contrary, I insist that our existing technology is not sophisticated enough by comparison with the smaller-scaled, more versatile ecotechnology that could be developed and to a large extent is already available in pilot form or on drawing boards. Such an ecotechnology would use the inexhaustible energy capacities of nature — the sun and wind, the tides and waterways, the temperature differentials of the earth and the abundance of hydrogen around us as fuels — to provide the ecocommunity with non-polluting materials or wastes that could be easily recycled. Indeed, decentralization would make it possible to avoid the concentrated solid waste problems created by our giant cities, wastes which can only be burned or dumped in massive quantities into our seas.

I would hope that ecocommunities and ecotechnologies, scaled to human dimensions, would open a new era in face-to-face relationships and direct democracy, providing the free time that would make it possible in Hellenic fashion for people to manage the affairs of society without the mediation of bureaucracies and professional political functionaries. The splits opened by hierarchical society ages ago would now be healed and transcended. The antagonistic division between sexes and age-groups, town and country, administration and community, mind and body would be reconciled and harmonized in a more humanistic and ecological synthesis. Out of this transcendence would emerge a new relationship between humanity and the natural world in which society itself would be conceived as an ecosystem based on unity in diversity, spontaneity, and non-hierarchical relationships. Once again we would seek to achieve in our own minds the respiritization of the natural world — not, to be sure, by abjectly returning to the myths of the archaic era, but by seeing in human consciousness a natural world rendered self-conscious and self-active, informed by a non-repressive rationality that seeks to foster the diversity and complexity of life. Out of this non-Promethean orientation would emerge a new sensibility, one that would yield in Marx's words the humanization of nature and the naturalization of humanity.

In counterposing environmentalism to ecology, I am not saying that we should desist from opposing the construction of nuclear power plant or highways and sit back passively to await the coming of an ecological millenium. On the contrary, the existing ground must be held on to fervently, everywhere along the way, to rescue what we still have so that we can reconstitute society on the least polluted and least damaged environment available to us. But the stark alternatives of ecotopia or ecological devastation must be kept in the foreground and a coherent theory must always be advanced lest we offer alternatives that are as meaningless as the prevailing society's perspectives are barbarous. We cannot tell the "Third World", for example, not to industrialize when they are faced with harsh material denial and poverty. With a coherent theory that reaches to the fundamentals of the social problem, however, we can offer to the developing nations those technological and community models we require for own society. Without a coherent theoretical framework, we have very little to say except for tiring platitudes, episodic struggles, and pious hopes that the public can with good reason ignore except insofar as its own narrow day-to-day interests are concerned.

I suppose I could discuss these issues endlessly. Let me conclude on a rather ruthless but honest observation. The unique freedom that could await us results ironically —or should I say, dialectically — from the fact that our choices are woefully limited. A century ago, Marx could validly argue that the alternatives to socialism are barbarism. Harsh as the worst of these alternatives may be, society could at least expect to recover from them. Today the situation has become far more serious. The ecological crisis of our time has graduated society's alternatives to a more decisive level of futuristic choices. Either we will create an ecotopia based on ecological principles, or we will simply go under as a species. In my view this is not apocalyptic ranting — it is a scientific judgement that is validated daily by the very law of life of the prevailing society.

March 1974

An open letter
to the
Ecological Movement

With the opening of the eighties, the ecology movement in both the United States and Europe is faced with a serious crisis. This crisis is literally one of its identity and goals, a crisis that painfully challenges the movement's capacity to fulfill its rich promise of advancing alternatives to the domineering sensibility, the hierarchical political and economic institutions, and the manipulative strategies for social change that have produced the catastrophic split between humanity and nature.

To speak bluntly: the coming decade may well determine whether the ecology movement will be reduced to a decorative appendage of an inherently diseased anti-ecological society, a society riddled by an unbridled need for control, domination and exploitation of humanity and nature — or, hopefully, whether the ecology movement will become the growing educational arena for a new ecological society based on mutual aid, decentralized communities, a people's technology, and non-hierarchical, libertarian relations that will yield not only a new harmony between human and human, but between humanity and nature.

Perhaps it may seem presumptuous for a single individual to address himself to a sizable constituency of people who have centered their activities around ecological concerns. But my concern for the future of the ecology movement is not an impersonal or ephemeral one. For nearly thirty years I have written extensively on our growing ecological dislocations. These writings have been reinforced by my activities against the growing use of pesticides and food additives as early as 1952, the problem of nuclear fallout that surfaced with the first hydrogen bomb test in the Pacific in 1954, the radioactive pollution issue that emerged with the Windscale nuclear reactor "incident" in 1956, and Con Edison's attempt to construct the world's largest nuclear reactor in the very heart of New York City in 1963. Since then, I have been involved in anti-nuke alliances such as Clamshell and Shad, not to speak of their predecessors Ecology Action East, whose manifesto, *The Power to Destroy, The Power to Create*, I wrote in 1969, and the Citizens Committee on Radiation Information, which played a crucial role in stopping the Ravenswood reactor in 1963. Hence, I can hardly be described as an interloper or new-comer to the ecology movement. My remarks in this letter are the product of a very extensive experience as well as my individual concern for ideas that have claimed my attention for decades.

It is my conviction that my work and experience in all of these areas would mean very little if they were limited merely to the issues themselves, however important each one may be in its own right. "No Nukes," or for that matter, no food additives, no agribusiness, or no nuclear bombs is simply not enough if our horizon is limited to each one issue alone. Of equal importance is the need to reveal the toxic social causes, values, and inhuman relations that have created a planet which is already vastly poisoned.

Ecology, in my view, has always meant *social* ecology: the conviction that the very concept of dominating nature stems from the domination of human by human, indeed, of women by men, of the young by their elders, of one ethnic group by another, of society by the state, of the individual by bureaucracy, as well as of one economic class by another or a colonized people by a colonial power. To my thinking, social ecology has to begin its quest for freedom not only in the factory but also in the family, not only in the economy but also in the psyche, not only in the material conditions of life but also in the spiritual ones. Without changing the most molecular relationships in society — notably, those between men and women, adults and children, whites and other ethnic groups, heterosexuals and gays (the list, in fact, is considerable) — society will be riddled by domination even in a socialistic "classless" and "nonexploitative" form. It would be infused by hierarchy even as it celebrated the dubious virtues of "people's democracies," "socialism" and the "public owner-ship" of "natural resources." And as long as hierarchy persists, as long as domination organizes humanity around a system of elites, the project of dominating nature will continue to exist and inevitably lead our planet to ecological extinction.

The emergence of the women's movement, even more so than the counterculture, the "appropriate" technology crusade and the anti-nuke alliances (I will omit the clean-up escapades of

"Earth Day"), points to the very heart of the hierarchical domination that underpins our ecological crisis. Only insofar as a counterculture, an alternate technology or anti-nuke movement rests on the non-hierarchical sensibilities and structures that are most evident in the truly radical tendencies in feminism can the ecology movement realize its rich potential for basic changes in our prevailing anti-ecological society and its values. Only insofar as the ecology movement *consciously* cultivates an anti-hierarchical and a non-domineering sensibility, structure, and strategy for social change can it retain its very *identity* as the voice for a new balance between humanity and nature and its *goal* for a truly ecological society.

This identity and this goal is now faced with serious erosion. Ecology is now fashionable, indeed, faddish — and with this sleazy popularity has emerged a new type of environmentalist hype. From an outlook and movement that at least held the promise of challenging hierarchy and domination have emerged a form of *environmentalism* that is based more on tinkering with existing institutions, social relations, technologies, and values than on changing them. I use the word "environmentalism" to contrast it with ecology, specifically with social ecology. Where social ecology, in my view, seeks to eliminate the concept of the domination of nature by humanity by eliminating the domination of human by human, environmentalism reflects an "instrumentalist" or technical sensibility in which nature is viewed merely as a passive habitat, an agglomeration of external objects and forces, that must be made more "serviceable" for human use, irrespective of what these uses may be. Environmentalism, in fact, is merely environmental engineering. It does not bring into question the underlying notions of the present society, notably that man must dominate nature. On the contrary, it seeks to facilitate that domination by developing techniques for diminishing the hazards caused by domination. The very notions of hierarchy and domination are obscured by a technical emphasis on "alternative" power sources, structural designs for "conserving" energy, "simple" lifestyles in the name of "limits to growth" that now represent an enormous growth industry in its own right — and, of course, a mushrooming of "ecology"-oriented candidates for political office and "ecology"-oriented parties that are designed not only to engineer nature but also public opinion into an accommodating relationship with the prevailing society.

Nathan Glazer's "ecological" 24-square-mile solar satellite, O'Neil's "ecological" spaceships, and the DOE's giant "ecological" windmills, to cite the more blatant examples of this environmentalistic mentality, are no more "ecological" than nuclear power plants or agribusiness. If anything, their "ecological" pretensions are all the more dangerous because they are more deceptive and disorienting to the general public. The hoopla about a new "Earth Day" or future "Sun Days" or "Wind Days," like the pious rhetoric of fast-talking solar contractors and patent — hungry "ecological" inventors, conceal the all-important fact that solar energy, wind power, organic agriculture, holistic health, and "voluntary simplicity" will alter very little in our grotesque imbalance with nature if they leave the patriarchal family, the multinational corporation, the bureaucratic and centralized political structure, the property system, and the prevailing technocratic rationality untouched. Solar power, wind power, methane, and geothermal power are merely *power* insofar as the devices for using them are needlessly complex, bureaucratically controlled, corporately owned or institutionally centralized. Admittedly, they are less dangerous to the physical health of human beings than power derived from nuclear and fossil fuels, but they are clearly dangerous to the spiritual, moral and social health of humanity if they are treated merely as *techniques* that do not involve new relations between people and nature and within society itself. The designer, the bureaucrat, the corporate executive, and the political careerist do not introduce anything new or ecological in society or in our sensibilities toward nature and people because they adopt "soft energy paths," like all "technotwits" (to use Amory Lovins' description of himself in a personal conversation with me), they merely cushion or conceal the dangers to the biosphere and to human life by placing ecological technologies in a straitjacket of hierarchical values rather than by challenging the values and the institutions they represent.

By the same token, even decentralization becomes meaningless if it denotes logistical advantages of supply and recycling rather than human scale. If our goal in decentralizing society (or, as the "ecology"-oriented politicians like to put it, striking a "balance" between "decentralization" and "centralization") is intended to acquire "fresh food" or to "recycle wastes" easily or to reduce "transportation costs" or to foster "more" popular control (not, be it noted, *complete* popular control) over social life, decentralization too is divested of its rich ecological and libertarian meaning as a network of free, naturally balanced communities based on direct face-to-face democracy and fully actualized selves who can really engage in the *self*-management and *self*-activity so vital for the achievement of an ecological society. Like alternate technology, decentralization is reduced to a mere technical stratagem for concealing hierarchy and domination. The "ecological" vision of "municipal control of power," "nationalization of industry," not to speak of vague terms like "economic democracy," may seemingly restrict utilities and corporations, but leaves their overall control of society largely unchallenged. Indeed, even a nationalized corporate structure remains a bureaucratic and hierarchical one.

As an individual who has been deeply involved in ecological issues for decades, I am trying to alert well-intentioned ecologically oriented people to a profoundly serious problem in our movement. To put my concerns in the most direct form possible: I am disturbed by a widespread technocratic mentality and political opportunism that threatens to replace social ecology by a new form of social engineering. For a time it seemed that the ecology movement might well fulfill its libertarian potential as a movement for a non-hierarchical society. Reinforced by the most advanced tendencies in the feminist, gay, community and socially radical movements, it seemed that the ecology movement might well begin to focus its efforts on changing the basic structure of our anti-ecological society, not merely on providing more palatable techniques for perpetuating it or institutional cosmetics for concealing its irremediable diseases. The rise of the anti-nuke alliances based on a decentralized network of affinity groups, on a directly democratic decision-making process, and on direct action seemed to support this hope. The problem that faced the movement seemed primarily one of self-education and public education — the need to *fully* understand the meaning of the affinity group structure as a lasting, family-type form, the full implications of direct democracy, the concept of direct action as more than a "strategy" but as a deeply rooted sensibility, an outlook that expresses the fact that *everyone* had the right to take *direct control* of society and of her or his everyday life.

Ironically, the opening of the eighties, so rich in its promise of sweeping changes in values and consciousness, has also seen the emergence of a new opportunism, one that threatens to reduce the ecology movement to a mere cosmetic for the present society. Many self-styled "founders" of the anti-nuke alliances (one thinks here especially of the Clamshell Alliance) have become what Andrew Kopkind has described as "managerial radicals" — the manipulators of a political consensus that operates *within* the system in the very name of opposing it.

The "managerial radical" is not a very new phenomenon. Jerry Brown, like the Kennedy dynasty, has practiced the art in the political field for years. What is striking about the current crop is the extent to which "managerial radicals" come from important radical social movements of the sixties and, more significantly, from the ecology movement of the seventies. The radicals and idealists of the 1930s required decades to reach the middle-aged cynicism needed for capitulation, and they had the honesty to admit it in public. Former members of SDS and ecology action groups capitulate in their late youth or early maturity — and write their "embittered" biographies at 25, 30, or 35 years of age, spiced with rationalizations for their surrender to the status quo. Tom Hayden hardly requires much criticism, as his arguments against direct action at Seabrook last fall attest. Perhaps worse is the emergence of Barry Commoner's "Citizen's Party," of new financial institutions like MUSE (Musicians United for Safe Energy), and the "Voluntary Simplicity" celebration of a dual society of swinging, jeans-clad, high-brow elitists from the middle classes and the conventionally clad, consumer-oriented, low-brow underdogs from the working classes, a dual society generated by the corporate-financed "think tanks" of the Stanford Research Institute.

In all of these cases, the radical implications of a decentralized society based on alternate technologies and closely knit communities are shrewdly placed in the service of a technocratic sensibility, of "managerial radicals," and opportunistic careerists.

The grave danger here lies in the failure of many idealistic individuals to deal with major social issues on their own terms — to recognize the blatant incompatibilities of goals that remain in deep-seated conflict with each other, goals that cannot possibly coexist without delivering the ecology movement to its worst enemies. More often than not, these enemies are its "leaders" and "founders" who have tried to manipulate it to conform with the very system and ideologies that block any social or ecological reconciliation in the form of an ecological society.

The lure of "influence," of "mainstream politics," of "effectiveness" strikingly exemplifies the lack of coherence and consciousness that afflicts the ecology movement today. Affinity groups, direct democracy, and direct action are not likely to be palatable — or, for that matter, even comprehensible — to millions of people who live as soloists in discotheques and singles bars. Tragically, these millions have surrendered their social power, indeed, their very personalities, to politicians and bureaucrats who live in a nexus of obedience and command in which they are normally expected to play subordinate roles. *Yet this is precisely the immediate cause of the ecological crisis of our time* — a cause that has its historic roots in the market society that engulfs us. To ask powerless people to regain power over their lives is even more important than to add a complicated, often incomprehensible, and costly solar collector to their houses. Until they regain a new sense of power over their lives, until they create their own system of self-management to oppose the present system of hierarchical management, until they develop new ecological values to replace current domineering values — a process which solar collectors, wind machines, and French-intensive gardens can *facilitate* but never replace — nothing they change in society will yield a new balance with the natural world.

Obviously, powerless people will not eagerly accept affinity groups, direct democracy, and direct action in the normal course of events. That they harbor basic impulses which make them very susceptible to these forms and activities — a fact which always surprises the "managerial radical" in periods of crisis and confrontation — represents a potential that has yet to be fully realized and furnished with intellectual coherence through painstaking education and repeated examples. It was precisely this education and example that certain feminist and anti-nuke groups began to provide. What is so incredibly regressive about the technical thrust and electoral politics of environmental technocrats and "managerial radicals" today is that they recreate in the name of "soft energy paths," a specious "decentralization," and inherently hierarchical party-type structures the worst forms and habits that foster passivity, obedience and vulnerability to the mass media in the American public. The spectatorial politics promoted by Brown, Hayden, Commoner, the Clamshell "founders" like Wasserman and Lovejoy, together with recent huge demonstrations in Washington and New York City breed masses, not citizens—the manipulated objects of mass media whether it is used by Exxon or by the CED (Campaign for Economic Democracy), the Citizen's Party, and MUSE.

Ecology is being used against an ecological sensibility, ecological forms of organization, and ecological practices to "win" large constituencies, not to educate them. The fear of "isolation," of "futility," of "ineffectiveness" yields a new kind of isolation, futility and ineffectiveness, namely, a complete surrender of one's most basic ideals and goals. "Power" is gained at the cost of losing the only power we really have that can change this insane society — our moral integrity, our ideals, and our principles. This may be a festive occasion for careerists who have used the ecology issue to advance their stardom and personal fortunes; it would become the obituary of a movement that has, latent within itself, the ideals of a new world in which masses become individuals and natural resources become nature, both to be respected for their uniqueness and spirituality.

An ecologically oriented feminist movement is now emerging and the contours of the libertarian anti-nuke alliances still exist. The fusing of the two together with new movements that are likely to emerge from the varied crises of our times may open one of the most exciting and liberating decades of our century. Neither sexism, ageism, ethnic oppression, the "energy crisis," corporate power, conventional medicine, bureaucratic manipulation, conscription, militarism, urban devastation or political centralism can be separated from the ecological issue. All of these issues turn around hierarchy and domination, the root conceptions of a radical social ecology.

It is necessary, I believe, for everyone in the ecology movement to make a crucial decision: will the eighties retain the visionary concept of an ecological future based on a libertarian commitment to decentralization, alternative technology, and a libertarian practice based on affinity groups, direct democracy, and direct action? Or will the decade be marked by a dismal retreat into ideological obscurantism and a "mainstream politics" that acquires "power" and "effectiveness" by following the very "stream" it should seek to divert? Will it pursue fictitious "mass constituencies" by imitating the very forms of mass manipulation, mass media, and mass culture it is committed to oppose? These two directions cannot be reconciled. Our use of "media," mobilizations, and actions must appeal to mind and to spirit, not to conditioned reflexes and shock tactics that leave no room for reason and humanity. In any case, the choice must be made now, before the ecology movement becomes institutionalized into a mere appendage of the very system whose structure and methods it professes to oppose. It must be made consciously and decisively—or the century itself, not only the decade, will be lost to us forever.

February 1980

Energy, "Ecotechnocracy" and Ecology

With the launching of the "energy crisis," a new mystique has developed around the phrase "alternate energy." In characteristic American fashion, this takes the form of ritualistic purification: guilt over the extravagant use of irreplacable energy resources, fear in response to the apocalyptic consequences of "shortages," repentance over the afflictions resulting from waste, and the millenarian commitment to "new" techniques for achieving a stable energy system, i.e., "alternate energy." The operational term here is "technique." Whether one chooses to focus on Gerald Ford's plan to afflict America with some 200 nuclear reactors by 1980 or Professor Heronemus' plan to string the northern Atlantic with giant wind generators, the phrase "alternate energy" runs the grave risk of being debased and its radical content diffused of its serious social implications.

The trick is familiar enough. One intentionally confuses a mere variation of the status quo with fundamentally opposing concepts of life style, technology, and community. Just as the word "state" was cunningly identified with society, "hierarchy" with organization, "centralization" with planning — as though the latter couldn't exist without the former, indeed, as though both words were synonymous — so projects that reflect a shrewd reworking of established techniques and outlooks are prefixed by the word "alternate." With this one magical word, they acquire the aura of the radically new, the different, the "revolutionary." The word "energy," in turn, becomes the solvent by which richly qualitative distinctions are reduced to the gray, undifferentiated substrate for a crude psychic, physical and "ecological" cybernetics — the ebb and flow, the blockage and release of quantified power. Accordingly, by dint of shrewd linguistic parasitism, the old in a seemingly "new" form becomes little more than an "alternative" to itself. Variety, qualitative difference and uniqueness, those precious traits of phenomena to which an authentic ecological sensibility must always be a response, are rarefied into a "cosmic" oneness, into a universal "night in which" (to borrow the mocking language of a great German thinker) "all cows are black.'"

If energy becomes a device for interpreting reality on the cosmic scale of the Chinese Qi or Reich's orgone, we will then have succumbed to a mechanism that is no less inadequate than Newton's image of the world as a clock. I use the word "inadequate" advisedly: there is certainly truth in all of these conceptions — Newton's no less than the Chinese and Reich's — but it is a one-sided truth, not truth in its wholeness and roundedness. If Newton's image was essentially mechanical, a vision of the world united in the ebb, flow and distribution of energy is essentially thermodynamical. Both reduce quality to quantity; both are "world views" in search of mathematical equations; both tend toward a shallow scientism that regards mere motion as development, changes as growth, and feedback as dialectic. Acupuncture and psychology aside, in ecology the Newton of this thermodynamics, or more properly, energetics, is Howard Odum. In Odum's work, systems-analysis reduces the ecosystem to an analytic category for dealing with energy flow as though life forms were mere reservoirs and conduits for calories, not variegated organisms that exist as ends in themselves and in vital developmental relationships with each other. Ironically, far too many well-intentioned people who are rightly dissatisfied with the linear thinking, the despiritizing formulas, and above all, the mechanical materialism of traditional science have unknowingly turned to its opposite face — a mechanical spiritualism that subtly betrays them with a different rhetoric to the very world view they have rejected.

In terms of outlook, the results of flipping from one face of the coin to the other — from mechanics to energetics — tend to produce an ideological omelet, as formless and scattered as the real article itself. Cosmic oneness achieved merely through energetics easily decomposes into an obsessive preoccupation with gadgetry. Here, the mechanical begins to subvert the spiritual. One cannot live in a universal night all the time. Even if the cows are black, there must be enough light to delineate them. Among many "eco-freaks" — and I can think of no other term to describe my sisters and brothers in the alternate technology community — daylight often means neither a mellow dawn nor a soft twilight but the harsh glare of high noon, when structural detail and technical proficiency become ends in themselves. Small domes graduate into big ones; horticulturists are lured by a burgeoning market for pure foods into a questionable form of organic agribusiness; solar collectors and wind generators acquire a certain technical precosity that finds its armor in the patent office. In itself, this development might even be valuable if it were the "spin-off" of a flourishing social perspective, distinctly critical of the entire social order, and formed by moral, spiritual, and ecological values of a clearly revolutionary character. But as long as energetics is the sole thread that unites outlook with practice, the "eco-freak" often drops into an eco-technocratic limbo in which means become ends and the end is simply technical proficiency at best — or a sizeable income at worst. What I am saying quite simply is that, lacking a solidity of social ideas, an authentic ecological sensibility, a life-oriented outlook, and moral integrity, scientism and frankly capitalism overtly recolonize even the rhetorical ground which was claimed by mechanical spiritualism. If the dream that guides the "eco-freak" is held together by energetics, ecology with its broadly philosophical outlook that seeks the harmonization of humanity with nature dissolves into "environmentalism" or what amounts to mere environmental engineering, an organic approach dissolves into systems analysis, and "alternate technology" becomes technocratic manipulation.

The landscape of alternate technology is already marred by this regressive drift, especially by mega-projects to "harness" the sun and winds. By far the lion's share of federal funds for solar energy research is being funneled into projects that would occupy vast areas of desert land. These projects are a mockery of "alternate technology." By virtue of their scale, they are classically traditional in terms of their gigantism and in the extent to which they would exacerbate an already diseased, bureaucratically centralized, national division of labour — one which renders the American continent dependent upon and vulnerable to a few specialized areas of production. The oceans too have become industrial real estate, not merely as a result of proposals for floating nuclear reactors but also long strings of massive wind generators. And as if these mega-projects were not enough,

Glaser's suggestions for mile-square space platforms to capture solar energy beyond the atmosphere and beam microwaves to earthbound collectors would redecorate the sky with science-fiction industrial installations. Doubtless, many of these mega-project designers are well-intentioned and high-minded in their goals. But in terms of size, scale and ecological insight, their thinking is hardly different from that of James Watt. Their perspectives are the product of the traditional Industrial Revolution rather than a new ecological revolution, however sophisticated their designs may be.

Human beings, plants, animals, soil, and the inorganic substrate of an ecosystem form a community not merely because they share or manifest a oneness in "cosmic energy," but because they are qualitatively *different* and thereby complement each other in the wealth of their diversity. Without giving due and sensitive recognition to the differences in life-forms, the unity of an ecosystem would be one-dimensional, flattened out by its lack of variety and the complexity of the food web which gives it stability. The horrendous crime of the prevailing social order and its industry is that it is undoing the complexity of the biosphere. It is simplifying complex food webs by replacing the organic with the inorganic — turning soil into sand, forests into lumber, and land into concrete. In so simplifying the biosphere, this social order is working against the thrust of animal and plant evolution over the past billion years, a thrust which has been to colonize almost every niche on the planet with variegated life-forms, each uniquely, often exquisitely, adapted to fairly intractable material conditions for life. Not only is "small beautiful," to use E.F. Schumacher's expression, but so is diversity. Our planet finds its unity in the diversity of species and in the richness, stability and interdependence this diversity imparts to the totality of life, not in the black-painted-on-black energetics of mechanical spiritualism.

"Alternate energy" is ecological insofar as it promotes this diversity, partly by fostering an outlook that respects diversity, partly by using diverse sources of energy that make us dependent on variegated resources. The prevailing social order teaches us to think in terms of "magic bullets," whether they be chemotherapeutic "solutions" to all disease or the "one" source of energy that will satisfy all our needs for power. Accordingly, the industrial counterpart to antibiotics is nuclear energy, just as Paul Ehrlich's salvarsan, the "magic bullet" of the turn of the century, found its counterpart in petroleum. A "magic bullet" simplifies all our problems. It overlooks the differences between things by prescribing one solution for widely dissimilar problems. It fosters the view that there is a common denominator to the variegated world of phenomena — biological, social, or psychological — that can be encompassed by a single formula or agent. A respect for diversity is thus undermined by a Promethean view of the world as so much "matter" and "energy" that can be "harnessed" to serve the maw of agribusiness and industry. Nature becomes "natural resources," cities become "urban resources," and eventually even people become "human resources" — all irreducible "substances" for exploitation and production. The language itself reveals the sinister transformation of the organic into the inorganic, the simplification of a richly diverse reality into uniform "matter" to feed a society based on production for the sake of production, growth for the sake of growth, and consumption for the sake of consumption.

To make solar energy alone, or wind power alone, or methane alone the exclusive "solution" to our energy problems would be as regressive as adopting nuclear energy. Let us grant that solar energy, for example, may prove to be environmentally far less harmful and more efficient than conventional forms. But to view it as the exclusive source of energy presupposes a mentality and sensibility that leaves untouched the industrial apparatus and the competitive, profit-oriented social relations that threaten the viability of the biosphere. In all other spheres of life, growth would still be pursued for its own sake, production for its own sake, and consumption for its own sake, followed eventually by the simplification of the planet to a point which would resemble a more remote geological age in the evolution of the organic world. Conceptually, the beauty of "alternate energy" has been not merely its efficiency and its diminution of pollutants, but the ecological *interaction* of solar collectors, wind generators, and methane digesters with each other and with many other sources of energy including wood, water — and yes, coal and petroleum where necessary — to produce a new energy *pattern*, one that is artistically tailored to the ecosystem in which it is located. Variety would be recovered in the use of energy just as it would be in the cultivation of the soil, not only because variety obviates the need to use harmful "buffers," but because it promotes an ecological sensibility in all spheres of technology. Without variety and diversity in technology as a whole, solar energy would merely be a substitute for coal, oil, and uranium rather than function as a stepping stone to an entirely new way of dealing with the natural world and with each other as human beings.

What is no less important, "alternate energy" — if it is to form the basis for a new *ecotechnology* — would have to be scaled to human dimensions. Simply put, this means that corporate gigantism with its immense, incomprehensible industrial installations would have to be replaced by small units which people could comprehend and directly manage by themselves. No longer would they require the intervention of industrial bureaucrats, political technocrats, and a species of "environmentalists" who seek merely to engineer "natural resources" to suit the demands of an inherently irrational and anti-ecological society. No longer would people be separated from the means whereby they satisfy their material needs by a suprahuman technology with its attendant "experts" and "managers"; they would acquire a *direct* grasp of a comprehensible ectotechnology and regain the power over everyday life in all its aspects which they lost ages ago to ruling hierarchies in the political and economic sphere.* Indeed, following from the attempt to achieve a variegated energy pattern and an ecotechnology scaled to human dimensions, they would be obliged to decentralize their cities as well as their industrial apparatus into new ecocom-

---

* At the risk of spicing these remarks with some politically debatable issues, I would like to remind some of my libertarian Marxist friends — the sects we can give up as hopeless — that even "workers' control of production," a very fashionable slogan these days, would not be any sort of "control" at all if technology were so centralized and suprahuman that workers could no longer comprehend the nature of the technological apparatus other than their own narrow sphere. For this reason alone, libertarian Marxists would be wise to examine social ecology in a new light and emphasize the need to alter the technology so that it is controllable, indeed, to alter work so that it is no longer mind-stunting as well as physically exhausting toil. Victor Ferkiss, in his latest book (*The Future of Technological Civilization*) has dubbed my views "ecoanarchism." If "ecoanarchism" means the technical — not only the spiritual and political — power of people to create an ecotechnology that is comprehensible to them, one that they can really "control," I accept the new label with eagerness.

munities — communities that would be based on direct face-to-face relations and mutual aid.

One can well imagine what a new sense of humanness this variety and human scale would yield — a new sense of self, of individuality, and of community. Instruments of production would cease to be instruments of domination and social antagonism: they would be transformed into instruments of liberation and social harmonization. The means by which we acquire the most fundamental necessities of life would cease to be an awesome engineering mystery that invites legends of the unearthly to compensate for our lack of control over technology and society. They would be restored to the everyday world of the familiar, of the *oikos*, like the traditional tools of the craftsman. Selfhood would be redefined in new dimensions of self-activity, self-management, and self-realization because the technical apparatus so essential to the perpetuation of life — and today, so instrumental in its destruction — would form a comprehensible arena in which people could directly manage society. The self would find a new material and existential expression in productive as well as social activity.

Finally, the sun, wind, waters, and other presumably "inorganic" aspects of nature would enter our lives in new ways and possibly result in what I called, nearly a decade ago, a "new animism." They would cease to be mere "resources," forces to be "harnessed" and "exploited," and would become manifestations of a larger natural totality, indeed, as respiritized nature, be it the musical whirring of wind-generator blades or the shimmer of light on solar-collector plates. Having heard these sounds and seen these images with my own ears and eyes at installations reared in Vermont at Goddard College and in Massachusetts at the research station of New Alchemy Institute East, I have no compunction in using esthetic metaphors to describe what might ordinarily be dismissed as "noise" and "glare" in the vernacular of conventional technology. If we cherish the flapping of sails on a boat and the shimmer of sunlight on the sea, there is no reason why we cannot cherish the flapping of sails on a wind rotor and the reflection of sunlight on a solar collector. Our minds have shut out these responses and denied them to our spirit because the conventional sounds and imagery of technology are the earsplitting clatter of an assembly line and the eye-searing flames of a foundry. This is a form of self-denial with a vengeance. Having seen both technological worlds, I may perhaps claim a certain sensitivity to the difference and hope to transmit it to the reader. If the current literature on alternate sources of energy is conceived merely as an unconventional version of the *Mechanical Engineering Handbook*, it will have failed completely to achieve its purpose. Mere gadgetry for its own sake, or in what philosophers call a "reified" form, exists everywhere and is to be desperately shunned. To be sure, one must know one's craft, no less so in ecotechnology than in conventional technology. This is the burden (if "burden" it be) of the sculptor as well as the mason, of the painter as well as the carpenter. But in ecotechnology one must deal with craftsmanship in a special way. Overinflated into a swollen balloon, it may well carry us away from the ground on which we originally stood, from our sense of *oikos*, the ecological terrain which initially shaped our interests and concerns. I have seen this occur among my sisters and brothers in the ecological movement only too often. Indeed, having received a considerable training in electronics decades ago, I also know only too well how insanely obsessed one can become with the unending, even mindless, improvisation of circuit diagrams until one is as enamored by drawing, say, the electronic trigger for a nuclear bomb as for a television set. It is from people obsessed with reified technology and science that the AEC recruits its weapons engineers, the FBI its wire-tappers, the CIA its "counter-insurgency" experts. Let us not deceive ourselves: "ecofreaks" are no more immune to "the man" from Honeywell and NASA than "electronic freaks" are to "the man" from General Electric and the AEC — that is, until they have become ecotechnologists, informed by a deeply spiritual and intellectual commitment to an ecological society.

This means, in my view, that they are committed not merely to an "efficient" alternate technology but to a deeply human alternate technology — human in scale, in its liberatory goals, in its community roots. This means, too, that they are committed to diversity, to a sense of qualitative distinction, to energy and technology as an artistically molded pattern, not as a "magic bullet." Finally, it means that they are ecologists, not "environmentalists," people who have an organic outlook, not an engineering outlook. They are motivated by a more sweeping drama than an appetite for mere gadgets and scientistic "curiosities." They can see the wound that opened up in society and in the human spirit when the archaic community began to divide internally into systems of hierarchy and domination — the elders constituting themselves into a privileged gerontocracy in order to dominate the young, the males forming privileged patriarchies in order to dominate women, lastly male elites collecting into economic ruling classes in order to exploit their fellow men. From this drama of division, hierarchy, and domination emerged the Promethean mentality, the archetypal myth that man could dominate nature. Not only did it divide humanity from nature into a cruel dualism that split town from country, but it divided the human spirit itself, rearing thought above passion, mind above body, intellect above sensuousness. When finally every group tie — from clan to guild — dissolved into the market place jungle of atomized buyers and sellers, each in mutual competition with the other; when finally the sacred gift became the avaricious bargain, the craze for domination became an end in itself. It brought us a formidable body of scientific knowledge and a stupendously powerful technology, one which, if properly reworked and rescaled, could finally eliminate scarcity, want, and denial, or one which could tear down the planet if used for profit, accumulation and mindless growth.

The authentic ecotechnologist knows that the wounds must be healed. Indeed, these wounds are part of her or his body. Ecotechnologies and ecocommunities are the mortar that will serve not only to unite age groups, sexes, and town and country with each other in a non-hierarchical society; they will also help to close the splits in the human spirit and between humanity and nature. Whether these splits were necessary or not to achieve the striking advances in technology of the past millennia; whether we had to lose the child-like innocence of tribal society in order to acquire the mature innocence of a future society, ripened by the painful wisdom of history — all of this is a matter of abstract interest. What should count when confronted by a technical work is that we are not beguiled from these immense themes — this sweeping drama in which we split from blind nature only to return again on a more advanced level as nature rendered self-conscious in the form of creative, intelligent, and spiritually renewed beings. To deal with alternate energy sources in a language that is alien to social ecology, to reify the literature on the subject as a compendium of gadgets — a mere encyclopedia of gimmicks — would be worse than an error. It would be a form of betrayal — not so much to those who have worked in this field as to oneself.

February 1975

The Concept of Ecotechnologies and Ecocommunities

The expression "human habitat" contains a paradox that should be examined if it is not to lead us into a certain measure of confusion. Clearly any man-made structure, indeed, any artifact that figures in an environment is "human" and part of a "human habitat." Viewed in terms of this all-embracing definition, a human habitat could include the scarring towers of New York City's World Trade Center and the low-slung town houses of Boston's Beacon Hill or the steel mills of Pittsburg and the artisan shops of Williamsburg. What is man-made in a habitat is "human," strictly speaking, and many serious writers see no discordancies in juxtaposing towers and town houses or mills and shops as components of a human habitat.

But this definition, while obviously secure in its technical accuracy, is somewhat disquieting. It seems to preclude the basis for judging whether certain man-made things are desirable or not — and it has been used to achieve this exclusion with telling effect. More than one horrendous urban design has been force-fed to the public on the grounds that it is no less "human," technically speaking, than a Florentine neighborhood square, and no pains have been spared to remind irate citizens that they are exercising inexcusable "value judgements" in describing the one as "inhuman" and the other as eminently "human." Yet we tend to resist the notion that the man-made origin of a thing suffices to characterize it as "human." We press the point that the word "human" should have considerably more than a technical meaning, that it should reflect deeply felt moral needs and ends.

This vexing paradox by no means confronts conventional technologists and planners alone. Even the new, so-called "countercultural" technologists and communitarians have confused technique with values or, more strictly speaking, the dimensions of a structure with its ethical or "human" qualities. It does not always improve our insight into this paradox to declare that "small is beautiful" or to describe "small" technologies as "soft," "intermediate," or "appropriate." Such adjectives are more neutral morally than E. F. Schumacher (who coined most of these terms) would have us believe. (1) As a critic of Schumacher has recently observed; if big is not good, small is not necessarily beautiful. (2) Indeed, much that is small—such as a suburban tract, a back-breaking plow, a tiring handloom, or the modest office of a local real estate broker—may be downright repellent and dehumanizing by any standards. Dimensions are no more substitutes for values than the technical origins of a particular thing, although they may certainly be a factor in launching an individual on a particular ethical trajectory that rejects "big" for one reason or "small" for another.

That social philosophers, researchers, and popular writers who identify "small" with "human" have touched a nerve in a sizable segment of the American public seems to be one of the more obvious facts of our times. Practical efforts to create a human habitat based on comparatively small communities, horticultural techniques of food cultivation, modest-sized complexes of solar-wind-methane energy installations, and craft technologies are widespread today and derive directly from the "countercultural" upsurge of the sixties. The constituency for these alternate technologies and communities is, in fact, much larger than the casual observor is likely to realize and its underlying philosophy, even if largely intuitive, has a coherence that has rarely been articulated in the conventional literature.

Nor can this movement be dismissed as episodic. Aside from the likelihood that it will have an existential impact comparable to the "counterculture" from which it derived, it has already pioneered in new technologies, service organizations, and community forms that have a tangibility, a reconstructive character, and a justly earned public recognition that can scarcely be compared with its almost formless and erratic antecedents of the last decade. Far from being episodic, this new quest for a "human habitat" articulates, even more than it fully recognizes, a well-formed and far-reaching historic tradition. Classical Hellenic thought initiated this tradition with its view of the polis as an ethical community; later, anarchist theorists such as Peter Kropotkin were to give it modernity with their concepts of face-to-face democracy and popular self-administration.

"HUMAN" AS HUMAN SCALE

It is important to emphasize the Hellenic (and largely western) origins of the new quest for a "human habitat" if only to place in clearer perspective the mystical Asian ambience that surrounds it. Despite the tendency of so many new technologists and communitarians to slight science as spiritually desiccating, they retain closer affinities to the western scientific outlook than they are likely to admit.[3] Quite often, in fact, the much-despised mechanical materialism associated with Newtonian science is simply replaced by an equally mechanical spiritualism that satisfies neither the needs of the new technologists for systematic research nor the needs of the new communitarians for a human-oriented value system.[4]

At the risk of seeming heretical, I would like to suggest that the Indian and Chinese philosophical works so much in vogue today provide no satisfactory melding of the disciplined rationalism, technical sophistication, social activism, and personalistic ethics that actually vitalize this quest. One must grossly misread Asian literature to find the rational, technical, and ethical inspiration for developing human-oriented technologies and communities.[5] Despite the widely expressed need for a sense of unity with nature that Asian philosophy is said to satisfy, the primacy this philosophy gives to "cosmic" concerns over mundane social and individual needs tends to conflict with the intense subjectivism of its western acolytes, their activism, and the practical wisdom they exercise in designing their technologies and communities.

If we must anchor the new quest for a human habitat in philosophical traditions of a pre-industrial era, it would seem that Hellenic rather than Asian thought is more relevant, even if it tends to receive scant attention. The fascinating Hellenic blend of metaphysical speculation with empirical study, of qualitative with quantitative science, and of natural with social phenomena is rarely equalled by Asian thinkers and religious teachers. We still "talk Greek," as it were, when we speak of "ecology," "technology," and "economics." We also "think Greek" when we impute "good" or "evil," "just" or "unjust," "human" or "inhuman" — in short, an ethical dimension — to data that conventional science views as hard facts. Although modern science can justly claim its origins in Hellenic philosophy, so too can the new technologists and communitarians who seek a human habitat, perhaps with even greater validity. For Greek "science," if such it can be called in the modern sense of the term, is rarely free of an ethical stance toward reality and experience. To Plato and Aristotle, the analysis of phenomena at all levels of reality is never exhausted by the strictly descriptive query, "how." Analysis must include an acknowledgement of functional interrelationship, indeed, of a metaphysical *telos*, which is expressed by the intentional query, "why".[6] Despite the high degree of secularism and factual systematization that Greek thought (expecially in Aristotle's extant writings) introduced into the western intellectual tradition, its center was eminently ethical and its orientation was human and social.

"Human," in Greek thought, means scaled to human dimensions, at least as far as social institutions and communities are concerned. Although it has been observed that Plato in *The Laws* computes the most satisfactory number of households in his "best polis" on the basis of Pythagorean numerology, a close study of that dialogue shows that his motives are strikingly pragmatic. The number, 5040, enjoys the alluring advantage that it contains the "largest number of consecutive divisors" and yet comprises a number that suffices "for purposes of war and every peacetime activity, all contracts and dealings, and for taxes and grants."[7] No figure could be so all-inclusive. In blending Pythagorean mysticism with pragmatic considerations, Plato affords his contemporaries a bridge to span the gap between the archaic world of the mythopoeic and the practical world of social organization, a characteristic example of "cosmic" and social parallelism that has proved so appealing to the new technologists and communitarians of our own time.

Aristotle is more secular: he replaces Plato's mysticism by strictly ethical premises. But these very premises provide him with his uniquely Hellenic stance — a moral conception of what we (borrowing our social terminology from zoology) designate as a "habitat." In a widely quoted passage, Aristotle tells us that the "best *polis*" must be one that "can be taken in at a single view."[8] His reasons for this scale, although rarely cited, form what is perhaps one of the most compelling arguments in social theory for decentralization. The population of a *polis* must suffice to achieve not only the "good life" and "self-sufficiency" in a "political community," but must be limited to a size which renders it possible for citizens to "know each other's personal characters, since where this does not happen to be the case the business of electing officials and trying law suits is bound to go badly; haphazard decision is unjust in both matters, and this must obviously prevail in an excessively numerous community."(9)

"Small," in Aristotle's view, is human because it allows for individual control over the affairs of the community and the exercise of individual human powers in the social realm. A "big" community may be more efficient for economic or military purposes, but it would be "unjust." Its citizens would be incapable of making decisions of profound social importance and would thereby fail to realize their distinctive human capacities for rational social judgement.(10) Hence the *polis* must be large enough to meet its material needs and achieve self-sufficiency, but small enough to be taken in at one view. Only in such a *polis* would human beings be able to realize their humanity, that is to say, to actualize their potentialities for rational judgement.

The Hellenic interpretation of "human" as self-consciousness and self-realization in the private sphere of life recurs throughout western thought from Descartes to the contemporary existentialists. A highly individualistic subjectivism is the intellectual hallmark of philosophy in the modern era. The Hellenic interpretation of "human" as self-activity and self-administration, in the public sphere, however, is surprisingly rare. The Protestant sects which were to gather together under the ample rubric of Puritan congregationalism seem to have articulated perhaps the earliest modern attempts to establish the administrative autonomy of small decentralized groups as opposed to the centralized hierarchies of the Catholic and Anglican clergy. In colonial America, the Puritan congregation was to be extended from the religious to the political sphere — if, indeed, Puritan ideology established any distinction between the two — by vesting considerable civil authority in town meetings.(11) The theme is picked up again by Rousseau in his critique of deputized power and representative government. His praise of the Greek popular assembly based on face-to-face democracy is all the more remarkable if one bears in mind that it was written at a high-point in the development of the centralized nation-state.(12) Finally, the concept of a human habitat as a modern *polis* acquires its clearest coherence and multidimensionality in the work of Peter Kropotkin, one of the major theorists of nineteenth-century anarchism and a distinguished biogeographer in his own right.(13) In *Fields, Factories and Workshops*, a classic that has exercised immense direct and indirect influence since its publication as a series of articles in the late 1880s, Kropotkin formulates the most impressive case for decentralized communities.(14) His concept of a human habitat is based on an ecological integration of town and countryside, a highly flexible technology and communications system, a revival of artisanship as a productive form of "aesthetic enjoyment," and direct local democracy freed of the social ills, notably slavery, patriarchialism, and class conflict, that subverted Greek democracy.

The revival of interest in Kropotkin's work, a revival that has been nourished by *The New Ecologist* in England and by what Victor Ferkiss describes as the "eco-anarchism" of many new technologists and communitarians in the United States, could well serve as a valuable point of departure for formulating an ethical dimension to the word "human." If our values are not to be entirely arbitrary and relativistic, they must be rooted in certain objective criteria about humanity itself. What clearly unites an Aristotle with a Kropotkin, despite a historic span of more than two millenia, is their emphasis on self-consciousness as the most distinctive of human attributes, notably, the capacity of human beings to engage in self-reflection, rational action, and foresee the consequences of their activities. Human action is not merely any action by human beings, but action that fosters reflexivity, rational practice, and foresight. Judging a habitat by this criterion, we would be obliged to look beyond the mere presence of human artifacts and inquire into whether or not the habitat promotes distinctively human traits and potentialities.

Clearly a habitat that is largely incomprehensible to the humans who inhabit it would be regarded as inhuman. Whether by reason of its size, its centralization, or the exclusivity of its decision-making process, it would deny the individual the opportunity to understand key social factors that affect his personal destiny. Such a habitat, by closing to the individual a strategic area for the formation of consciousness, would challenge the integrity of consciousness itself. That this trend, so apparent in the years following World War II, can evoke popular resistance is suggested by the often violent social unrest, particularly among American youth, of the 1960s. The official "habitat," marked by a formidable degree of centralization and bureaucratization, seems to have generated, in reaction, the "subhabitats" or "sub-cultures" of the last decade from which so many of the new technologists and communitarians were to emerge.

But the same trend toward gigantism and centralization can produce a mind-numbing quiescence. An inhuman habitat tends to produce a dehumanizing one — dehumanizing in the sense that the degradation inflicted on the public sphere eventually invades the private sphere. The individual who is denied the opportunity to exercise self-administration in the public sphere suffers an attrition not only of self-consciousness but also of self-hood. The primacy of subjectivity, which philosophy since the Renaissance placed above all other considerations in the western intellectual tradition, is vitiated by the erosion of the ego. The shrivelling of the public sphere is followed by the shrivelling of the private sphere — that inviolable area which is presumably the last refuge of the individual in an overly centralized and bureaucratized society. The ego, increasingly desiccated by the aridity of the social sphere, becomes fit material for mass culture, stereotyped responses, and a preoccupation with trivia.[15]

A human habitat minimally presupposes human scale, that is to say, a scale that lends itself to public comprehension, individual participation, and face-to-face relationships. But a caveat must be sounded: it is not enough to deal with such a habitat exclusively in terms of its artifacts or their dimensions. Even the most delicately wrought "garden cities" do not make a human habitat if the term "human" is to mean more than pleasant vistas, comfortable homes, and efficient logistics. The "big" literally dwarfs the ego, but the "small" does not in itself elevate it. Beyond "big" or "small" are the compelling problems of the "just" and "good" in the Hellenic and libertarian sense of these terms: the "good life" as a materially secure and reflexive one, the "good society" as an ethical community based on justice, public participation, and mutual concern. It is patently impossible to describe such a habitat strictly in terms of its physical attributes, however important they may be. Eventually, any such description must include the political infrastructure, institutions, interpersonal relations, and guiding values that justify the use of the word "human." In the absence of these political, institutional, psychological, and moral elements, the description becomes a mere inventory of things and structures, an artifactual aggregate that may secure the individual's self-preservation and creature comforts, but explains nothing about the development of his selfhood and moral outlook.

ECOLOGY AND ENVIRONMENTALISM

The extent to which a designer accepts this multidimensional notion of human scale generally tells us whether his work can be regarded as qualitatively "new" or merely an extension of the conventional technical wisdom into new fields of research.

A considerable amount of research is currently underway in non-nuclear "alternate" sources of energy such as solar, wind, and methane installations, in food cultivation, and in energy-saving dwellings and communities. From a strictly artifactual standpoint, this research is often difficult to distinguish. To cite a few examples: it is not unusual to read accounts of the "new technology" that contain fast-and-loose comparisons between the Meinel design for monumental "solar farms" and Steve Baer's small, delightfully playful solar-heated "drumwall" house. One finds William E. Heronemus's scheme for stringing large windmill installations across prairies and stretches of ocean juxtaposed with Hans Meyer's 12-foot-high wind generator. R. Buckminster Fuller's "Tetrahedral City," a soaring pyramidal structure designed to accomodate a million residents may be found together with a description of Moshe Safdie's compact modular "Habitat," both of which are adduced as evidence of "organic" design and structural growth. (16)

But can such sharply contrasting proposals and projects be grouped together because they employ similar technical principles or profess adherence to an "organic" design concept? The Meinel, Heronemus, and Fuller proposals differ not only in their physical dimensions from the installations designed by Baer, Meyer, and Safdie; they differ even more significantly in their conceptualization of a human habitat, whether this difference is explicitly stated, presupposed or, in Fuller's case, grossly misstated. The habitats that would emerge from the Meinel, Heronemus, and Fuller proposals would differ from a New York City, a Chicago, or a Pittsburgh primarily by virtue of their capacity to use inexhaustible resources such as solar and wind power, and an inexhaustible form of "real estate," notably the upward reaches of space. None of these proposals involves any appreciable structural modifications of existing habitats; none of them is likely to arrest the trend toward urban gigantism, political and economic centralization, bureaucratic manipulation, and the ethic of brute self-interest. Perhaps the only significant claim they can make is long-run efficiency in the use of key resources — a claim that has been seriously challenged by friendly critics as well as opponents.(17)

Such an approach might well be described as "environmentalistic" if, by this term we mean a morally neutral but more efficient technical administration of nature for concrete pragmatic ends. Environmentalism can thus be regarded simply as a form of natural engineering. The objectives of the environmentalist presuppose no uniquely beneficient relationship between man and nature that is implicit in so many statements of an "ecological ethic," notably a respect for the biosphere, a conscious effort to function within its parameters, and an attempt to achieve harmony between society and the natural world. Indeed, it is doubtful if words such as "nature" and "harmony" have any meaning for the environmentalist. "Nature" would be regarded as an inventory of "natural resources" and "harmony" as a poetic metaphor for "adaptation." Environmentalism advances the goal of using these resources efficiently and prudently, with minimal harm to public health and with due regard to the conservation of raw materials for future generations.

Although Baer, Meyer, and Safdie are likely to agree with the environmentalist emphasis on efficiency and prudence, they can hardly be regarded as mere technicians. It is fair to assume from their designs and sense of human scale that they are committed to an ecological ethic, not merely involved in the concerns of technical proficiency. Baer's sense of outrage over the social indifference of some of his colleagues, Meyer's almost rhapsodic commitment to a naturalistic sensibility, and Safdie's organic and communitarian vision, despite its puzzling eclecticism, reflect a decentralistic concept of habitats, a fervent regard for human beings as ends in themselves, and a holistic attitude toward nature. In their quest for technologies and communities that will serve to harmonize man with man and human society with nature, they might well be called "social ecologists" rather than designers, a term the late E.A. Gutkind coined a quarter of a century ago in a masterful discussion on community.[18] Their technologies and communities, in turn, could be described as "ecotechnologies" and "ecocommunities," terms that are meant to impart an ecological ethic to conventional notions of technics and urbanism.[19]

If Baer, Meyer, and Safdie seem to reflect a largely intuitive commitment to social ecology, The New Alchemy Institute and urban service groups such as the Institute for Local Self-Reliance exhibit a high degres of ideological sophistication. The assumption that John Todd, director of The New Alchemy Institute, is guided by a "practical, how-to-do it approach" (as a journalist recently reported in a major New York daily) is grossly misleading.[19] The New Alchemy Institute, which Todd did so much to establish, scores a major advance over many new technologists by integrating ecotechnologies into functionally interrelated systems that stand in marked contrast to the mutually exclusive units one so often encounters at other research installations. The Institute's windmills, solar collectors, aquacultural units and, very significantly, its extensive gardens — all taken together — could be described as a highly unique ecosystem. Todd, it is worth noting, explicitly acknowledges the influence of Kropotkin and other libertarian thinkers on his decentralistic and integrative outlook. He views his work as a project to alter social consciousness and human sensibility as well as technical practice.[20]

This emphasis on the integration of small-scale ecotechnologies acquires a distinct communitarian thrust in the work of the Institute for Local Self-Reliance. The Institute, while occupied with more modest installations than New Alchemy, promotes rooftop gardens, solar energy units, waste recycling, and retro-fitting projects in the very midst of Washington, D.C. Eco-technologies are expressly viewed by the Institute's members as a means for achieving a new kind of urban community based on popular control of the resources and institutions that affect the urban dweller's life. They stress full public participation in local governance and finance, neighborhood control of food and energy resources, decentralization, and mutual aid. Accordingly, technology is not the sole focus of the Institute but rather one of many means for achieving active participation in community life. Like New Alchemy, the Institute for Local Self-Reliance has been consciously influenced by Kropotkin and libertarian ideas. The tendency to report the approach of The New Alchemy Institute and the Institute for Local Self-Reliance as a "practical, how-to-do it" one reflects the intractability of the conventional mind to notions of a human habitat as an ethical community.[21] Even when these notions are cast in a familiar ecological jargon, they tend to be debased to technical "nuts-and-bolts" terms.

Ecotechnology, in fact, can scarcely be exemplified by a statuesque solar collector or a dramatic wind generator reared in splendid isolation from the ecosystem in which it is located. If the word "ecotechnology" is to have more than a strictly tech-nical meaning, it must be seen as the very ensemble itself, functionally integrated with human communities as part of a shared biosphere of people and nonhuman life forms. This ensemble has the distinct goal of not only meeting human needs in an ecologically sound manner — one which favours diversity within an ecosystem — but of consciously promoting the integ-rity of the biosphere. The Promethean quest of using technol-ogy to "dominate nature" is replaced by the ecological ethic of using technology to harmonize humanity's relationship with nature.

Human consciousness, in effect, is placed in the service of both human needs and ecological diversity. Inasmuch as human beings are themselves products of the natural world, human self-consciousness could be described in philosophical terms as nature rendered "self-conscious," a natural world guided by human rationality toward balanced or harmonious ecological as well as social ends. This philosophical vision has a historical pedigree in the western intellectual tradition. It reaches back to Hellenic philosophy as the concept of a world *nous*, a concept which, in Fichte's stirring prose, envisions consciousness "no longer as that stranger in Nature whose connection with existence is so incomprehensible; it is native to it, and indeed one of its necessary manifestation."(22)

Ecocommunity, in turn, could scarcely be exemplified by any urban aggregate or, for that matter, any rural houshold that happens to acquire its resources from solar and wind installations. If the word "ecocommunity" is to have more than a strictly logistical and technical meaning, it must describe a decentralized community that allows for direct popular administration, the efficient return of wastes to the countryside, the maximum use of local resources — and yet it must be large enough to foster cultural diversity and psychological uniqueness. The community, like its technology, is itself the ensemble of its libertarian institutions, humanly-scaled structures, the diverse productive tasks that expose the individual to industrial, craft, and horticultural work, in short, the rounded community that the Hellenic *polis* was meant to be in the eyes of its great democratic statesmen. It is within such a decentralized community, sensitively tailored to its natural ecosystem, that we could hope to develop a new sensibility toward the world of life and a new level of self-consciousness, rational action, and foresight.

Just as we are warned by many scholars that merely structural terms like "city-state" do not fully capture the meaning of a civic fraternity like the *polis*, so morally neutral words like "intermediate technology" and "environment" do not capture the meaning of ethically-charged concepts like "ecotechnology" and "ecocommunity." A blending of ecotechnologies and ecocommunities would more closely resemble a balanced, rationally-guided ecosystem than a passive ensemble of physical surroundings with the "appropriate technology" to sustain it. Indeed, until our estranged species with its increasing sense of alienation toward any earthly surrroundings can achieve this balanced, rationally guided ecosystem, it is doubtful if we can meaningfully describe any environment as a suitable habitat for people, much less a truly human one.

December 1976

FOOTNOTES

1. E.F. Schumacher, *Small is Beautiful* (Harper & Row, New York, 1974).

2. To rephrase the title of Tony Mullaney's two-part article, "If Big is Not Good, Small is Not Beautiful," *Peacework* (a New England publication of the American Friends Service Committee), December 1975 (No. 37) and January 1976 (No. 38). Mullaney's criticism is very trenchant but, unfortunately, it overstates the case for centralism and planning in the Third World with the result that it tends to veer over to the position of Marxian criticisms of Schumacher.

3. Murray Bookchin, "Energy, 'Ecotechnocracy' and Ecology," *Liberation*, Vol. 19, No. 2 (1975), pp. 29-33, and published elsewhere in this book.

4. See Chogyam Trungpa, *Cutting Through Spiritual Materialism* (Shambhala, Berkeley, Ca., 1973).

5. See C.K. Yang, "The Functional Relationship between Confucian Thought and Chinese Religion," in *Chinese Thought and Institutions* (edited by John K. Fairbanks (The University of Chicago Press, Chicago, 1957), pp. 270-71, for the larger context of rationalism and Asian philosophy.

6. R. G. Collingwood, *The Idea of Nature* (Oxford University Press, New York, 1945), pp. 29-92.

7. Plato, *The Laws*, V, 737e, 738a (Trevor J. Saunders translation).

8. Aristotle, *The Politics*, VIII, 5, 1326b25 (B. Jowett translation).

9. Aristotle, *The Politics*, VIII, 5, 1326b15 (H. Racham translation in Loeb Classical library). The latter translation has been selected, here, for its greater accuracy.

10. In Aristotle, this intimacy of association advances beyond mere institutional relationships to the level of friendship. "Political friendship is not an agreement of opinion as it might occur between strangers, or an agreement on scientific propositions," observes Eric Vogelin; "it is an agreement between citizens as to their interests, an agreement on policies and their execution." Eric Vogelin, *Plato and Aristotle* (Lousiane State University Press, Baton Rouge, La., 1957), p. 321.

11. See Summer Chilton Powell, *The Puritan Village* (Wesleyan University Press, Middletown, Conn., 1963); Michael Zucherman, *Peaceable Kingdoms* (Vintage Books, New York, 1970); Kenneth Lockridge, *A New England Town* (W. W. Norton & Co., New York, 1970).

12. J. J. Rousseau, *The Social Contract* (Modern Library, New York, 1950), pp. 94-96. "In Greece, all that the people had to do, it did for itself; it was constantly assembled in the public square," Rousseau observes. "... the moment a people allows itself to be represented," he adds, "it is no longer free: it no longer exists."

13. Kropotkin did not actually model his image of a decentralized society on the Hellenic polis, but rather on the medieval communes. The author owes a debt to the German radical theorist, the late Josef Weber, who used the expression "the new or modern polis" in personal discussions that date back to the 1950s.

14. Peter Kropotkin, *Fields, Factories and Workshops* (Benjamin Blom Publishers, New York, 1968 reissue of 1913 edition). An abridged version, updated by commentaries, has been prepared by Colin Ward and published by Harper & Row, New York, 1974.

15. Max Horkheimer and Theodor W. Adorno, The *Dialectic of Enlightenment* (Seabury Press, New York, 1972), pp. 151-52, 155, 166-67. The discussion is masterful in its profundity and, considering the year in which it was written (1944), its predictive insights.

16. Aden and Marjorie Meinel, "A Briefing on Solar Power Farms," presented before the Task Force on Energy of the House of Representatives Committee on Science and Astronautics, Washington, D.C., 6 March 1972; Steve Baer, *Sunspots* (Zomeworks Corp., Albuquerque, N. M., 1975), p. 97; William E. Heronemus, "The United States Energy Crisis: Some Proposed Gentle Solutions," presented before a joint conference of The American Society of Mechanical Engineers and The Institute of Electrical and Electronic Engineers, West Springfield, Mass., 12 January 1972; R. Buckminister Fuller: Tetrahedral City, 1966 in Justus Dahinden, *Urban Structures for the Future* (Praeger Publishers, New York, 1972), pp. 162-63; Moshe Safdie, *Beyond Habitat* (The MIT Press, Cambridge, Mass., 1970).

17. Wilson Clark, *Energy for Survival* (Anchor Books, New York, 1974), pp. 412-16, 426-27.

18. E. Al Gutkind, *Community and Environment* (Philosophical Library, New York, 1954), p. 9. For a lengthy discussion of the distinction between ecology and environementalism, see Murray Bookchin, "Toward an Ecological Society," *Philosophica*, Vol. 13, No. 1 (1974), pp. 73-85. This paper, originally delivered as a lecture at the University of Michigan in 1973, explores the concept of "ecotechnology" and "ecocommunity," terms which the author coined in the 1960s and which have entered into the vernacular of the new technologists in forms that have no relation to their original meaning. The essay appears in this book.

19. Ted Morgan, "Looking for: Epoch B," *The New York Times Magazine*, 29 February 1976, p. 32.

20. John Todd (interview) in *What Do We Use For Lifeboats?* published as part of a collection of interviews by Harper & Row, New York, 1976, p. 76.

21. Conversations between the author and John Todd of The New Alchemy Institute and Gil Friend of The Institute of Local Self-Reliance, 5 March 1976.

22. Johann Gottlieb Fichte, *Lie Bestimmung des Menschen* (1800), translated by R. M. Chisholm as *The Vocation of Man* (The Bobbs-Merrill Co., New York, 1956), p. 20.

Reprinted with permission from *Habitat International* Pergamon Press, Ltd.

Self-Management and the New Technology

Self-management in all its rich and varied meanings has always been closely wedded to technical developments — often to an extent that has not received the explicit attention it deserves. By emphasizing the association between the two, I do not mean to advance a crude, reductionist theory of technological determinism. People are completely social beings. They develop values, institutions, and cultural relationships that either foster or inhibit the evolution of technics. It need hardly be emphasized that basic technical inventions such as the steam engine, so vital to capitalist, indeed to early industrial society were known to the Hellenistic world more than two millenia ago. That this major source of power was never used as more than a plaything attests to the enormous hold of ancient values and culture on the evolution of technics generally and specifically on eras that were not assimilated to a market-oriented rationality.

But it would be equally crude and in its own way reductionist to deny the extent to which technics, once it is established in one form or another, contributes to humanity's definitions and interpretations of self-management. This is evident today when self-management is conceived primarily in economic terms such as "workers' control," "industrial democracy," "workers participation," indeed, even as radical anarchosyndicalist demands for "*economic* collectivization." The fact that this unadorned economic interpretation of self-management has pre-empted other interpretations of the term, notably forms reminiscent of the municipal confederations of medieval society, the French revolutionary sections of 1793, and the Paris Commune, will be discussed later. This much is clear: when we speak of "self-management," today, we usually mean one or another form of syndicalism. We mean an economic formation that involves the way in which labour is organized, tools and machines deployed, and material resources rationally allocated. In short, we mean technics.

Once we bring technics into the situation, however, we open the way to a number of paradoxes that cannot be dismissed by bellicose rhetoric and moral platitudes. If the role of technics in shaping society and thinking has often been overstated by writers as disparate in their social views as Marshall MacLuhan and Jacques Ellul, its influence in forming social institutions and cultural attitudes cannot be dismissed. The highly economistic meaning we so often impart of the term "self-management" is itself damning evidence of the extent to which industrial society "industrializes" the meaning to terms.* The words "self-management" become intellectually dissociated into their components and ideologically opposed to each other. "Management" tends to pre-empt "self"; administration tends to assume sovereignty over individual autonomy. Owing to the influence of technocratic values over thinking, self-hood — so crucial to the meaning of libertarian management in all aspects of life — is subtly displaced by the virtues of efficient administrative strategies. Accordingly, "self-management" is increasingly promoted for functional rather than liberatory reasons, even by the most committed syndicalists. We are urged to think that "small is beautiful" because it yields the conservation of "energy" rather than a human scale that renders society comprehensible and controllable by all. Self-activity and self-management are seen as aspects of industrial logistics that resolve economic and technical problems rather than moral and social ones. Thus the very technocratic society that denies selfhood to humanity establishes the terms of discourse for those who wish to replace it by a libertarian one. It reaches into the sensibility of its most radical opponents by establishing the parameters for their critique and practice, in short, by "industrializing" syndicalism.

No less paradoxical is the limited nature of "self-management"

---

* Consider the degree to which cybernetics has entered into commonplace linguistic usage, for example, as evidence of this development. We no longer ask for an interlocutor's "advice" but for his or her "feedback" and we no longer engage in a "dialogue" but solicit an individual's "input." This sinister invasion of the world of "logos," in its wide-ranging meaning as speech and reason, by the electronic terminology of modern technocracy represents not only the subversion of human interaction at every level of social experience but of personality itself as an organic and developmental phenomenon. LaMettrie's *Man a Machine* enters his modern estate as a cybernetic system — not merely in his physical attributes but in his very subjectivity.

itself when it leaves its technical premises unquestioned. Can we comfortably assume that collectivized enterprises controlled by workers have changed the social, cultural, and intellectual status of workers to a decisive degree? Do factories, mines and large-scale agricultural enterprises become domains of freedom because their operations are now managed — however anarchistically — by workers' collectives? By eliminating economic exploitation have we actually eliminated social domination? By removing class rule have we removed hierarchical rule? To state the issue bluntly: can present-day technics remain substantially the way it is while the men and women who operate it are expected to undergo significant transformation as human beings?

Here, notions such as "workers' control," "industrial democracy," and "workers' participation" face the challenge of an exploitative technics in its sharpest form. Perhaps no more compelling argument has been advanced against syndicalist notions of economic organization than the fact that modern technology is intrinsically authoritarian. Such arguments, as we shall see, come not merely from overtly bourgeois ideologists but from seemingly "radical" ones as well. What underpins these arguments from all parts of the political spectrum is a shared assumption that technics is socially neutral. The functional view that technics is merely the instrumental means for humanity's "metabolism" with nature is broadly accepted as given. That factories are the loci of authority is reduced to a "natural fact" — in short, a fact beyond the purview of ethics and social consideration.

Tragically, when ethical views of technics are removed from their historic and social context, the functional view tends to prevail for precisely the same reason that the ethical view fails — for both views assume that technology is always a matter of mere design, a "given" that is either efficient or not. Only recently have we begun to see a popular questioning of technics as merely "given," notably with respect to nuclear power installations. The notion that even the "peaceful atom" is *intrinsically* a "demonic atom" has become very widespread as a result of the Three-Mile-Island meltdown at Harrisburg. What is perhaps most significant about this nuclear "incident" is that critics of nuclear power have focused public attention on new, ecologically sound, and implicitly more *humanistic* technologies that await development and application. The distinction between "good" and "bad" technics — that is, an *ethical* evaluation of technical development — has taken root on a scale that is unknown at any time in the past since the early Industrial Revolution.

What I propose to emphasize, here, is the need for proponents of self-management to deal with technics in the same *ethical* context that anti-nuclear groups deal with energy resources. I propose to ask if the factory, mine, and modern agricultural enterprises can legitimately be regarded as an acceptable arena for a libertarian concept of self-management — and if not, what alternatives exist that can legitimate that concept on a new ethical, social, and cultural level. This responsibility becomes all the more crucial today because "self-management" has increasingly been denatured to mean a mere technical problem in industrial management, one that renders it palatable to sophisticated sections of the bourgeoisie and to neo-Marxian tendencies. "Workers' control" may even become fashionable management strategy as long as workers consent to remain merely workers. Their "decisions" may be viewed as desirable — indeed, "productive" — if they contribute to the technical rationalization of industrial operations, however "radical" the rhetoric and colourful the institutions within which they "manage" industry.

Yet if self-management remains no more than another form of management of existing forms of technics; if toil is socialized or collectivized rather than transmuted into meaningful self-expression — and if these feeble, indeed, insidious, modifications of the material conditions of life are equated with "freedom" — self-management becomes a hollow goal. Viewed from this perspective, the very concept of self-management requires reexamination if freedom is itself to be rescued from the semantics of technocracy. We would do well to examine some basic conceptions of "self" and "management" — particularly in relation to technological development — before the two words are recoupled again as a liberatory social ideal.

Selfhood has its authentic origins in the Hellenic notion of *autonomia,* of "self-rule." The word "rule" deserves emphasis. That *autonomia* or "autonomy" has come, in our own time, to mean merely "independence" is evidence of our gross simplification of terms that often had a rich ethical meaning in pre-market eras. Greek "selfhood" was intimately associated with rule, *social* rule, the capacity of the individual to directly participate in governing society even before he could manage his economic affairs. The very term "economics," in fact, denoted the management of the household — the *oikos* — rather than society, a somewhat inferior, even if necessary, activity by comparison with participation in the community or *polis.*

Selfhood, I would claim, was thus associated with individual claims *to power within society* rather than the management of material life. To be sure, the ability to exercise power within society — and thereby to be an *individual,* a "self" — presupposed the leisure and material freedom afforded by a well-managed household. But once this *oikos* was granted, "selfhood" presupposed considerably more, and these presuppositions are tremendously significant for our own age, when the self has become grossly powerless and individuality has become little more than a euphemism for egotism.

To begin with, selfhood implied the recognition of individual competence. Autonomia or "self-rule" would have been completely meaningless if the fraternity of selves that composed the Hellenic *polis* (notably, the Athenian democracy) was not constituted of men of strong character who could discharge the formidable responsibilities of "rule." The *polis,* in short, rested on the premise that its citizens could be entrusted with "power" because they possessed the personal capacity to use power in a trustworthy fashion. The education of citizens into rule was therefore an education into personal competence, intelligence, moral probity, and social commitment. The *ecclesia* of Athens, a popular assembly of the citizen body that met at least forty times a year, was the testing ground of this education into self-rule; the *agora,* the public square where Athenians transacted almost every aspect of their affairs, was its authentic school. Selfhood, in effect, originated first and foremost in a politics of personality, not in processes of production.* It is almost meaningless etymologically to dissociate the word "self" from the capacity to exercise control over social life, to "rule" in the Greek sense of the term. Denied its characterological meaning — its connotations of personal fortitude and moral probity — selfhood dissolves into mere "egohood," that hollow, often neurotic shell of human personality that lies strewn amidst the wastes of bourgeois society like the debris of its industrial operations.

To divest selfhood of these personal traits is to be irresponsibly footloose with any term to which the word "self" is appended. "Self-activity," to use another common expression, implies the activation of these strong character traits in social processes. It, too, rests on the demanding foundations of a politics of personality that is educative of the individual, formative of his or her capacity to intervene and directly alter social events, and, carried into action itself, to enter into a shared social practice. Without the personal judgement, moral force, will, and sensibility to be active in this *full* and *direct* sense of the term, such a self would atrophy and its activity would be reduced to a relationship based on obedience and command. Self-activity, in this sense, can only be *direct* action. But direct action, like rule, can only be understood as the predicates of a self that is engaged in the social processes these terms denote. Self, the education toward selfhood, and the exercise of selfhood — almost as a daily gymnastic in the making of individuality — is an end in itself, the culmination of what we so flippantly call "self-actualization."

Anarchist organization and its policy of direct action is, by definition, the educational instrument for achieving these time-honoured goals. It is the *agora*, as it were, for a politics of personality. The "affinity group" form, at its best, is a unique form of consociation based on a mutual recognition of competence in all its members or, at least, the need to attain competence. Where such groups cease to educate toward this goal, they become mere euphemisms. Worse, they "produce" militants rather than anarchists, subordinates rather than selves. Optimally, the

---

* It should be evident to the reader that I use the word "politics" in the Hellenic meaning of the terms, as the administration of the *polis*, not in any electoral sense. The administration of the *polis* was seen by the Athenians as a continual educative process as well as a vital social activity in which each citizen was expected to participate.

anarchist affinity group is an ethical union of free, morally strong individuals who can directly participate in consensual rule because they are competent and live in a mutual recognition of each other's competence. Only when they have attained this condition and thereby sufficiently revolutionized *themselves* as selves can they profess to be revolutionaries — to be the citizens of a future libertarian society.

I have dwelt upon these aspects of the term "self" — and only space prevents me from dealing with it in the detail it deserves — because it has become the weakest link in the concept of "self-management." Until such selves are minimally attained, self-management becomes a contradiction in terms. Self-management without the "self" that is expected to engage in this "managing," in fact, turns into its very opposite: hierarchy based on obedience and command. The abolition of class rule in no way challenges the existence of such hierarchical relations. They may exist within the family between sex and age groups, among disparate ethnic groups, within bureaucracies and in administrative social groups that profess to be executing the policies of a libertarian organization or a libertarian society. There is no way to immunize *any* social formation, even the most dedicated anarchist groups, from hierarchical relations except through the wisdom of "self-consciousness" that comes from the "self-actualization" of the individual's potentiality for selfhood. This has been the message of western philosophy from Socrates to Hegel. Its plea for wisdom and self-consciousness as the sole guide to truth and insight remains even more compelling today than it did in earlier, more articulated social eras.

Before turning to the challenge posed by technics in the process of "self-formation," it is important to remember that self-rule — *autonomia* — historically precedes the modern notion of "self-management." Ironically, the fact that *autonomia* denotes "independence" with its implications of a free-wheeling materialistic bourgeois ego rather than a socially involved individual is significant. Self-rule applies to society as a whole, not merely to the economy. Hellenic selfhood found its fullest expression in the *polis* rather than the *oikos*, in the social community rather than the technical. Once we cross the threshold of history, self-management is the management of villages, neighbourhoods, towns, and cities. The technical sphere of life is conspicuously secondary to the social. In the two revolutions that open the modern era of secular politics—the American and French—self-management emerges in the libertarian town meetings that swept from Boston to Charleston and the popular sections that assembled in Parisian *quatiers*. The intensely *civic* nature of self-management stands in marked contrast to its crassly *economic* nature today. It would be redundant, given Kropotkin's impressive work in this field, to explore earlier social periods for evidence of this juxtaposition or enter into additional details. The fact remains that self-management had a broader meaning in libertarian practice than it has at the present time.

Here, technics must be assigned a greater role in producing this change than it ordinarily receives. The tool-using artisan nature of pre-capitalist societies always provided a material space for a subterranean libertarian development, even when politically centralized states had attained a considerable degree of growth. Beneath the imperial institutions of European and Asian states lay the clannic, village, and guild systems of consociation that neither army nor tax farmer could effectively demolish. Both Marx and Kropotkin include classic descriptions of this archaic social network—an ancient, seemingly faceless world impervious to change or destruction. The Hellenic *polis* and the Christian congregation added the rich tints of individuality—of selfhood and self-consciousness—to this tapestry until self-management acquired the resplendent colours of a highly individuated world. In the urban democracies of central Europe and Italy, as in the *polis* of the Greek promontory, municipal self-management in towns scaled to comprehensible human dimensions reached a colourful, if brief, effloresence in the fullest sense of the term. The norms of a socially committed individualism were established that were to haunt the American and French revolutions centuries later and define the most advanced concepts of self and management into our own time.

There can be no return to these periods—either socially or technically. Their limits are only too clear to excuse an atavistic yearning for the past. But the social and technical forces that were to destroy them are even more transitory than we tend to believe. I will focus, here, on the technical dimension to the exclusion of the institutional. Of the technical changes that separate our own era from past ones, no single "device" was more important than the least "mechanical" of all — the factory. At the risk of casting all caution to the winds, I will aver that neither Watt's steam engine nor Bessemer's steel furnace was more significant than the simple process of rationalizing labour into an industrial engine for the production of commodities. Machinery, in the conventional sense of the term, heightened this process vastly — but the systematic rationalization of labour to serve labour in ever-specialized tasks totally demolished the technical structure of self-managed societies and ultimately of workmanship — the "selfhood" of the economic realm.

We must pause to weigh the meaning of these remarks. Artisanship relies on skill and a surprisingly small toolkit. Skill, in fact, is its real premise: training and long experience in a rich variety of expressive, often artistic tasks; highly purposeful, often intellectual activity; dexterity of fingers and coordination of body; the challenge of a rich variety of stimuli and subtle expressions of self. Its background is the work song, its spirituality the pleasure of articulating in raw materials their own latent possibilities for acquiring a pleasing and useful form. Not surprisingly, Plato's deity is literally a craftsman who imprints the forms on matter. The presuppositions that support these artisan traits are obvious — a roundedness and fullness of personal virtuosity that is ethical, spiritual, and esthetic as well as technical. True craftsmanship is loving work, not onerous toil. It arouses the senses, not dulls them. It adds dignity to humanity, not demeans it. It gives free range to the spirit, not aborts it. Within the technical sphere it is the expression of selfhood *par excellence* — of individuation, consciousness, and freedom. These words dance throughout every account of well-crafted objects and artistic works.

The factory worker lives merely on the memory of such traits. The din of the factory drowns out every thought, not to speak of any song; the division of labour denies the worker any relationship to the commodity; the rationalization of labour dulls his or her senses and exhausts his or her body. There is no room whatever for any of the artisan's modes of expression — from artistry to spirituality — other than an interaction with objects that reduces the worker to a mere object. The distinction between artisan and worker hardly requires elucidation. But two significant facts stand out that turn the transformation from craft to factory into a social and characterological disaster. The first fact is the dehumanization of the worker into a mass being; the second is the worker's reduction into a hierarchical being.

There is a certain significance in the fact that this devolution of the artisan into a mere toiler was adduced by Marx and Engels as evidence of the proletariat's intrinsically revolutionary traits. And it is precisely in this gross misjudgment of the proletariat's destiny that syndicalism often follows in the wake of Marxism. Both ideologies share the notion that the factory is the "school" of revolution (in the case of syndicalism, of social reconstruction) rather than its undoing. Both share a common commitment to the factory's structural role as a source of social mobilization.

For better or worse, Marx and Engels express these views more clearly than syndicalist — and anarchosyndicalist — theorists. Conceived as a mass being or a class being, Marx's proletariat becomes a mere instrument of history. Its very depersonalization into a category of political economy ironically frees it of every human trait but need, "urgent, no longer disguisable, absolutely imperative *need*..." As pure "class" or social "agent," comparable to the pure, disenchanted social world produced by capitalism, it has no *personal* will but only a *historical* one. It is an instrument of history in the strictest sense of the term. Thus, to Marx, "The question is not what this or that proletarian, or even the whole proletariat *considers* as its aim. The question is *what the proletariat is,* and what, consequent on that *being,* it will be compelled to do."

Here, being is separated from person, action from will, social activity from selfhood. Indeed, it is the very divestiture of the proletariat's selfhood — its dehumanization — that gives it the quality of a "universal" social agent, one that gives it almost transcendental social qualities. My quotations, taken from *The Holy Family* of the early 1840s, were to permeate Marx's writings for decades to follow. Without bearing them in mind during readings of Marx in his later works, these works become unintelligible — all rhetoric about the moral superiority of the proletariat notwithstanding to the contrary.

Accordingly, it is not surprising to find that for Marx the factory provides a virtually ecclesiastical arena for the schooling of this social "agent." Here, technics functions not only as a means for humanity's metabolism with nature but for humanity's metabolism with itself. Together with the centralization of industry through competition and expropriation, "the mass of misery, oppression, slavery, degradation and exploitation grows; but with this there also grows the revolt of the working class, a class constantly increasing in numbers, and *trained, united and organized by the very mechanism of the capitalist process of production*," declares Marx in the closing pages of volume one of *Capital*. "The monopoly of capital becomes a fetter upon the mode of production which has flourished alongside and under it... This integument is burst asunder. The knell of capitalist private property sounds. The expropriators are expropriated." (My emphasis — M.B.)

The importance of these famous lines by Marx lies in the revolutionary function they assign to the factory, its role in training, uniting, and organizing the proletariat "by the very mechanism of the capitalist process of production." The factory, one might very well say, almost "fabricates" revolution with the same impersonality that it "fabricates" commodities. But even more significant is the fact that is "fabricates" the proletariat itself. This specific view is intrinsic to syndicalism as well. Paradoxically, the factory structure in both cases is not merely a technical structure; it is also a social structure. Marx tends to disdain it historically as a domain of necessity, one whose invasion into life must ultimately be attenuated by the free-time required for communism. Syndicalism hypostasizes this structure; it forms the contours for a libertarian society. Both, however, underscore its significance as a technical arena for social organization, whether it be for the proletariat as a class or for society as a whole.

We arrive at the troubling fact that this structure, far from functioning as a force for social change, actually functions as a force for social regression. Marxism and syndicalism alike, by virtue of their commitment to the factory as a revolutionary social arena, must recast self-management to mean the industrial management of the self. For Marxism this poses no problem. Selfhood can never exist within the factory walls. The factory serves not only to mobilize and train the proletariat but to dehumanize it. Freedom is to be found not within the factory but rather outside it. For freedom "cannot consist of anything else but of the fact that socialized man, the associated producers, regulate their interchange with nature rationally, bring it under their common control, instead of being ruled by it as by some blind power..." Marx observes in volume three of *Capital*. "But it always remains a realm of necessity. Beyond it begins that development of human power, which is its own end, the true realm of freedom, which, however, can flourish only upon that realm of necessity as its basis. The shortening of the working day is its fundamental premise."

Obviously, the factory conceived as a "realm of necessity" requires no need for self-management. Indeed, it is the very antithesis of a school for self-formation like the *agora* and the Hellenic notion of education. For contemporary Marxists to ape their syndicalist opponents by demanding "workers' control" of industry is a travesty of the very spirit of Marx's concept of freedom. It is to demean a great thinker in his own name on terms that are completely alien to his ideas. Appropriately, Engels, in his essay "On Authority," draws Marx's critique of anarchism to its harshest conclusions precisely on the basis of factory operations. Authority, conceived as "the imposition of the will of another upon ours," as "subordination," is unavoidable in any industrial society, including communism. It is a *natural* fact of modern technics, as indispensable (in Engels' view) as the factory itself. Engels then proceeds to detail this view against the anarchists with the philistine exactitude of the Victorian mind. Coordination of industrial operations presupposes subordination to command; indeed, to the "despotism" of automatic machinery and the "necessity of authority,... of *imperious* authority" to managerial command. (My emphasis — M.B.) Engels never fails us in our narrowest prejudices on this score. He deftly skips from the commanding role of cotton-spinning machinery to the "instantaneous and absolute obedience" required by the captain of a ship. Coordination is dutifully confused with command, organization with hierarchy, agreement with domination — indeed, "imperious" domination.

What is more interesting than the fallacies of Engels' essay is its insidious truths. The factory is, in fact, a realm of necessity — not a realm of freedom. It is a school for hierarchy, for obedience and command, not for a liberatory revolution. It reproduces the servility of the proletariat and undermines its selfhood, its capacity to transcend need. Accordingly, insofar as self-management, self-activity, and selfhood are the very essence of the "realm of freedom," they must be denied at the "material base" of society while they are presumably affirmed in its "superstructure" — at least as long as the factory and the technics of capitalist production are conceived *merely* as technics, as natural facts of production.

On the other hand, viewed as a social arena, we must further conceive that this dehumanized realm of necessity — riddled by "imperious authority" — can somehow enlarge the class consciousness of a dehumanized working being into a universal social consciousness; that this being, divested of all selfhood in its daily life of toil can recover the social commitment and competence puresupposed by a sweeping social revolution and a truly free society based on self-management in the broadest sense of the term. Finally, we must conceive that this free society can remove hierarchy in one realm while "imperiously" fostering it in another, perhaps more basic one. Carried to its fullest logic, the paradox assumes absurd proportions. Hierarchy, like overalls, becomes a garment that one discards in the "realm of freedom" only to don it again in the "realm of necessity." Like a see-saw, freedom rises and falls at the point where we place our social fulcrum — possibly at the center of the plank in one "stage" of history, closer to one end or another at other "stages, but in any event strictly measurable by the length of the "working day."

Syndicalism shares this fatal paradox no less than Marxism. Its redeeming virtue lies in its implicit awareness — virtually explicit in the works of Charles Fourier — that technics must be divested of its hierarchical and joyless character if society is to be freed of these burdens. With syndicalism, however, this awareness is often warped by its acceptance of the factory as the infrastructure of the new society within the old, as a model for working class organization, and as a school for the humanization of the proletariat and its mobilization as a revolutionary social force. Hence, technics raises a startling dilemma for libertarian concepts of self-management. From what source are workers — indeed, all dominated people such as women, young and elderly people, ethnic groups, and cultural communities — to acquire the subjectivity that fosters selfhood? What technologies can supplant the hierarchical mobilization of labour into factories? And finally, what constitutes "management" that involves the fostering of authentic competence, moral probity, and wisdom?

The answer to each of these questions would require a sizable work in itself. In this article, I will confine myself in cursory fashion to the second question: the new, potentially non-hierarchical technologies that could supplant the factory as the technics for a libertarian society — one which I identify with anarchocommunism.

Technics is no more a "natural fact" than our chemically treated food crops and our synthetically fermented beverages. Even Marx is obliged to treat it in a social context when he sees it in term of its class functions. Far from being a "given," it is potentially the most malleable of humanity's modes of "metabolizing" with nature. The institutions, values, and cultural shibboleths with which humans engage in a "metabolic" relationship with the natural world are often less amenable to change than the tools and machines that give them material tangibility. Their "primacy" over social relations, technological determinists notwithstanding to the contrary, is mythic. They are immersed in a social world of human intentions, needs, wills, and interactions.

The factory exhibits this social dimension with a vengeance. Its appearance in the world was determined not by strictly mechanical factors but organic ones. It was a means for *rationalizing* labour, not for *implementing* labour with tools. Once this fact is fully weighed, the factory ceases to enjoy the autonomy it acquires from Engels and his acolytes. It is a "realm of necessity" only insofar as a need remains for its existence. But this need is not strictly technical; to the contrary, it is largely social. The factory is the realm of hierarchy and domination, not the battleground of "man's" conflict with nature. Once its functions as an instrument of human domination are questioned, we can reasonably ask how valid is the "need" for its perpetuation. By the same token, money, weapons, and nuclear power plants are instruments of a society gone mad. Once the insanity of society is lifted, we can also ask how valid is the "need" for their perpetuation. "Need" itself is a socially conditioned phenomenon — a fact not unknown to Marx by any means — that may be intrinsically rational or irrational. *The "realm of necessity" thus has highly elastic, perhaps ineffable boundaries; in fact, it is as "necessary" socially as the vision one has of freedom. To separate one from the other inexorably is sheer ideology, for it may well be that freedom does not "base" itself on the "realm of necessity" but really determines it.*

To Fourier, this conclusion was implicit in the best lines of his writings. The two "realms" of necessity and freedom were resynthesized into a higher level of societal behavior and values in which joy, creativity, and pleasure were ends in themselves. Freedom had subsumed necessity and joy has subsumed toil. But such sweeping notions cannot be advanced abstractly. They must be established concretely — or else the rich possibilities of reality become elusive categories that deny the claims of imagination. Hence the enormous power of utopian thinking at its best : the ability to show almost visually what so often remains the abstractions of competing ideologies. Consider concretely, indeed utopistically, the alternatives that may turn arduous work into festive play : a harvest that is marked by dancing, feasting, singing, and loving contrasted with the monotony of gang labour or deadening mechanization. One form of harvesting reinforces community ; the other, isolation and a sense of oppression. The same task performed esthetics may be a work of art ; performed under the lash of domination, it becomes an ignominious burden. The identical task under conditions of freedom is an esthetic experience ; under conditions of domination, it becomes onerous toil. To assume that every arduous task must be a tormenting one is a social judgement that is determined by the social structure itself, not simply the technical conditions of work. The employer who demands silence from his employees is, in fact, an employer. The same work may be performed playfully, creatively, imaginatively, even artistically in the absence of social constraints that identify responsability with renunciation and efficiency with sobriety.

Elsewhere, I have assessed and inventoried the technical alternatives that are available to existing forms of technology.* Since this assessment, there is much I would add and much I would reject in the technical aspects of my account. Perhaps more important than any details which can now be found in such outstanding books like *Radical Technology* by British anarchists are the principles I would want to emphasize here. A new technology is emerging — a technology no less significant for the future than the factory is for the present. Potentially, it lends itself to a sifting of existing technics in terms of their ecological integrity and their impact on human freedom. On its own terms, it can be a highly decentralized technics that is human in scale, simple in construction, and naturalistic in orientation. It can acquire its energy from the sun and wind, from recycled wastes and replenishable "resources" such as timber. It affords the possibility of making food cultivation into a spiritually and materially rewarding form of gardening. It is restorative of the environment and, perhaps more significantly, of personal and communal autonomy.

This new technology may rightly be called a "people's technology." The French-intensive community gardens spontaneously opened by ghetto dwellers in gutted neighbourhoods of New York, the hand-crafted solar panels that are gradually appearing on the rooftops of tenements, the small windmills that have been reared aloft beside them to generale electric power — all, taken together, express new initiatives by ordinarily passive communities to reclaim control over the material conditions of their lives. What counts is not whether a food cooperative can replace a giant supermarket or a community garden the produce supplied by agribusiness or a wind-powered generator the electricity supplied by a smothering public utility. The cooperatives, gardens, and windmills are the technical *symbols* of a resurgence of selfhood that is ordinarily denied to the ghetto "masses" and a growing sense of competence that is ordinarily denied to a client citizenry. The factory image of the city, even of citizenship, has

---

* See "Toward a Liberatory Technology" in my *Post-Scarcity Anarchism* (Black Rose Books, 1977)

already gone so far in repressing the smallest sparks of public life that technical and institutional alternatives may be able to go far enough to restore a sense of self-management in its traditional civic forms.

If one grants the silence that exists in factories today, the most important voices for self-management in any popular sense are heard from the neighbourhoods of municipalities (perhaps its most traditional source), from feminist and ecological movements, from "masses" that have acquired a new stake in personal, cultural, sexual, and civic autonomy. The new technology to which I have alluded has not initiated this development. If anything, it may well be the result of a new sensibility of selfhood and competence that an overbearing technocratic society has produced as a result of its own repressive excesses. Solar and wind power and community gardens are vastly older technical strategies than the factory. That they have been revived as a people's technology suggests a driving need to disengage from a social system whose greatest weakness and strength is its all-encompassing nature. But these alternative technics provide a new, perhaps historic context for social change. They impart the *tangible* possibility for a recovery of self-management with all the rich nuances of the past, albeit without a return to the past. Their concreteness makes them thoroughly utopian, even realistically rather than visionary. Finally, as educative devices for community, they tend to create a politics of personality that compares only with the anarchist "affinity group" as an educative arena.

Alternatives are today in conflict on a scale comparable only to the breakdown of traditional society on the eve of the capitalist era. The same new technology can also become a corporate technology — the bases for solar power utilities, space satellites, and an "organic" agribusiness comparable only to the highly chemicalized one so prevalent today. The decentralized gardens, solar panels, windmills, and recycling centers can be centralized, industrialized, and structured along rationalized hierarchical lines. Neither Marxism nor syndicalism can comprehend the nature of these alternatives, much less their subtle implications. Yet rarely has there been a greater need for theoretical insight into the possibilities that lie before us, indeed, the historically new directions which humanity may follow. In the absence of a libertarian interpretation of these directions, of a libertarian *consciousness* that articulates the logic of this new technical framework, we may well witness the integration of a people's technology into a managerial and technocratic society. In which case, we will have been reduced like a Greek chorus to lamentations and incantations to a fate that leaves the future predetermined and cruelly destined to efface the entire human experience. This may be a heroic posture — but it is also a futile one.

June 1979

The myth of
city planning

City planning today lives within the tension of an historic contradiction: the idealization of urbanity as the *summum bonum* of social life and the crass realities of urban decay. In theory, at least, the city is revered as the authentic domain of culture, the strictly man-made social substance from which humanity fashions the essential achievements of consociation. In this tradition, the city is viewed as society distinguished from nature, territory from kinship, rationality from custom and myth, the civic compact of individuals from the archaic group cemented by the blood oath. Ideally conceived, the city is the arena for a mode of human propinquity that is freed from the deadening grip of custom, irrationality, the vicissitudes of natural contingency; in sum, the social domain in which the sovereign citizen is free to fashion her or his selfhood and personal destiny. Herein lies the utopian content of urban theory; and in truth, from an historic perspective, it would be difficult to dispute Max Horkheimer's assertion that the "fortunes of the individual have always been bound up with the development of urban society. The city dweller is the individual par excellence."[1]

Yet contemporary urban reality presents an entirely different picture. Today, urban history at its best grins scornfully at the modern city, and its ideals, tarnished beyond recognition, lie buried in the rubble of their own high precepts. No longer is the city nature domesticated, the arena of unfettered human propinquity, the space for individuality and rationality. The modern city reverts beyond even the archaic blood group to a herd territory of alienated humanity and to all that is demonic in human society. The city in our time is the secular altar on which propinquity and community are sacrificed to a lonely anonymity and privatized atomization; its culture is the debased creature of commodity production and the advertising agency, not the gathered wisdom of the mind; and its claims to freedom and individuality are mocked by the institutionalized manipulation of unknowing masses among whom crass egotism is the last residue of the selfhood that once formed the city's most precious human goals. Even the city's form — or lack of form — bespeaks the dissolution of its civic integrity. To say with Marx that the modern city urbanizes the land is testimony not so much to its dominance as to its loss of identity. For the city, by the very nature of the case, disappears when it becomes the whole, when it lacks the specificity provided by differentiation and delineability of form.

Caught in the contradiction between ideal and real, city planning emerges not merely as ideology but as myth. The myth originates in the very term "city planning," in the nomenclature and pedigree which this seeming discipline appropriates for itself. Juxtaposed to the megalopolis, to the formless urbanity that sprawls across the land and devours it, the word "city" has already become a euphemism, an erstwhile reality digested by what Lewis Mumford so justly calls the "anti-city." In dealing with the putative as fact, city planning enthrones the shadow of the real city in a futile effort to stake out a legacy to what is forever gone. Even more basely, it subtly devalues this memory in the very act of invoking it, for if the shadow must be presented as the real, the real must be degraded. Accordingly, city planning reduces all that is vital in the traditional city, including the ideal itself, to a deadening caricature — the megalopolis as "city," the non-city as the representation of its very antithesis. All the high standards of urbanity, as these have been developed over the centuries, are degraded to establish a false continuity between past and present, to offer up the death of the city as the token of its life.

The word "planning" merely compounds this grotesque act of violation. To the modern mind, "planning" implies rationality, a conceptual purposiveness that brings order to disorder, that reorganizes chance and contingency into humanly meaningful design. Behind the seeming rationality imparted to this word lies an inherent social irrationality. Under capitalism, "planning" is basically the conscious organization of scarcity amidst abundance, the attempt to impose a social nexus of want, denial, and toil on a technological system that, potentially at least, could remove all of these dehumanizing conditions from social life. Thus, "planning" emerges not only as the validation of the given — as opposed to revolution — but as the rationalization of the irrational. City planning does not escape from the contradictory nature of contemporary social planning as a whole. To the contrary, it is the application of rational technique to urbanity gone mad, the effort systematically to piece together a fragmentation that constitutes the very law of life of modern urbanity. Reinforcing the myth that the megalopolis is a city is the myth that planning can transcend its unquestioned social premises, that technique is a value in itself apart from the ends to which it is captive.

The critique of city planning can be true to itself only if it becomes a totalistic process of demystification, if it reaches into the social whole that yields the negation of the city. Its point of departure cannot be the techniques which the planner tries to place in the forefront of the discussion, a procedure which retains the illusory notion that design can be a substitute for the basic processes of social life. Critique must scrupulously examine the hidden premises which urban design assimilates. Accordingly, the megalopolis can no longer be examined in separation from the larger context of social development and the emergence of its urban ideals. To treat the city as an autonomous entity, apart from the social conditions which produce it, is to participate in the city planner's typical reification of urbanity, to isolate and objectify a habitat that is itself contingent and formed by other factors. Behind the physical structure of the city lies the social community — its workaday life, values, culture, familial ties, class relations, and personal bonds. To fail to consider how this hidden dimension of urbanity forms the structure of the city is as valueless, indeed misleading, as to ignore the role of the structure in reinforcing or undermining the social community. As a design isolate, the city is nothing but an archeological artifact; as the expression of a social community, it could well sum up the totality of a society's life processes.

These seemingly obvious considerations require emphasis because city planning is cursed by the nature of its origins: it usually emerges as a distinct discipline when the city has already become problematical. Before the city acquires a structural consciousness of itself as the unique object of self-study, its design and development are invariably functions of social processes other than urbanism. Not surprisingly, city planning wears a mien of introspection rather than innovation, all its futuristic pretensions aside. The problematically given predetermines the elaboration of the planner's techniques and designs. City planning, in effect, tries to "solve" problems, not remove them. It thereby retains the status quo in its solutions even when it seems most occupied in altering the urban structure, hence the mystifying role its ideology plays in modern social life. Critique must puncture this myth — not by denying the validity of design, but by relating it critically and in a revolutionary fashion to the social conditions of life.

Perhaps the first step in formulating a critique of city planning is to recover some sense of the urban tradition at its best, a tradition against which we can compare the thrust of contemporary planning and urban development. Without some notion of what was achieved by the city in the past, we tend to lose our perspective toward the extent to which it has declined in the present. This is not to say that any specific early city forms a paradigm on which we must model our own urban future; merely, that certain high standards were achieved and formulated that are valuable in themselves and which we may usefully regard as criteria for judging the direction that urban society has followed in our own time. A "model city" that might have existed prior to the modern city is a fiction, yet examples exist in the past that have an imperishable value of their own, examples which comprise, by their mere existence, a devastating critique of the degradation that afflicts contemporary cities.

What obviously makes urban space unique is that it provides a strictly human basis for association. Economic and social life ceases to depend exclusively on a sexual division of labour and kinship ties — the biological matrix of social life that segregates the labour process according to brute physical capacities and views the stranger as enemy — but rather is organized along territorial lines that open the possibility for social life as a function of self-worth and uniquely individual capacities, thereby establishing the basis for a community that is properly human and social. This development was a long and complex process of disengagement from specifically non-urban, indeed, highly biologically conditioned social organisms, a slow crystallization of civil society out of the family, clan, and tribe based on blood ties and a sexual division of labour. In this respect, the early cities with which we are most familiar were not authentically urban entities. Like Tenochtitlan in Indian Amercia, the city was essentially the religious and administrative center of a clan and tribal society, hierarchical, to be sure, and drifting toward bureaucratic modes of civic management, but nevertheless anchored in archaic naturalistic forms of social organization and based materially on a rural economy with dominant strata whose primary social interests were agrarian in character.

Looking toward the centers of our own civilization, this essentially agrarian type of city persists as the prehistory of urban society for thousands of years in the Near East and Asia. It becomes increasingly elaborated into administrative hierarchies and a more complex division of labour, without changing its intrinsically rural character. The city may divest the clan of any administrative function in civic management; it may collect thousands of artisans, priests, bureaucrats, nobles, and soldiers within its confines; indeed, it may resemble the modern city structurally and in terms of its size and density of population. Yet this kind of city belongs to urban prehistory in the sense that its social wealth consists primarily of agricultural surpluses and its rulers are defined by their roots in the countryside rather than the town. Accordingly, its internal market is poorly developed and its merchant class is a subordinated stratum in the service of agrarian rulers. The countryside dominates the town just as thousands of years later, in our own era, the town will dominate the countryside. In their monumental architectural forms these cities express the power of agrarian interests. Their civic structure and social relations, reinforced by religious precepts and tradition, imply the denial of individuality, indeed, the incapacity of the individual to find self-expression in a psychological space of her or his own, apart from the suzerainty of the supreme ruler. The ruler's sole claim to personality as the embodiment of the archaic communal conditions of life effaces the right of personality to the obedient mass below. Hegel quite appropriately describes the "gorgeous edifices" of this era as the expressions of a world "in which we find all rational ordinances and arrangements, but in such a way, that individuals remain as mere accidents." These ordinances and arrangements "revolve round a centre, round the sovereign, who, as patriarch — not as despot in the sense of the *Roman* Imperial Constitution — stands at the head." As Hegel goes on to note: "The glory of Oriental conception is the One Individual as that substantial being to which all belongs, so that no other individual has a separate existence, or mirrors himself in his subjective freedom."[2]

Not until we arrive at the Hellenic *polis* do we find a mode of civic life that acquires its own mainsprings of development and an urban organism that acknowledges the individuality of all its citizens, indeed, that promotes individuality without denying its base in an integrated social community. I do not want to romanticize or idealize the *polis*. The Hellenic city was reared in no small measure on the harsh confinement of women to the domestic sphere and its degradingly mundane chores. The leisure that made it possible for the citizen to fully participate in civic affairs depended partly upon slave labour. The *polis* was also a class society even within the citizen body itself, which conferred material benefits on the few that were largely denied to the many. Moreover, it was the closed fraternity of the *demos*, of the ancestral citizen, which, although guaranteeing safety and legal protection to the stranger, denied him any role in the management of its political life.

Yet, after all these qualifications are noted — and they are characteristic of the ancient world as a whole — we cannot help but admire the extent to which Hellenic civic rationality contained, and in many ways surmounted, its own archaic roots. That women were confined to the household, that the muscles of slaves made it possible for the citizen to acquire the free time for reflection and civic activity, that the stranger performed those commercial functions which temporarily insulated the *demos* from the debasing effects of trade and self-interest, are the consequences not merely of an archaic tradition that reaches back to tribal life, but perhaps more compellingly, of an undeveloped technological base and meagre agricultural resources. Tradition, in fact, often becomes a thin rationalization for a real poverty of material resources — and Greek thought reveals a surprisingly secular candor about the relationship between the two, as one can glean from a reading of Thucydides and Aristotle. Yet, paradoxically, the very agricultural poverty of Greece made the *polis* possible as a fairly independent urban entity. The poor soil of the Hellenic promontory and the isolation fostered by its rugged, mountainous terrain precluded the development of the strong centralized agrarian power we encounter in the fertile, agriculturally rich river valleys of the Near East and Orient. Accordingly, to a degree virtually unknown up to the classical era, the *polis* could create and enlarge a uniquely urban space of its own — not as a society in which the land dominated the city or the city the land, but as an almost artistic equipoise of town and country, and psychologically, a balance that reflected the outlook of the yeoman farmer and urban citizen harmoniously united in a single personality.

From these conditions of life, I believe, emerges the Hellenic notion of *autarchia* which, apart from its popular economic connotations of material self-sufficiency, implies for the Greek a balance between mind and body, needs and resources, individual and society. Neither collectivity nor subjectivity are unconditional; the Hellenic individual is, in microcosm, the society of which he is a part. But this relationship implies no denial of individual uniqueness; merely, that the wholeness and roundedness of the individual is a function of the *polis*, a civic entity that includes not only the city proper but its rural environs. The relationship, in effect, is reciprocal and mutually reinforcing. To speak of the priority of the community or the individual over each other is to project our own sense of social alienation back to Hellenic times, for the very essence of the *polis* is its integration of the two. Greek individuality is an integrated constellation of the personal and social, not a separation of the two components into an antagonistic dualism. The *polis*, far from establishing a priority over personality, is at once its constitutive material and the laboratory for its elaboration. We grossly misread Hellenic dualism when we permeate it with our own anxious sense of "apartness" and polarity, for this dualism is always synthesized by Hellenic culture, hence the enormous difficulties we encounter in classifying Greek philosophy into "materialistic" and "idealistic" schools of thought.

The integration of individual and society is clearly revealed by the very structure of the *polis* itself and its theoretical conception of urbanism. The underlying theory of civic management is amateurism — the accessibility of virtually all organs of power to the citizen, the conscious despecialization of municipal agencies, the formulation of policy in face-to-face assemblies, and the use of the lot in the selection of public officials. The civic structure both affirms individuality and contains it. By the unimpaired expression which this structure gives to the citizen, it individuates him along social lines. Thus, life is to be lived not in the home but in the *agora* — the municipal square and market place — where matters of state become subjects of personal talk. Ironically, the fact that politics becomes "gossip" does not degrade politics but personalizes it and gives it a vitally existential dimension. The remarkable power of Aristophanic mockery is its capacity to interpret immense themes in the rough jargon of the public square. This desanctification of great themes, their rough-and-ready vernacularization, implies not a debasement of important ideas, but a largeness of mind in the community itself, an acknowledgement of its capacity to discuss them and a conscious despecialization of thought as the preserve of an elite. The *agora*, in turn, prepares the way for the *ecclesia*, the assembly of all citizens which convenes each tenth of the year. Here, in the open hillside of the *pnyx*, the citizen body assembles to debate the policies of the community. The practice of formulating policy in the open reveals the essential commitment of the *polis* to public purview and face-to-face relationships.

We find, here, a transcendence of the city that is not often made in the historical literature on urban society. Until the Hellenic era, the city had a typically magical or cosmological orientation; structurally, in the layout of its streets and in the symbolism of its architecture, it provided testimony to the authority of natural forces and suprahuman powers. Technochtitlan is laid out according to a traditional orientation along the cardinal points, an orientation we find not only throughout Eastern cities but even in Rome. By contrast, the Hellenic mind turned its civic outlook from nature and cosmology to man by adding a vividly humanistic dimension to the largely religious concepts of Eastern urbanism. Athens, like the free people who nurtured it, was a spontaneous civic creation. The apparent "anarchy" of the city's residential quarters marks a sharp break with an earlier urban outlook that placed nature and the cosmos above human beings. Dwellings are located where they are simply because the locations are places where *people* live — not "planned" according to recipes contrived by a priesthood. Location is a function of life and sociability, of community and intercourse freely and spontaneously expressed, not of magic or religious cosmology. The Hellenic sense of space is completely humanistic and communitarian; its pell-mell character suggests that the Greeks found their civic fulfillment more in themselves and in their interrelationships than in the privatized domain of their dwellings and work places.

If territoriality is conceived merely as the historic solvent of blood ties, then the Greek sense of space added a uniquely positive dimension to this conception that transcends it. A territory defined by human propinquity and intercourse implies the complete subordination of territoriality to the people who occupy an area — the humanized space of a true community that is internalized and acquires a subjective character, not merely a geographic one. Thus, as Zimmern observes, wherever the ancient Greeks came together there was a *polis*, that is, a free community, and it mattered little where it was located. When the *polis* finally passed into the shadows of history, it mattered little if or where they came together: the *polis* was gone forever. The abstract externalized sense of territoriality that marks the modern city, like the priority it gives to design over community, is in every sense an urban atavism. If the priests of pre-Hellenic urbanism were architects who imposed a cosmological design on the city, the architects of modern urbanism are priests whose designs are crassly utilitarian. Both are architects of the mythic insofar as they subserve the human essence of the city — its communitarian dimension — to suprahuman or inhuman ends.

A *polis* so large that it transcended a scale comprehensible to the citizen meant that it became merely territorial and vitiated its goal as a community. Accordingly, Aristotle establishes the rule that the *polis* should properly house "the largest number which suffices for the purposes of life and can be taken in at a single view."(3) In sharp contrast to the modern metropolitan impulse to unlimited growth — an impulse that Hegel would call a "bad infinity" — the Hellenic impulse always emphasized limit, and the *polis* was always limited by what the Greek could take in "at a single view." This high regard for limit, E. A. Gutkind observes, "dominates Greek town planning to such a degree that, to give only one example, Syracuse at the time of its greatest expansion consisted of five different towns, each surrounded by its own wall. Strabo called it Pentapolis."(4)

Space limitations do not make it possible to discuss the reasons why the *polis* declined except to remind the reader that it was a class society and hence an inherently contradictory one. Eventually it fell victim to a growing Mediterranean commerce that undermined its most precious civic values while precluding its development along authentically bourgeois lines. The urban values of the *polis* appear again, more than a millenium later, in the medieval town — but only intuitively, without the clear rationality that the Greeks brought to their social life. Like the *polis*, the medieval town emerged in the space left for urban development by a weak agrarian society, decentralized by geography and by internal conflict. Again like the *polis*, the medieval town and outlying countryside achieved a certain balance that is reflected in the modest dimensions of the town itself and its early democratic structure. Both were scaled to human dimensions and could be taken in "at a single view." But between the *polis* and the medieval town there are significant differences that partly account for the diverging historical developments they followed. The *polis* was not structured civically around the family but rather around the *agora*, which was more public square than market place. The medieval town merged work with the family in a domestic economy that turned the public square as much into a market place as an arena for social intercourse. The intense political interests of the Greeks, indeed, the fact that they were farmers as well as urban dwellers, relegated commercial activity to a secondary place in their lives; actually, the Greek tended to disdain commerce and left it in the hands of resident non-citizens. The medieval burgher, by contrast, was mainly an artisan or merchant, and only incidentally a food cultivator in the garden behind his home. His principal interest focused on trade and not surprisingly he pioneered the path toward capitalism and the bourgeois city.

Trade is the reduction and quantification of the world to commodity equivalents, the leveller of quality, skill, and concrete labour to numerical units that can be measured by time and money, by clocks and gold. What sets this abstract quantified world in motion is competition — the struggle for self-preservation on the market place. Capitalism, the domain of competition *par excellence*, has its fair share of violence, plunder, piracy, and enslavement; but in the normal course of events its mode of self-preservation is a quiet process of economic cannibalization — the devouring of one capitalist by another and the ever-greater centralization of capital in fewer hands. This takes place as a ritual peculiar to the capitalist mode of production — notably, as production for the sake of production, as growth for the sake of growth. The bourgeois maxim, "grow or die," becomes capitalism's very law of life. The inevitable impact of this unceasing expansion on the city can only be appreciated fully in our own time by the limitless expansion of the modern megalopolis, as the arena both for the endless production of commodities and their sale. If the Greeks subordinated the market place to the city, the emerging bourgeoisie subordinated the city to the market place — indeed, it eventually turned the city itself into a market place. This development marked not only the end of the small, sharply contoured medieval town, but the emergence of the sprawling capitalist megalopolis, a maw which devours every viable element of urbanity. Precapitalist cities were limited by the countryside, not only externally in the sense that the growth of free cities inevitably came up against social, cultural, and material barriers reared by entrenched agrarian interests, but also internally, insofar as the city reflected the social relations on the land. Except in the case of the late medieval cities, exchange relations were never completely autonomous; to one degree or another, they were placed in the service of the land. But once exchange relations begin to dominate the land and finally transform agrarian society, the city develops according to the workings of a suprasocial law. Production for the sake of production, translated into urban terms, means the growth of the city for its own sake — without any intrinsic urban criteria or even human criteria to arrest that growth. Limit becomes the enemy of growth; the human scale, the enemy of the commercial scale; quality, the enemy of quantity; the synthesis of dualism, the enemy of the buyer-seller dichotomy. Paradoxically, capitalism yields an urbanized world without cities — a world of urban belts that lack internal structure, definition, and civic uniqueness.

Bourgeois society, which abolishes urban limit and dissolves urban form, acquires an historic dynamic that has very far-reaching civic and psychic consequences. Competition tends to transform the numerous small enterprises that marked the inception of the industrial era into fewer and fewer highly centralized corporate giants. All the elements of society begin to change their dimensions. Civic and political gigantism parallel industrial and commercial gigantism. The city acquires dimensions so far removed from the human scale and human control that it ceases to appear as the shelter of individuality. Urban space reaches not only outward over the land but upward into the sky, blotting out the horizon as well as the countryside. The faceless geometric architecture of soaring skyscrapers and immense complexes of high-rise dwellings bespeaks a monumentalism that reflects the authority not of superhuman persons but of suprahuman bureaucratic institutions. No natural or human forms adorn these structures, forms on which the imagination can fasten in awe or defiance. Their cold geometry and functional design instill a sense of powerlessness in the urban dweller that precludes the presence of human meaning, for these structures appear no longer as the works of man but of institutions. They even tend to bear the names of the corporations that erected them. Before such gigantic, undefinable, bureaucratic entities, the urban dweller feels psychically as well as physically dwarfed. Unlike the monumental structures of the Baroque city, whose ornamentation was evidence of personified power, the institutional monumentalism of the megalopolis becomes a source of bewilderment and disorientation. Confronted every day by this architectural nullity, the urban dweller finds no monarch against whom she or he can rebel, no gods to defy, no priests and courtiers to overthrow. There is nothing, in fact, but an interminable bureaucratic nexus that traps the individual in an impersonal skein of agencies and corporations. These soaring geometric structures exude social power in its most reified form: power for the sake of power, domination for the sake of domination.

The urban ego, driven back from the social basis of individuality, must desperately learn to fend for itself. In this highly privatized world of isolated monads, the great crowds that surround the individual in the megalopolis lack any communitarian content. Louis Wirth, a generation ago, could remark upon the superficiality of urban relationships, of acquaintanceships that "stand in a relationship of utility" to each other and the disappearance of "the spontaneous self-expression, the morale, and the sense of participation that comes with living in an integrated society."(5) The gay Parisian crowds in which Baudelaire loved to immerse himself a century earlier had become, by Wirth's time, the blasé crowds whose spontaneity was carefully regulated and whose contacts were coolly superficial. Spontaneity of intercourse had been replaced by a prudent courtesy. The megalopolis carries this degradation to its most primal depths. Cornered in a sense of isolation that is accentuated by the massive, unknowing, impersonal crowds that surround the urban dweller, the individual ceases to be gay or even blasé, but fearful. The egoistic, calculating mentality which the bourgeois market normally generates in its isolated monads and by which it corrodes the sense of community that marked precapitalist urbanity is heightened by the megalopolis into a hostility that verges on mutual terror.

The megalopolis, in effect, atavistically travels the full circle of urban history back to the primitive community's dread of the stranger — but now, without the solidarity that the primitive community afforded to its own kind. The freedom which urban territoriality increasingly provided for the outsider, the individuality which the city eventually generated in all who inhabited its environs, the right of the urban dweller to be taken on her or his own merits apart from kinship ties and blood lineages, and perhaps more fundamentally, the solidarity the city forged among its citizens *qua* individuals into a purely social community unified by propinquity and an urbanely rational heritage — all of this is dissolved by the megalopolis into an alienating, crassly utilitarian, externalized mode of sociation in which everyone now reverts to the status of the outsider, to the primal stranger as real or potential foe. The barbarism of the past returns to settle over the forest of skyscrapers and high-rise dwellings like a sickening miasma. If the medieval town celebrated the fact that city air is "free air," the bourgeois megalopolis chokes on a polluted air that is poisoned not only by the toxicants of its industries, motor vehicles, and energy installations, but by a darkening cloud of hostility and fear. By virtue of a dialectical irony unique to itself, the city at its "height" in the most urbanized of urban worlds regenerates the mythic traditions of a humanity that has barely advanced beyond animality, yet without the redeeming innocence that marked this primal age.

The tribalism of the past reappears in the megalopolis as mocking caricature — as a ubiquitous process of ghettoization. To the degree that dread replaces spontaneous intercourse and its degradation into courtesy, panic unites normally alienated people of the same area and status in a hierarchy of fears against those who are sequentially more different and more removed from the familiar conditions of their lives. Tribalism appears in the degenerated form of the urban enclave. The ghetto is not merely the condition of the blacks and the poor who occupy the central districts of the megalopolis: as the beleaguered enclave of suburbia, exurbia, and the residential pockets of the well-to-do-in the inner city, the ghetto becomes the condition of everyone who is caught in the megalopolitan skein. The outward radiation of modern urban society from its civic nuclei reads like a spectrum of either increasingly deprived or seemingly privileged ghettoes: the materially denied black and Puerto Rican ghettoes in the central parts of the city (marbled, to be sure, by well-policed enclaves of fearful whites); the materially more affluent but spiritually denied suburbanite fringe, united merely by its aversion for the city proper; and finally that pathetic caricature of all privilege in bourgeois society, the beleagured exurbanite fringe, inwardly paralyzed by a suspicion of invaders from the central city and suburbs. Just as the bourgeois market place makes each individual a stranger to another, so the bourgeois city estranges these central and fringe areas from each other. The paradox of the megalopolis is that it unites these areas internally not in the felicitous heterogeneity of unity in diversity that marked the medieval commune — a heterogeneity unified by mutual aid and a common municipal tradition — but rather in the suspicions, anxieties, and hatreds of the stranger from the "other" ghetto. The city, once the refuge of the stranger from archaic parochialism, is now the primary source of estrangement. Ghetto boundaries comprise the unseen internal walls within the city that once, as real walls, secured the city and distinguished it from the countryside. The bourgeois city assimilates archaic parochialism as a permanent and festering urban condition. No longer are the elements of the city cemented by mutual aid, a shared culture, and a sense of community; rather, they are cemented by a social dynamite that threatens to explode the urban tradition into its very antithesis.

To these historic contradictions and tendencies, city planning and its disciplinary cousin, urban sociology, oppose the platitudes of analytical and technical accomodation. Leonard Reissman does not speak for himself alone when he affirms that, while "there have been recurrent crises" in urban history, "there is little chance for a perfect solution..." The thrust of this thinking is strictly ideological: the megalopolis is here to stay, and the sooner we learn to live with it, the better. A dysutopian mentality increasingly pervades contemporary city planning and urban sociology, an outlook misleadingly formulated in terms of a regression to rural parochialism or adjustment to an "urbanized world." Radical critique tends to be denigrated. Typically, Reissman belabours "rural sociologists" for seeking "a rural idyll or an urban utopia." Such thinking, he scornfully adds, is "super-critical," with the result that "we continue to criticize the city more often than we praise it, to magnify its faults more often than we stress its advantages." These remarks conclude with the pragmatically triumphant note that "In any case, such discussions have hardly slowed the pace of urban growth."(6)

Reissman is unique in that he examines the assumptions of urban sociology. More often than not, these assumptions are simply taken for granted. Urban sociology presupposes that the city can be taken as a social isolate — often, quite apart from other social factors that define it — and examined on its own terms. Economics becomes "urban economics"; social relations, "urban relations"; politics, "urban politics"; and the city dweller, an "urban man" in an "urbanized world." "Urbanism," in effect, replaces capitalism as the legitimate object of social investigation. On this derivative level, urban sociology becomes descriptive rather than critical, analytical rather than censorious.

To the more vulgar urban sociologist, the problems of the megalopolis are to be explained as the work of the self-seeking, the greedy, and the indifferent. Even Reissman is not above this level of discourse; "the economics of avarice, the politics of ignorance," we are told, "make the perfect city only a utopia."[7] These villainous traits are imputed not only to land speculators, construction barons, government bureaucrats, landlords and banking interests, but rather flippantly to the general public. People, we are told, do not care enough about their urban environment to do anything for it. An abstract "we" is distilled from the medley of conflicting social interests, a target of insidious propaganda that demands concern, but denies the power of action to those who are most concerned — the ordinary urban dwellers who must endure the megalopolis not only as a place of work but also as a way of life.

In city planning the counterpart of this abstract "we" is the abstract design: the architectural sketch that will resolve the gravest urban problems with the most sophisticated "know-how." "One question about city planning," observes Frank Fisher, "must have come to the mind of anyone who has fingered the magnificent volumes in which the proposals of planners are generally presented. Why do those green spaces, those carefully placed skyscrapers, those pleasant residential districts, and equally pleasant factory and working areas, still remain dreams for the most part? Why are our cities hardly any less ugly and unpleasant than they were at the height of the 19th century's Industrial Revolution?"[8] Fisher's questions, quite humane in themselves, are nevertheless loaded with presuppositions about the nature of residence, work, the relationship of town to country, and structural size that require critical examination before "the magnificent volumes" can be compiled. For the purposes of our discussion, however, the most important of these presuppositions is that a rational city is primarily a product of good designing — that "green spaces," "pleasant residential districts," "equally pleasant factory and working areas," not to speak of "carefully placed skyscrapers," in themselves produce human, rational, or even viable cities.

The priority that city planning assigns to structural design represents a fairly recent development. Western notions of the city, certainly as we know them from earlier visionaries of urban reconstruction, were clearly linked to a larger, often sharply critical, conception of the nature of society itself. Plato's *Republic* advances a notion of the *polis* not only in terms of what it *ought* to be, but how class relations, education, social attitudes, modes of administration, and ownership of property form its very essence and determine its size and configuration. To the degree that design factors enter into the dialogue, they are seen as a function of social life. However unpalatable the hierarchical bias of the dialogue may be, Plato follows a tradition that discusses the city as the result of a distinctive social configuration, not as an autonomous entity that can be isolated and reserved for analysis and design on its own terms.

This tradition is perpetuated by Aristotle, More, Campanella, Andreae, indeed, by virtually all the visionaries of the city well into the early nineteenth century. A high point is reached in the works of Fourier, who combines social critique and reconstruction in a strikingly revolutionary manner. In contrast even to Owen, the English utopian, Fourier conceives of the phalanstery not merely as a sober community of labour, but a shelter of sensuous pleasure. A delightfully unguarded hedonism pervades his notions of work, of the relationship between the sexes, of food and adornment, even of the design of the phalanstery itself which will provide "elegant communication with all parts of the building and its dependencies."(9) Here, Rabelais' Abbey of Thélème is thorougly democratized. The right to "Do what thou wouldst," which forms the rule of the "Thélèmite order," ceases to be the privilege of a Renaissance elite and becomes the prerogative of society at large.

The notion that design dictates urban conditions of life becomes dominant in an ambience of social protest, when cities in Europe and America had undergone appalling decay under the impact of the Industrial Revolution. Although the emergence of the modern city planning movement is usually dated with the publication in 1898 of Ebenezer Howard's *Tomorrow: A Peaceful Path to Real Reform* (later retitled *Garden Cities of Tomorrow*), Howard's efforts had been preceded by L'Enfant's plan for the city of Washington and, in the case of a more sinister enterprise, by Haussman's remodeling of Paris, an immense effort visibly designed to deal effectively with the insurrections that had plagued the French ruling classes. No less significantly, the middle years of the century were marked by legislation and regulations to cope with the disastrous hygienic conditions of the time. Major cholera epidemics threatened not only the poorer quarters of European and American cities but also the wealthy ones, and these could be brought under control only by serious efforts to improve urban sanitation and living conditions. Moreover, the 1840s reminded the European bourgeoisie that it had a restive, increasingly class-conscious proletariat on its hands. Accordingly, the middle part of the century opened a period of bourgeois paternalism toward working-class dwellings, as witnessed by the construction of Louis Napoleon's *cités ouvrières*, state-subsidized "model villages" for English workers, and the Krupp settlements in the Ruhr. On the whole, however, these programs did not appreciably affect the established cities, nor did they greatly alter the urban landscape of Europe and the United States. As to the latter country, Mel Scott not unjustly observes that as late as "that painful decade now ironically called the Gay Nineties there were few urban Americans who would have subscribed to the belief, or hope, that entire cities and metropolitan regions can be developed and renewed by a continuous process of decision-making based on long-range planning."[10]

Howard's impact on this state of mind, both by means of his book and his practical endeavours in creating the first "garden city" of Letchworth, is almost legendary. "*Garden Cities of Tomorrow,*" Mumford rightly observes, "has done more than any single book to guide the modern town planning movement and to alter its objectives."[11] In many respects, it originated this movement, for the idea that town planning should be a cause, an ideal around which to mobilize popular interest, state resources, and social opinion, must be ascribed more to Howard than to any of his predecessors and successors. Yet Howard can also be regarded as fathering, however unintentionally, the myth that structural design is equatable with social rationality. Although deeply influenced by Henry George and Peter Kropotkin, Howard's social ideals are repeatedly vitiated by the exigencies of design and by a British proclivity for a compromising "realism."

As F. J. Osborn, one of his closest associates, emphasizes, Howard "was not a political theorist, not a dreamer, but an inventor." The curious juxtaposition of these words and the pragmatic, indeed technical bias it reveals tells us much about the "garden city" movement as a whole. As Osborn explains: "The inventor proceeds by first conceiving an idea of a possible new product or instrument, next by evolving a design on paper with patient thought for the adaptation of the structure to the conditions it has to fulfill, and finally by experimentation with models to test the design in practice."[12]

This crudely Baconian mentality pervades modern city planning. To Aristotle, the city was a way of life: its achievement was gauged not by its size, population, or logistical efficiency, but by the extent to which it enabled its citizens "to live temperately and liberally in the enjoyment of leisure."[13] To Le Corbusier, by contrast, the city is a "tool," a logistical device.[14] Even Frank Lloyd Wright once described the city as "the only possible ideal machine..."[15] This mechanistic orientation has its conceptual antecedents in the functionalist theories of the bourgeois Enlightenment architects — figures such as Lodoli, who provocatively expressed a greater admiration for the sewers of Rome than the sacristy of St. Peter's. Speculative thought tends to be replaced by pragmatic realism, human values by operationalism, ends by the hypostasization of means. With Lodoli, as Alexander Tzonis observes, we see an end to the period when "theories of architecture considered the design of a building to be determined by a set of independent objectives, whether the Vitruvian triad ('Accomodation, Handsomeness and Lastingness') or Perrault's dichotomy between 'Positive' and 'Arbitrary' values."[16]

Modern city planning is the stepchild of this degraded rationalism and functionalism. Inspired as Howard's intentions may be, he assigns to design the task of achieving goals that involve sweeping revolutionary changes in the economic, social, and cultural fabric of bourgeois society. Compared to the megalopolis, Howard's garden city is attractive enough: a compact urban entity of some thirty thousand people, scaled to human dimensions, and surrounded by a green belt to limit growth and provide open land for recreational and agricultural purposes.

Suitable areas of the green belt are to be occupied by farmers (Howard limited this agricultural population to two thousand); the larger urban population of thirty thousand is to engage in manufacturing, commerce, and services. All land is to be held in trust and leased to occupants on a rental basis. Howard spelled out many design and fiscal details of this proposal, but he was careful to emphasize at the very outset of his book that these were "merely suggestive, and will probably be much departed from."[17]

But even the most generous modifications of Howard's garden city do not alter the fact that the project is a structural design — and, as such, neither more nor less than what such a design can perform. The design may provide the basis for greater human contiguity, the structural instruments for community, and easy communication with places of work, with shopping centers, and with service enterprises. Nevertheless it leaves undefined the nature of human contiguity, community, and the relationship between the urban dweller and the rural environs. Most importantly, it leaves undefined the nature of work in garden city, the control of the means of production, the problem of distributing goods and services equitably, and it leaves unanalyzed the conflicting social interests that collect around these issues. Actually, Howard's "invention" does provide an orientation toward all of these problems — namely, a system of benevolent capitalism that presumably avoids the "extremes" of "communism" and "individualism."[18] Howard's *Garden Cities of Tomorrow* is permeated by an underlying assumption that a compromise can be struck between an inherently irrational social reality and a moral ideology of high-minded conciliation.

Yet the offices, industrial factories, and shopping centers that are intended to provide garden city with the means of life are themselves battlegrounds of conflicting social interests. Within these entities we find the sources of alienated labour, of income differentials, and of disparities between work time and free time. By itself, no structural design can reconcile the conflicting interests and social differences that gather beneath the surface of garden city. These interests and differences must be dealt with largely on their own terms — by far-reaching changes in social and economic relations. Which is not to say that a social resolution of the problems created by the bourgeois factory, office, and shopping center obviates the need for a structural design that will promote community and a balance between town and country; rather that one without the other is a truncated solution, and hence, no solution at all.

Howard's garden city, it is worth noting, falls far short of the highly progressive criteria advanced by earlier utopias and historical experiences in dealing with problems of social management and modes of work. In contrast to the Greek *polis*, which administered its affairs on the basis of a face-to-face democracy, Howard merely proposes a Central Council and a departmental structure based on elections. Garden city has none of the recall mechanisms that were established by the Paris Commune of 1871. Unlike More's Utopia, there is no proposal for rotating agricultural and industrial work. In garden city, the mode of social labour is decided simply by the needs of capital. Inasmuch as Howard's economic horizon is not substantially broader than that of any benevolent bourgeois of his day, notions of industrial self-management are simply absent from his work.

The intrinsic limits of Howard's garden city, indeed, of the thirty-odd "new towns" that have been constructed in England and those that are aborning in the United States, are that these communities do not encompass anywhere near the full range and possibilities of human experience. Neighborliness is mistaken for organic social intercourse and mutual aid; well-manicured parks for the harmonization of humanity with nature; the proximity of work places for the development of a new meaning for work and its integration with play; an eclectic mix of ranch-houses, slab-like apartment buildings, and bachelor-type flats for spontaneous architectural variety; shopping-mart plazas and a vast expanse of lawn for the *agora*; lecture halls for cultural centers; hobby classes for vocational variety; benevolent trusts or municipal councils for self-administration. One can add endlessly to this list of warped criteria that serve to obfuscate rather than clarify the high attainments of the urban tradition. Although people may earn their income without leaving these communities — and a substantial portion must travel for considerable distances to the central city to do so — the nature of their work and the income-differentials that group them into alien social classes are not a matter of community concern. A crucial area of life is thus removed from the community and delivered to a socio-economic system that exists apart from it even as it exists within it. Indeed, the appearance of community serves the ideological function of concealing the incompleteness of an intimate and shared social life. Key elements of the self are formed outside the parameters of the design by forces that stem from economic competition, class antagonisms, social hierarchy and domination, and economic exploitation. Although people are brought together to enjoy certain conveniences and pleasantries, they remain as truncated and culturally impoverished in garden cities and "new towns" as they were in the megalopolis, with the difference that in the big cities the stark reality of urban decay removes any veil of appearances from the incompleteness and contradictions of social life.

These internal contradictions have not been faced with candour by either the supporters or opponents of the garden city concept. That the "new towns" of England, the United States, and other countries modeled on the garden city design have not awakened "the soft notes of brotherliness and goodwill" Howard described as their essential goal; that they have not placed "in strong hands implements of peace and construction, so that implements of war and destruction may drop uselessly down" — all of this is painfully obvious fact. (19) Nor has there been any promise that they will remotely approximate such far-reaching goals. In the best of cases, the new towns differ from the suburbs by virtue of the ease with which people can reach their work places and acquire services within the community. In the worst of cases, these communities are little more than bedroom suburbs of the big cities and add enormously to their congestion during working hours.

Nor has reality been any kinder to the devotees of the metropolis. The old cities keep growing even as the number of "new towns" multiply, each urban form slowly encroaching on the other and creating urban belts that threaten to undermine the integrity of both. Jane Jacob's spirited defense of traditional neighborhood life partakes of all the illusions that mar Frederic J. Osborn's defense of Howard's vision. Culturally, this neighborhood world if faced with extinction: the same forces that truncate the inhabitant of the "new town" are delivering the small shop over to the supermarket and the old tenement complex to the aseptic high-rise superblock. Colourful enclaves of neighborhood culture will doubtless continue to exist as urban showpieces — contemporary counterparts of the existing medieval and Renaissance towns that attract tourists to Europe for visual respite from the urban monotony that is rapidly prevailing in most cities of the world.

To the degreee that the urban dweller becomes disenchanted with an undisguisedly functional design rationality, city planning begins to flirt with a design exotica that rehabilitates this very rationality in a mystified form. A pop ideology of urbanism — half science fiction, half fraud — tends to defuse the urban dweller's frustration by evoking design elements that are unique only in the nightmarish dimensions they add to prevailing modes of city planning. In Buckminster Fuller, Paoli Soleri, Constantinos Doxiades, Yona Friedman, Nicolas Schöffer, and a bouquet of newly arrived Japanese designers, the system tries to recover its social credibility with the shamanistic and occult. Fuller, to examine the most prominent of these shamans, finds no inconsistency in trying to reconcile an appeal for individual spontaneity with a suprahuman tetrahedronal structure that will house a million people. Perhaps more absurdly, he tries to combine an ecological perspective with an air-conditioned dome over Manhattan Island.

Fuller, in fact, is an artist in advancing an outlook so "cosmic" in its insensibility to qualitative distinctions that individuality and community dissolve into mere digits in a computerized "world game." His inflated, oversized vision lacks not only human scale but even natural scale. Yet once we strip away the "mega"-verbiage he borrows from cybernetics, systems analysis, and the aerospace industry, what remains of his thinking is a mechanistic reductionism embodying the crudest features of the prevailing functional rationality. "The environment," we are told, "always consists of energy — energy as matter, energy as radiation, energy as gravity and energy as 'events.'" An environment so divested of qualitative distinctions beggars even the machine-like Cartesian world of mere matter and motion. In this universe, everything is interchangeable. Accordingly, Fuller adds:

"Housing is an energetic environment-controlling mechanism. Thinking correctly of all housing as machinery (one is tempted to ask, not as *home* or *community*? — M.B.) we begin to realize the complete continuity of interrelationship of such technological evolution as that of the home bedroom into the railway sleeping car, into the automobile with seat-to-bed conversions, into the filling-station toilets, which are accessories of the parlour-on wheels; the trailer, the motels, hotels, and ocean liners."[20] Portability replaces community and mobility a sense of rootedness and place. The individual becomes a camper who belongs everywhere — and nowhere. Perhaps more appropriately, Fullerian social theory envisions the individual as an astronaut who pilots the earth as a mechanical spaceship. Here, hypostasized design leaves even the mundane world of conventional planning for the interstellar space of Kubrick's *2001*. This magic is essentially cinematic — as synthetic as the film on which it unfolds.

That Fuller's work arouses popular interest can be explained by default — that is, as a result of the vacuum left by the absence of a searching radical theory of the city and community. Why, it may be asked, did Fourier's interpretations of community fail to acquire relevance for so many of the generations that followed his own? At what point — and for what reasons — did the generous utopian visions that surfaced in the early nineteenth century lose continuity with later periods that so desperately required their elaboration and fulfillment? The rupture can be dated from the ascendency of Marxism as a social movement. Largely under the impetus of Marx's class theory, the city ceased to be a matter of serious concern to radical analysts and the notion of community a goal in social reconstruction. Radicalism found an almost exclusive locus in the factory and proletariat. Just as bourgeois urban sociology neglected the work place for the city, so radical social theory neglected the city for the work place. That the two arenas could have been integrated as a unified realm of critique and reconstruction occurred to only a few radical theorists of the last century, notably Kropotkin and William Morris.

Yet even the worker does not exist merely in a factory milieu and her or his social experiences are not exhausted at the point of production. The proletarian is not only a class being but also an urban being. Capitalism generates a broad social crisis that often makes workers more accessible to revolutionary visions as urban dwellers—as victims of pollution, congestion, isolation, real estate extortion, neighborhood decay, bad transportation, civic manipulation, and the spiritually dehumanizing effects of megalopolitan life—than as exploited producers of surplus value. Marx and Engels were far less oblivious to this fact than the epigones who were to speak in their names. In *The Housing Question*, written in 1872, Engels creditably links his views with the most vital concepts of Owen and Fourier; to resolve the housing problem—and, one may add, the urban problem as a whole— Engels argues that the big cities must be decentralized and the antithesis between town and country overcome. The same theme is taken up 13 years later in Engels' highly influential work, *Anti-Duhring*. With the vulgarization of Marxism and its transformation into a powerful political ideology, this tradition receded into the background. The notion of "scientific socialism" fostered a distinct bias against Marx's utopian predecessors and the communitarian visions that permeated their works. By the turn of the century, urban problems ceased to be an issue of any real significance in Marxist theory. Even the notion of decentralization was airily dismissed as a "utopian" absurdity.

Not until the late 1960s do we begin to see design emerge as a function of an entirely new way of life. That this approach had its isolated devotees in the long interim between Fourier's day and our own is evident enough from any reading of urban history. The Sixties are unique, however, in that the concept of community began to develop on a broad popular scale—indeed, a largely generational scale—when young people in considerable numbers, disenchanted with the prevailing society, reoriented themselves toward reconstructive utopistic projects of their own. New values were formulated that often involved a total break with the commodity system as a whole and charted the way to new forms of sociation.

The young people who began to formulate these new values and forms of sociation—values and forms that have since been grouped under the rubric of "the counterculture"—unquestionably comprised a privileged social stratum. For the most part, they came from the affluent, white, middle-class suburbs and the better universities of the United States, the enclaves and training grounds of the new American technocracy. To adduce their privileged status as evidence for the trifling nature of the movement itself sidesteps a key question: why did privilege lead to a rejection of the social and material values that had spawned these very privileges in the first place? Why, in fact, didn't these young people, like so many before them in previous generations, take up the basic values of their parents and expand the arena of privilege they had inherited?

These questions reveal an historic change in the material premises for the radical social movements in the advanced capitalist countries. By the Sixties, the so-called "First World" had undergone unprecedented technological changes. Technology had advanced to a point where the values spawned by material scarcity, particularly those values fostered by the bourgeois era, no longer seemed morally or culturally relevant. The work ethic, the moral authority imputed to material denial, parsimony, and sensual renunciation, the high social valuation placed on competition and "free enterprise," the emphasis on privatization and individuation based on egotism, seemed obsolete in the light of technological achievements that afforded entirely contrary alternatives — freedom from a lifetime of toil and a materially secure social disposition oriented toward community and the full expression of individual human powers. The new alternatives opened by technological advances made the cherished values of the past seem not only obsolete but odious. There is no paradox in the fact that the weakest link in the old society turned out to be that very stratum which enjoyed the real privilege of rejecting false privilege.

Which is not to say that the technological context of the counterculture was consciously grasped and elaborated into a coherent perspective for society as a whole. Indeed, the outlook of most middle-class dropout youth and students remained largely intuitive and often fell easy prey to the faddism nurtured by the established society. The erratic features of the new movement, its feverish and its quixotic oscillations, can be partly explained by this lack of adequate consciousness. Often, young people were easily victimized and crudely exploited by commercial interests that shrewdly pandered to the more superficial aspects of the new culture. Large numbers of this dropout youth, exultant in their newly discovered sense of liberation, lacked an awareness of the harsh fact that complete freedom is impossible in a prevailing system of unfreedom. Insofar as they hoped rapidly to replace the dominant culture by their own merely on the strength of example and moral suasion, they failed. But insofar as they began to see themselves as the most advanced sector of a larger movement to revolutionize society as a whole, their culture has a compelling relevance as part of an historic enlightenment that eventually may change every aspect of social life.

The most striking feature of this culture is the emphasis it places on personal relations as the locus of abstract social ideals, its attempt to translate freedom and love into existential realities of everyday life. This personalistic yet socially involved approach has yielded not only an increasingly explicit critique of doctrinaire socialist theory, but also of design-oriented city planning. Much has been written about the "retreat" of dropout youth to rural communes. Far less has been written about the extent to which ecologically minded young people began to subject city planning to a devastating critique, often advancing alternative proposals to dehumanizing urban "revitalization" and "rehabilitation" projects. Generally, these alternatives stemmed from a perspective toward design that was radically different from that of conventional city planners. For the countercultural planners, the point of departure for any design was not the extent to which the city expedites traffic, communications, and economic activities. Rather, they were primarily occupied with the relationship of design to the fostering of personal intimacy, many-sided social relationships, nonhierarchical modes of organization, communistic living arrangements, and material independence from the market economy. Design, here, took its point of departure not from abstract concepts of space and efficiency, but from an explicit critique of the status quo and a conception, rooted in developing life-styles, of the free human relationships that were to replace it. The design elements of the plan followed from radically new social alternatives that were already being practiced as subcultures in many communities throughout the country. To use an expression that was very much in the air: the attempt was made to replace hierarchical space by liberated space.

Among the many plans of this kind to be developed in the late Sixties and early Seventies, perhaps the most impressive was formulated in Berkeley by an ad hoc group from People's Architecture, the local Tenant's Union, and members of the local food cooperative. The plan shows a remarkably high degree of radical social consciousness. It draws its inspiration from the "People's Park" episode in May 1969, when dropout youth, students, and later ordinary citizens of Berkeley fought with police for more than a week to retain a lovely park and playground which they had spontaneously created out of a neglected, garbage-strewn lot owned by the University of California. The park, eventually reclaimed by its university proprietors at the cost of a young man's life, many severe injuries, and massive arrests, is at this writing a parking lot and paved soccer field. But the memory of the episode has waned slowly. To the young Berkeley planners, "People's Park was the beginning of the Revolutionary Ecology Movement" — a movement, unfortunately, that has yet to live up to these high hopes. The thrust of the plan, entitled *Blueprint for a Communal Environment*, is radically countercultural. "The revolutionary culture," declare the writers of the *Blueprint*, "gives us new communal, eco-viable ways of organizing our lives, while people's politics gives us the means to resist the System."(21) The *Blueprint* is a project not only for reconstruction but also for struggle on a wide social terrain against the established order.

This document of the Berkeley planners aims at more than the structural redesigning of an existing communty; it avows and explores a new way of life at the most elementary level of human intercourse. The new way of life is communal and seeks as much as possible to divorce itself from commodity relationships. The goal of the design is "Communal ways of organizing our lives (to) help to cut down on consumption, to provide for basic human needs more efficiently, to resist the system, to support ourselves and overcome the misery of atomized living." The social and private are thoroughly fused in this one sentence. Design gives expression to a new life-style that stands opposed to the repressive organization of society.(22)

Shelter is redesigned to "overcome the fragmentation of our lives... to encourage communication and break down privatization." The plan's authors observe that with "women's liberation, and a new communal morality, the nuclear family is becoming obsolete." Accordingly, floor plans are proposed which allow for larger multi-purpose rooms which promote more interaction, "such as communal dining rooms, meeting spaces and work areas." Methods are suggested for creating roof openings and converting exterior upper walls into communicating links with neighboring houses as well as between rooms and upper stories.(23)

"All land in Berkeley is treated as a marketable commodity" observe the young planners. "Space is parcelled into neat consumer packages. In between rows of land parcels are transportation 'corridors' to keep people flowing from workplace to market." The *Blueprint* proposes the dismantling of backyard and sideyard fences to open land as interior parks and gardens. Platform "bridgeways" between houses are suggested to break down the strict division between indoor and outdoor space. The purpose of these suggestions is not merely to restore nature to the urban dweller's world, but to open avenues of intimate communication. The plan focuses not merely on public plazas and parks, but the immediate neighborhoods in which people live their daily lives. Indeed, with magnificent insouciance, the plan tosses all considerations of private property to the winds by suggesting that vacant lots be appropriated by neighborhoods and turned into communal space.(24)

Half the streets of Berkeley, the plan notes, could easily be closed off to stimulate collective transportation experiments and reduce traffic congestion in residential areas. This would "free *ten times* more land area for public use than we now have in park acreage. Intersections could become parks, gardens, plazas, with paving material recovered and used to make artificial hills." The plan recommends that Berkeley residents should walk or bicycle to places whenever feasible. If motor vehicles must be used, they should be pooled and maintained on a communal basis. People should drive together to common destinations in order to reduce the number of vehicles in use and to share the human experience of common travel. Community services will make a "quantum leap," observe the planners, when "small groups of neighbors mobilize resources and energy in order to cement fragmented neighborhoods back together and begin to take care of business (from child care to education) on a local level and in an integrated way." In this connection, the *Blueprint* suggests that men and women should rotate the use of their homes for child-care centers. First-aid skills and knowledge of more advanced medical techniques should be mobilized on a neighborhood basis. Finally, wastes should be collectively recycled to avoid pollution and the destruction of recyclable resources.(25)

The *Blueprint* advances a refreshingly imaginative program for ruralizing the city and fostering the material independence of its inhabitants. It suggests communally worked backyard gardens for the cultivation of organic food, even entering into the specifics of composting, mulching, and the preparation of seedlings. It proposes the establishment of a "People's Market... which will receive the organic products of rural communes and small farmers, and distribute them to the neighborhood (food) conspiracies. Such a market place will have other uses — craftspeople can sell their wares there." The "People's Market" is visualized as a "solid example of creative thinking about communal use of space. Its structure will be portable, and will be built in such a way as to serve neighborhood kids as play equipment on non-market days."(26)

The *Blueprint* leaves no illusion that this ensemble of reconstructive ideas will "liberate" Berkeley or other communities. It sees the realization of these concepts as the first steps toward reorienting the individual self from a passive acceptance of isolation and dependence on bureaucratic institutions to popular initiatives that will recreate communal contacts and face-to-face networks of mutual aid. Ultimately, society as a whole will have to be reorganized by the great majority who are now forced into hierarchical subservience to the few. Yet until these revolutionary changes are achieved, a new state of mind, nourished by working community ties, must be fashioned so that people will be able to fuse their deepest personal needs with broader social ideals. Indeed, unless this fusion is achieved, these very ideals will remain abstractions and will not be realized at all.

Many of the *Blueprint's* structural suggestions are not new. The idea of using roof openings to link houses is obviously borrowed from Pueblo Indian villages, the urban gardens from medieval communes and precapitalist towns generally, the pedestrian streets and plazas from the Renaissance cities and earlier urban forms. What makes the plan unique, however, is that it derives its design concepts from radically new life-styles that are antithetical to an increasingly bureaucratic society. Doubtless, each of its design elements could be assimilated in piecemeal fashion to conventional ways of life as has been the case with so many radical ideas in the past. The plan is sensitive to this possibility. From the outset, it adopts a revolutionary stance. Its premise in advance of any design is a culture that is counter to the prevailing one — one that emphasizes community rather than isolation, the sharing of resources and skills rather than their privatized possession, independence from rather than dependence on the bourgeois market place, loving relations and mutual aid rather than egotism and competition. The *Blueprint* clearly articulates the social preconditions for a free community that other, ostensibly radical, plans leave unexamined. It is humanistic, not "iconoclastic"; it is radical, not "original." And whether or not the planners were fully conscious of their historic antecedents, they were presenting a Hellenic vision of urban life. The truly human city, to them, is a way of life (not a mere "design") that fosters the integration of individual with society, of town with country, of personal needs with social ones without denying the integrity of each.

The Sixties have passed — and with them many of the high hopes raised by dropout youth and radical students. An insecure, so-called "middle American" adult public, seeking respite from challenges to traditional values, is trying to entrench itself in the status quo, indeed, to evoke an "innocence" imputed to the past that is apocryphal in any case. Where the counterculture has managed to hold its own against overtly hostile forces, it has had to contend with a political mode of dope-peddling in the form of sectarian Marxism and "Third World" voyeurism. Here, archaic ideologies and modes of organization assume the semblance of "radicalism" and, like toxic germs, fester in the wounds opened by public malaise and political repression.

Yet even this ebbing phase of what is surely a much larger cultural and social development could be valuable as a sobering period of maturation. A new world will not be gained merely by strewing the pathway to the future with flowers. The largely intuitive impulses that exploded with such naive enthusiasm in the Sixties, only to become bitter, harsh, and dehumanizing in the pseudo-radicalism that closed the decade, were never adequate to the long-range historic project of developing a wider public consciousness of the need for social change. By the late Sixties, the counterculture ceased to speak to America with under-standing and in relevant terms. Its politicization took the worst form possible — arrogance and a senselessly violent rhetoric. Far more than the flowers of the mid-Sixties, the angry clenched fists of the late Sixties served to alarm and utterly alienate an uncomprehending public.

Yet many of the demands raised by this movement of young people are imperishable. No matter how far the movement may recede from its earlier eminence, these demands must inevitably be recovered and advanced if there is to be any social future. In calling for a melding of the more abstract ideals of social liberation with personal liberation, in seeking to form the nuclear libertarian communistic relationships so necessary to the rearing of a truly emancipated society, in trying to subvert the influence of the commodity nexus on the individual self and its relationship with other selves, in emphasizing the need for a spontaneous expres-sion of sensuality and a humanistic sensibility, in challenging hierarchy and domination in all its forms and manifestations, in trying to synthesize new decentralized communities based on an ecological balance with the natural world — in raising all of these demands as a single ensemble, the counterculture gave a modern expression to a long historic mainstream of human dreams and aspirations. And however intuitively, it did so on the basis of the historic challenge posed by technological advances unprece-dented in history. These demands can never be fully submerged by political repression; they have become the voice of an increasingly self-conscious reason that is sedimented into the very perspective of humanity toward its future. What were only recently the hotly debated views of a small minority of the young are almost unconsciously accepted by millions of people in all age groups.

What strongly favours the growth of these demands is the harsh fact that society is left with very few choices today. The city has completed its historic evolution. Its dialectic from the village, temple area, fortress, or administrative center, each dominated by agrarian interests, to the megalopolis which completely dominates the countryside, marks the absolute negation of the city as we have known it in history. With the modern city, we can no longer speak of a clearly defined urban entity with a collective urban interest of its own. Just as each phase or "moment" of the city in history is marked by its own internal limits, so the megalopolis represents the limits of the city as such — of *civitas* as distinguished from *communitas*. The political principle in the form of the state dissolves all the elements of the social principle, replacing community ties by bureaucratic ones. Personified space dissolves into institutional space — and with the violent ghettoization of the modern city, into what Oscar Newman crassly describes as "defensible space." The human scale is enveloped by urban gigantism. This "anti-city," neither urban nor rural, affords no arena for the development of community or even humanistic sociation. At most, the megalopolis is pieced together by mutually hostile enclaves each of which is internally "united" by its hostility to the stranger on the perimeter. At its worst, this urban cancer is in physical, moral and logistical decay. It ceases even to function on its own terms, as an efficient arena for the production and marketing of commodities.

City planning validates the urban crisis by dealing with it as a problem of logistics and design. The conventional planner's concern for efficient movement involves the reduction of human beings to little more than commodities that circulate through the capitalist economy as exchange values. The triumph of computer-simulation techniques in city planning reflects the degradation of the urban dweller from the status of "brother" in the medieval commune to that of "citizen" in the traditional bourgeois city and ultimately to that of a mere ,digit in the megalopolis. If the traditional city emancipated human sociation from blood ties, the megalopolis dissolves sociation as such and reduces it to digital aggregation. City planning presents this dissolution as ideology. In the dynamic design, people become "population" and their relations mere movement guided by the needs and constraints of the prevailing system.

We see, here, the profound difference between the sensibility of the young Berkeley planners and their conventional counter-parts. The Berkeley planners start from the premise that urbanity does not emancipate human sociation from the blood tie merely to deliver the individual to the alienated and privatized world of the bourgeois market place. In the *Blueprint*, sociation is recovered in the commune, in ties freely formed by human affinity rather than ancestral lineage. Urbanity, in effect, is fulfilled as a commune composed of communes. Conventional city planning, by accepting the city as it is, prevents us from understanding what humanized territory could be — namely, a new *polis* that would be a commune made up of communes, of nuclear groups united by choice and selective affinity, not simply by kinship and blood ties. Accordingly, just as people become mere "population," territo-rialism becomes mere "space" through which people, vehicles, and commodities flow. City planning becomes the mechanical organization of space by design, not the ecological colonization of territory by people. *Civitas* completely assimilates *communitas*; the political principle, the social principle.

To restore urbanity as a humanized terrain for sociation, the megalopolis must be ruthlessly dissolved and its place taken by new decentralized ecocommunities, each carefully tailored to the carrying capacity of the natural ecosystem in which it is located. One might reasonably say that these ecocommunities will possess the best features of the *polis* and medieval commune, supported by rounded ecotechnologies that rescale the most advanced elements of modern technology to local dimensions. The equilibrium between town and country will be restored — not as a sprawling suburb that mistakes a lawn or a woodlot for "nature," but as an interactive functional ecocommunity that unites industry with agriculture, mental work with physical. No longer a mere spectatorial object to be seen from a window or during a stroll, nature will become an integral part of all aspects of the human experience, from work to play. Only in this way can the needs of the natural world become integrated with those of the social to yield an authentic ecological consciousness that transcends the instrumentalist "environmental" mentality of the sanitary engineer.

Our place in the history of the city is unique. Precapitalist cities, owing to an incomplete technological development that perpetuated material scarcity, either stagnated within their limits or exploded destructively beyond them, only to fall back again to their original dimensions or disappear entirely. Where the city was not frozen (as in Asia and the Near East) by hereditary castes and agrarian hierarchies, its unity was dissolved by the commodity system and market place. This was the fate of the *polis.* Modern technology has now reached so advanced a level of development that it permits humanity to reconstruct urban life along lines that could foster a balanced, well-rounded, and harmonious community of interests between human beings and between humanity and the natural world. This ecocommunity would be more than what we have always meant by a city; it would be a social work of art, a community fashioned by human creativity, reason, and ecological insight.

Alternatively, we are confronted by an urban development that is almost certain to disintegrate into bureaucratic mobilization, chronic social war, and a condition of permanent violence. If the earliest hieroglyph of the city was a wall intersected by two roads, the symbol of the megalopolis may well become a police badge on which a gun is superimposed. In this kind of "city," the revenge of social irrationality will claim its toll in the form of an absolute division of human from human. This is the very negation of urbanity. Perhaps more significantly, the limits of the megalopolis can be formulated as nothing less than the limits of society itself as an instrument of hierarchy and domination. Left to its own development, the megalopolis spells the doom not only of the city as such but of human sociation. For in such an urban world, technology, subserved to irrational and demonic forces, becomes not the instrument of harmony and security, but the means for systematically plundering the human spirit and the natural world.

May 1973

FOOTNOTES

1. Max Horkheimer, *The Eclipse of Reason* (New York: Oxford University Press, 1947), p. 131.
2. G.W.F. Hegel, *The Philosophy of History* (New York: Dover Publications, 1956), p. 105.
3. Aristotle, "Politica" in *The Basic Works of Aristotle* (New York: Random House, 1941), p. 1284, Book VII, 4:25.

4. E.A. Gutkind, *The Twilight of Cities* (New York: The Free Press of Glencoe, 1962), p. 17.

5. Louis Wirth, "Urbanism as a Way of Life" in *Community, Life and Social Policy* (Chicago: University of Chicago Press, 1956), p. 120.

6. Leonard Reissman, *The Urban Process* (New York: The Free Press of Glencoe, 1964), p. 10.

7. *Ibid.*, p. 7.

8. Frank Fisher, "Where City Planning Stands Today," *Commentary*, January 1954, p. 75.

9. Charles Fourier, *Selections* (London: S. Sonnenschein & Co., 1901), p. 138.

10. Mel Scott, *American City Planning* (Berkeley: University of California Press, 1971), p. 1.

11. Lewis Mumford, "The Garden City Idea and Modern Planning," in Ebenezer Howard, *Garden Cities of Tomorrow* (Cambridge: The M.I.T. Press, 1965), p. 29.

12. F.J. Osborn (preface), *Ibid.*, p. 21.

13. Aristotle, *op. cit.*, p. 1284, Book VII, 5:32.

14. Le Corbusier, *The City of Tomorrow* (Cambridge: The M.I.T. Press, 1971), p. 1.

15. Frank Lloyd Wright, "The City as Machine," in *Metropolis: Values in Conflict*, ed. C.E. Elias, Jr., *et al.* (Belmont, Ca.: Wadsworth Publishing Co., Inc., 1964), p. 94.

16. Alexander Tzonis, *Towards a Non-Oppressive Environment* (Boston: i Press, Inc., 1972), p. 66.

17. Ebenezer Howard, *op. cit.*, p. 51.

18. *Ibid.*, see especially pp. 90, 113-15.

19. *Ibid.*, p. 150.

20. R. Buckminster Fuller, *Utopia or Oblivion* (New York: Bantam Books, 1969), p. 360.

21. "Blueprint for a Communal Environment," in *Sources*, ed. Theodore Roszak (New York: Harper Colophon Books, 1972), p. 393.

22. *Ibid.*, p. 394.

23. *Ibid.*, p. 395.

24. *Ibid.*, pp. 399, 400.

25. *Ibid.*, pp. 411-12.

26. *Ibid.*, p. 405.

Toward a Vision
of the
Urban Future

"**W**ithout testament," observed Hannah Arendt in *Between Past and Future*, "... without tradition — which selects and names, which hands down and preserves, which indicates where the treasures are and what their worth is — there seems to be no willed continuity in time and hence, humanly speaking, neither past nor future, only sempiternal change of the world and the biological cycle of creatures in it."[1]

If the city can be added to the lost treasures which Arendt laments in her deeply sensitive essays, this loss is due in no small measure to the modern stance of "contemporaneity," a stance which virtually denies an urban past in its deadening claim to sempiternal change, to an eternality of problems that have neither the retrospect of uniqueness nor the prospect of visionary solutions. To the degree that the very word "city" is still applied to the formless urban agglomerations that blot the human landscape, we live with the shallow myth that the problems of the civic present are equatable with those of the civic past — and hence, in a sinister sense, with the civic future. Accordingly, we know neither past nor future but only a present that lacks even the self-consciousness of its social preconditions, limitations, and historic fragility.

Our very language betrays the limitations within which we operate — more precisely, the preconceptions with which we define the functions of the modern city and our "solutions" to its problems. However operational it may be, the most unspoken preconception that guides our view of the modern city is an entirely entrepreneurial one. Indeed, all shabby moral platitudes aside, we simply view the city as a business enterprise. Our underlying urban problems are commonly described in fiscal terms and often attributed to "poor management," "financial irresponsibility," and "imbalanced budgets." Judging from this terminology, it would seem that a "good city" is a fiscally secure city, and the job of civic institutions is to manage the city as a "sound business." Presumably, the "best city" is not only one that balances its budget and is self-financing but even earns a sizable profit.

To anyone who has even a glancing acquaintance with urban history, this is a breathtaking notion of the city, indeed, a notion that could arise only in the most unadorned and mediocre of bourgeois epochs. Yet lacking a sense of both past and future, we would do well to recall that the city has variously been seen as a ceremonial center (the temple city), an administrative center (the palace city), a civic fraternity (the polis), and a guild city (the medieval commune). Heavenly or secular, it has always been uniquely a social space, the terrain in which the suspect "stranger" became transformed into the citizen — this, as distinguished from the biological parochialism of the clan and tribe with its roots in blood ties, the sexual division of labour, and age groups. As the Greeks so well knew, the "good city" represented the triumph of society over biology, of reason over impulse, of humanity over folkdom. That capitalism with its principle of unlimited growth and its own economic emphasis on "sempiternal change" began to expand the medieval marketplace beyond any comprehensible human scale is a problem that has been more than adequately explored; but where this tendency would take us was still conjectural. (2) The last century saw the city defer to — and even model itself — on the factory. (3) The opening years of the present century witnessed the conceptual reduction of the city to a "machine," a notion which was accepted by such presumably disparate architects and planners as Le Corbusier and Frank Lloyd Wright. McLuhan brought us into the multinational corporate world with his catchy phrase "the global village," and Doxiades presumably afforded us the "multidisciplinary" tools for making the multinational city seem like an international one. (4)

If the schemes of Le Corbusier, Wright, McLuhan, and Doxiades seem remote at present, if they have been pre-empted by the bookkeeping of Abe Beame, the shift is not without its irony. Beame plodded his way to the center of New York politics as a comptroller, not as a social reformer or city planner. His concept of community is probably exhausted by the New York Democratic Party's headquarters and backrooms. He lacks even the Dickensian eccentricities of a Scrooge. Only his gray hair, aging face, and diminutive stature rescue him from appearing as a corporate technocrat. He is, oddly enough, a man of the LaGuardia generation who, like the Abbe Sieyes of the French Revolution, could claim a supreme credential for having lived in a colourful, dramatic, and dynamic era: he managed to survive. By virtue of his very appearance and professional background, Beame personifies the transformation of New York's urban problems from those of social reform into those of fiscal manipulation.

Lest this transformation be taken too much for granted, it has implications that go far beyond any mere headlines. The change means that our modern capitalist society has not only subverted the city's historic role as a medium for socializing parochial fold into worldly humans; it has completely degraded the city into a mere business venture to be gauged by monetary rather than social or cultural criteria. It has, in effect, added a vulgar dimension to Arendt's worst fears of "sempiternal change" by removing the city from the history books and placing it in account books. The city has become a problem not in social theory, community, or psychology but in bookkeeping. It has ceased to be a human creation and has become a commodity. Its achievement is to be judged not by architectural beauty, cultural inspiration, and human association but by economic productivity, taxable resources, and fiscal success. The most startling aspect of this development — long in the making when the city was subordinated to the factory and to commerce — is that urban theory must cease to pretend that its revered social and cultural criteria apply to the modern city. Architecture, sociology, anthropology, planning, and cultural history tell us nothing about the city as it exists today. Urban ideology is business ideology. Its tools are not Doxiades' ekistics but double-entry bookkeeping.

The extent to which we have removed the city from the history books and placed it in the account books is evidenced not only by the declining cities of the northeast but by the burgeoning cities of the sunbelt. Success, here, is a quixotic form of failure — for the historic urban trend of our day has not been toward cities but rather a curious form of urbanization without cities.(5) The devolution of the sunbelt cities almost entirely into industrial and commercial "mousetraps" (to quote a *Fortune* journalist) has yielded a devastating form of "success." Business has become a cult; growth, a deity; money, a talisman. The mythic has reappeared in its most mundane quantified form to create one of the most dehumanizing ideologies in urban history. In the plastic, unadorned subdivisions, high-rises, and slab office buildings of Los Angeles, Phoenix, Dallas, and Houston eastward to Tampa and Miami, life and culture have been sacrificed to the most robotized forms of mass production, mass merchandizing, and mass culture. The faceless structures that sprawl across the "southern rim" lack the seasoning of history, of authentic cultural intercourse, of urban development and centering. The cities themselves have moved, for the most part, by huge leaps, not by evolution, and the propelling force of the leaps has been some sort of "resource," be it copper or petroleum, aerospace or electronics, range empires or agribusiness. The "gold fever" has never left the sunbelt; it has merely produced gold in different, often more feverish ways. If the American empire found its original colonies on the western frontier, the sunbelt cities have been its traditional outposts and provided the nodal points for its most aggressive domestic impulses.

Accordingly, these nodal points — now, sprawling Standard Metropolitan Statistic Areas — are economically "relevant." They form the centers of the "new" industries spawned by World War II, of intensively worked factory "farms," of fuels for high-technology, of shopping malls and retail emporiums. Big government, particulary the Federal government, occupies every niche that has not been filled by big business and the two inevitably interlink to form big bureaucracy. Municipal autonomy has rarely been a strategic concept in the SMSA's of the sunbelt. The earliest cities were often cavalry fortresses, not the new "Jerusalems" established by radical, often anarchistic religious and political dissenters. Although the frontier nourished the myth of rugged individualism, community, and vigilantism, its daily life and tenacious greed nourished self-interest and privatism. Not surprisingly, regional administration tends to supplant municipal administration, digesting not only neighborhoods but entire cities in the entrails of huge administrative bureaucracies. Citizenship, in turn, tends to be gauged more by the capacity to attract investment, make money, and engage in big-spending than by civic activism and social reform.

The northeastern cities are significantly different. New York, whose urban agony has made it paradigmatic for the cities of the entire region, was the most important point of entry for immigrants into the continent and their first point of contact with the realities of the "American Dream." The city achieved its elevated status not merely as a major port and financial center, but as the crucible in which the polyglot immigrants of Europe were melded into a usable labour force. American business itself accorded the city a special status, however resentfully and boorishly. Whether by virtue of high investments, political privileges or, more significantly, social reforms, the city had to be supported as the demographic and cultural placenta to Europe. More cosmopolitan than any other city in the land, it formed a lifeline to the old world with its material and intellectual riches. If a single part of the United States was the American "melting pot," it was New York City, and if America needed a space to achieve a measure of demographic and cultural homogeneity from which to draw Europe's labour and skills, it was through New York City.

The present "fiscal crisis" in New York means, quite frankly, that the city has been abandoned. Its traditional function is no longer necessary. Today, New York does not receive the bulk of its immigrants from Europe but from within the United States and its Hispanic "posessions." At a time when technology requires less muscle and more skill, New York has ceased to be an historic port of entry for needed "human resources" and has become the dumping ground for superfluous "human waste." The Statue of Liberty exhibits its backside to domestic refugees from religious and political persecution. With its growing proportion of blacks, Hispanics, and aged, the city has turned into an economic anachronism and a political menace. Its "minorities," who now comprise residential majorities in many parts of the city, are seen as impediments to a highly corporate, mechanized, and planned economy. Like the "masterless men" who appeared all over Europe during the decline of feudalism, these minorities have become marginal people in an era of technocratic state capitalism. From the bad conscience of the system, the city rears itself up as a spectre from the past that must be exorcised. Physically it must be set adrift, abandoned to its squalor, archaisms, and leprous process of decay.

It is not a satisfactory argument to rake up the trite explanations, such as "fiscal mismanagement" and an "eroding tax base," that Washington has flung at New York to justify its neglect of the city. One could reasonably ask if Washington itself has a more sound fiscal or economic base than the cosmopolis to the north. That Washington is largely a subsidized city, indeed subsidized partly by the massive taxes it drains from New York, suggests that the viability of any city in an era of oligopoly and state controls can no longer be explained by the precepts of "free enterprise" economics. Washington is artificially sustained because it is needed as a national administrative center. To the degree that any city is a heavy recepient of direct or indirect Federal funds, exorbitant revenues from oligopolistic practices, or loot drained by leisured high-income counties from exploited low-income ones, it is artificially sustained by the country as a whole. Accordingly, Washington lives on tax revenues requisitioned on a national scale, the sunbelt cities on aeronautic, and military subsidies, oil money, and real-estate hustles, the wealthy communities of southern California on riches plundered from the poorer countries of the north and east, the Imperial Valley on artifically inflated food prices by which New Yorkers, Bostonians, and Chicagoans are bled daily. That New York has been the object of opprobrium rather than support at all levels of the Federal government and the financial world is evidence not so much of its "fiscal mismanagement" but its lack of economic relevancy. Its eminence as a center of immigrant labour has waned and the immigrants it currently receives are viewed as despised social flotsam.

Perhaps no less significantly, the city has become politically dangerous. One could easily visualize that New York, which once provided the space for melding needed immigrant labour, could again be favored as a space in which "dispensable" sectors of the population could be dumped. It might seem plausible that, as "friendly fascism" oozes over the social landscape, it might leave oases in which the ethnically abused, the indigent, even the eccentrics, might find a home in the interests of social pacification. The most sinister feature of the trend toward corporate and state capitalism is that such oases are basically incompatible with a totalitarian trend, even of the "friendly" variety. The sixties have vividly demonstrated that "affluence" does not placate the restless but awakens them. In the language of modern sociologese, improved material conditions arouse "high expectations" and ultimately a rebellious ambience throughout the country. Viewed from this standpoint, current attempts to subvert New York City's traditional reformistic policies are not without political cunning. The centralized state's growing police functions and its increasing manipulation of the economy have been followed by its growing control over local administrative authority. New York's loss of municipal self-administration to the central government could portend a far-reaching destruction of municipal institutions everywhere. Rearing up before us would be an immense political behemoth that could engulf the last administrative structures of American towns and cities.

In the sunbelt cities, the emergence of such a behemoth already has acquired considerable reality. The tremendous weight that is given to economic expansion, to business operations, to governmentally fostered projects has served not only to promote mindless urban expansion but an appalling degree of civic passivity. The extent to which these cities have surrendered to industrial, commercial, and governmental operations is comparable only to the squalid decay of cities during the Industrial Revolution. The consequences of this surrender can be expressed as a form of municipal growth that occurs in inverse proportion to civic attrition — civic in the sense that that city once comprised a vital body politic. Homogeneity has effaced neighborhoods, regionalization has effaced municipalities, and immense enterprises, fed by the bequests of big government, have effaced the existence of a socially active citizenry. The basic concerns of the sunbelt cities are growth, not reform; the basic concerns of its citizens are services, not social participation. Politically, the residents of the sunbelt cities constitute a client population, bereft of citizenship and social activism by the very success of their economic growth. To the degree that meaningful politics is practiced in these cities, it is bureaucratically orchestrated by business and government.

If the great Hellenic standards of urbanism have meaning any longer for students of the city and its development, the disappearance of an active body politic, of an authentic, socially involved citizenry is equivalent to the death of the city itself. Greek social thought viewed the city as a public arena, a realm of discourse and rational administration that presupposed a public opinion, public institutions, and a public man. In the absence of such a public, there was no polis, no citizens, no community. The sunbelt cities have replaced public life by publicity, by a spectacular, typically American form of "dialogue" that involves the promotion of political and economic entities. In the spectacularized world of publicity, even the classical market of free entrepreneurs is converted into oligopolistically managed shopping malls, democratic political institutions into appointed bureaucracies, and citizens into taxpayers. What remains of the city is merely its high residential density, not its urbane populace.

If the municipal success of the sunbelt cities is marked by civic failure, the municipal failures of the older cities have been marked by a certain degree of civic success. Owing to the decline of municipal services in the older cities of the northeast, a vacuum is developing between the traditional institutions that managed the city and the urban population itself. These institutions, in effect, have been compelled to surrender a considerable degree of their authority to the citizenry. Understaffed municipal agencies can no longer pretend to adequately meet such basic needs as sanitation, education, health, and public safety. An eerie municipal "no-man's-land" is emerging between the institutional apparatus of the older cities and the people it professes to service. This "no-man's-land" — this urban vacuum, to be more precise — is slowly being filled by the ordinary people themselves. Far more striking than New York's fiscal crisis is the public response it has evoked. Libraries, schools, even hospitals and fire houses, have been occupied by aroused citizens, a trend that is significant not because amateurs can often exhibit a technical capacity to replace the services of professionals but rather the high degree of social activism that the crisis has aroused at a grass roots level. From the seeming decline of the older cities, taxpayers are slowly being transformed into citizens, privatized districts into authentic neighborhoods, and a passive populace into an active public.

If would be naive to overstate this trend and view it as a practical solution to the crises that beleaguer the northeastern cities. The awakening of public life in these cities will not end the erosion of their economic and fiscal bases. If the destiny of the American city is to be determined largely by its industrial and commercial "growth potential," this very criterion implies a redefinition of the city as a business enterprise, not a social and cultural space. So conceived, the city will have ceased to exist precisely because of its strictly economic preconditions and its standards of successful performance.

If the real historic basis of the city, on the other hand, is seen to be an active body politic and a spirited public life, then New York is more successful as an authentic municipality than Dallas or Houston. The evidence for this reawakening of citizen activity amidst urban decay is often compelling. For example, a convocation last year of block-association representatives by the Citizens Committee for New York City and the Federation of Citywide Block Associations, yielded 1,300 activists who, according to a *New York Times* report, "debated community with the zest, and frequently the contentiousness, of an election-year political convention." The report notes that the "neighborhood activists" were guided by the "conviction that civic betterment starts on the block where on lives." However oppressive the problems discussed — "crime, sanitation, housing improvements, fund-raising, recycling, day care and 'fighting City Hall'" — the mood of the activists "was anything but grim. There was almost an evangelical, upbeat spirit as block leaders told of ways they had successfully dealt with safety problems or found new techniques of raising money for tree planting."[5]

It matters little that the issues raised may often be trivial and inconsequential. What is far more important than the agenda of such forms is the extraparliamentary nature of the form itself and the participatory features of the association. Convocations of molecular civic groups like "block associations" that resemble a "political convention" in a normal year mark a rupture with institutionalized governmental processes. They comprise, in Martin Buber's sense, social structures as distinguished from political ones.[6] Power acquires a public, indeed a personal, character which, to the bureaucrat, is a kind of social "vigilantism" and "anarchy" and to the participant is a "town meeting." The energy that buoys up the convocation, the anti-hierarchical character that often marks its organization, and the verve of its participants implies a renewed sense of power as distinguished from the powerlessness that constitutes the social malaise of our times.

The trivialities of the agenda should not blind us to the historic importance of municipal reawakenings at this level of action. The role of civic activism as means for far-reaching social change dates back to the American and French revolutions, and formed the basis for revolutionary change in the Paris Commune of 1871. In revolutionary America, "the nature of city government came in for heated discussion," observes Merril Jensen in a fascinating discussion of the period. Town meetings, whether legal or informal, "had been a focal point of revolutionary activity." The antidemocratic reaction that set in after the American revolution was marked by efforts to do away with town meeting governments that had spread well beyond New England to the mid-Atlantic and Southern states. Attempts by conservative elements were made to establish a "corporate form (of municipal government) whereby the towns could be government by mayors and councils" elected from urban wards. Judging from New Jersey, the merchants "backed incorporation consistently in the efforts to escape town meetings." Such efforts were successful not only in cities and towns of that state but also in Charleston, New Haven, and eventually even Boston. Jensen, addressing himself to the incorporated form of municipal government and restricted suffrage that replaced the more democratic assembly form of the revolutionaries of 1776 in Philadelphia, expresses a judgement that could apply to all the successful efforts on behalf of municipal incorporation following the revolution: "The counter-revolution in Philadelphia was complete."[7]

A decade later, the French revolutionaries faced much the same problem when the *sans culottes* and enragés tried to affirm the power of the Parisian local popular assemblies or "sections" over the centralized Convention and Committee of Public Safety controlled by Robespierrists. Ironically, the final victory of the Convention over the sections was to cost Robespierre his life and end the influence of the Jacobins over subsequent developments.

The municipal movement, indeed a rich classical heritage of the city as community that had nourished the social outlook of German idealism and later utopian socialist and anarchist theories, dropped from sight with the emergence of Marxism and its narrow "class analysis" of history. Yet it can hardly be ignored that the Paris Commune of 1871, which provided Marxism and anarchism with its earliest models of a liberated society, was precisely a revolutionary municipal movement whose goal of a "social republic" had been developed within a confederalist framework of free municipalities or "communes."

Although the older northeastern cities of the United States hardly bear comparison with their own ancestral communities of two centuries ago, much less revolutionary Paris, it would be myopic to ignore certain fascinating similarities. The block committees of New York City are not the town meetings of Boston or the sections of Paris; they do not profess any historic goals for the most part nor have they advanced any programmatic expression in support of major social change. But they clearly score a new advance in the demands of their participants — primarily, a claim to governance in the administration of their "blocks," a proclivity for federation, and in the best of cases, an emerging body politic. The city itself is riddled by tenants associations, ad hoc committees and councils to achieve specific neighborhood goals, a stable Neighborhood Housing Movement, and broad-spectrum organizations that propound an ideology of "neighborhood government."[8] These groups, often networks, that advance a concept of decentralized self-management, however intuitive their views, stand out in refreshing relief against a decades-long history of municipal centralization and neighborhood erosion.[9] Even demands of "municipal liberty" are being heard in terms that are more suggestive of an earlier civic radicalism than its proponents are prepared to admit.

In a number of instances, such "block" and neighborhood organisations have gone beyond the proprieties of convocations, fundraising, sanitation, public safety, and even demonstrations to take over unused or abandoned property and stake out a moral right to cooperative ownership. Apart from episodic occupations of closed libraries, schools, and a "peoples" firehouse, the most important of these occupations have been neglected or unhabitable buildings. One such action, now called the "East Eleventh Street Movement" has achieved a national reputation. Initially, the Movement was a Puerto Rican neighborhood organization, one of several in the Lower Eastside of Manhattan, which formed an alliance with some young radical intellectuals to rehabilitate an abandoned tenement that had been gutted completely by fire. The block itself, one of the worst in the Hispanic ghetto, had become a hangout for drug addicts, car-strippers, muggers, and arsonists. Unlike most buildings which are taken over by squatters, 519 East 11 St. was a city-acquired ruin, a mere shell of a structure that had been boarded up after it had been totally destroyed by fire. This building was to be totally rebuilt by co-opers, composed for the most part of Puerto Ricans and some whites, by funds acquired from a city "program" that accepts labour as equity for loans — the now famous "sweat equity program."(10) The Movement's attempts to acquire the building, to fund it, to expand its activities to other abandoned structures were to become a cause celebre that has since inspired similar efforts both in the Lower Eastside and other ghetto areas. To a certain degree, the building was taken over before "sweat equity" negotiations with the city had been completed. The city was patently reluctant to assist the co-opers and apparently yielded to strong local pressure before supplying aid. The building itself was not only rebuilt but also "retrofitted" with energy-saving devices, insulation, solar panels for preheating water and a Jacobs wind generator for some of its electric power. An account of the conflicts between the "East Eleventh Street Movement," the city bureaucracy, and finally Consolidated Edision would comprise a sizable article in itself. What is perhaps the most significant feature of the project is its libertarian ambience. The project was not only a fascinating structural enterprise; it was an extraordinary cooperative effort in every sense of the term. Politically, the Movement was "fighting City Hall" — and it did so with an awareness that it was promoting decentralized local rights over big municipal as well as big State and Federal government. Economically, it was fighting the financial establishment by advancing a concept of labour — "sweat equity" — over the usual capital and monetary premises of investment. Socially, it was fighting the pre-eminence which bureau-racy has claimed over the community by intervening and often disrupting the maddening regulatory machinery that has so often, in itself, defeated almost every grass-roots movement for structural and neighborhood rehabilitation.

All of these conflicts were conducted with a minimal degree of hierarchy and a strong emphasis on egalitarian organizational forms. Participants were encouraged to voice their views and freely assume responsability for the building itself and the group's conflicts with municipal agencies and utilities. This organizational form has been preserved after the rebuilding of 519 East 11 Street was completed and occupied. The entire block was — and, in part, remains — involved in varying degreees with the group's activities and its efforts to reclaim other buildings in the area. Many participants have acquired a heightened sense of social awareness as a result of their own efforts to achieve a degree of "municipal liberty," if only for their own physical space and nearby blocks. Activists who remain involved with the larger aspects of the project — its explosive political, social, and economic implications — have a radical consciousness of their goals. What began as a desperate effort of housing co-opers to rescue their own homes, in effect, has become a social movement.

Such movements, in some cases involving "illegal" seizures of abandoned buildings, are growing in number in New York and other older cities. Although they have not always exhibited the staying power and libertarian ambience of the "East Eleventh Street Movement," they must be seen in terms of the context they have themselves created. "Municipal liberty" in the older cities, to be sure, does not mean the "liberty, equality, and fraternity" which the more radical Parisian sections tried to foster; nor does it have the mobilizing and solidarizing qualities of the more radical American town meetings. The projects than can be related to this new civic trend — be they housing co-opers, "sweat equity" programs, block committees, tenants groups, neighborhood "alliances, or cooperative day-care, educational, cultural, and even food projects — vary enormously in their longevity, stability, social consciousness, and scope. In some cases, they are blatantly elitist and civically exclusionary. To a large extent, they form a constellation of new subcultures that have evolved from the broader countercultural movement of the sixties, a constellation that has been greatly modified by ethnic disparaties, urban disarray, a broad disengagement of municipal government from its own constituency, an emerging "free space" for popular, often libertarian, civic entities, and the civic bases for a new body politic.

But a living trend they remain — and the most important trend to emerge in American cities today. In contrast to the bureaucratically managed and municipally regimented sunbelt cities, they represent a largely regional development. The very fact that they have been fueled by urban decay conceals their significance as the most significant trend in generations to reclaim the city as the public space for an authentic citizenry. If they are not a "vision" of the future, they may well be one of its harbingers. Certainly they are one of the most exciting links American cities have yet produced between the urban past and the urban future — a new "treasure," as Arendt might have put it, in the development of human community and the human spirit.

A vision of the urban future — if it is to be conceived as a city and not a sprawling agglomeration of man-made structures — is haunted by the past. The assumption that we cannot "return" to the past can become a trite excuse for ignorance of that very past or an unconditional renunciation of what we can learn from it. To the serious student of urban life, the most fascinating point of departure for relating past to future is the Hellenic polis. That we live in a world of nation-states and multinational corporations is no excuse to continue do so. The urban future must be viewed from a standpoint that may sharply contradict the immediate future of our present SMSAs, a future that seems to consist of more business, more structural as well as economic growth, and more centralization, whether in the name of "regionalization" or "federalism." That future must be above all a new conception of the "city of man" that fulfills our most advanced concepts of humanity's potentialities: freedom and self-consciousness, the two terms that form the historic message of Western civilization.

Self-consciousness, at the very least, implies a new self: a self that *can* be conscious. Consciousness, certainly in the fulness of its truth, presupposes an environment in which the individual can conceptually grasp the conditions that influence his or her life and exercise control over them. Indeed, insofar as an individual lacks these dual elements of consciousness, he or she is neither free nor fully human in the self-actualized sense of the term. Denied intellectual and institutional access to the economic resources that sustain us, to the culture that nourishes our mental and spiritual growth, and to the social forms that frame our behaviour as civilized beings, we are not only denied our freedom and our ability to function rationally but our very selfhood. The great cultural critics of society have voiced this conclusion for centuries. This conclusion has even more relevance today — an era of social decay that seems almost cosmic in its scale — than at any time in the past.

In terms of the city, such a conclusion means that a vision of the urban future can be regarded as rational and humanly viable only insofar as the city lends itself to individual comprehension — notably, that it is an entity that can be understood by the individual and modified by individual action. That the city whose population "can be taken in at a single view" (Aristotle) — that is, scaled physically and numerically to human dimensions — remained essential to the Hellenic ideal of the polis is merely another way of saying that a city without a citizenry, an active body politic, is not a city, indeed unworthy of anything but barbarians.[11] Human scale is a necessary condition for human self-fulfillment and social fulfillment. A humanistic vision of the future city must rest on the premise that the authentic "city of man" is comprehensible to its citizens or else they will cease to be citizens and public life itself will disappear. A vision of the urban future is thus meaningless if it does not include from its very outset the decentralization of the great SMSAs, the restoration of city life as a comprehensible form of public life.

Still another vision of the future must include the recovery of face-to-face form of civic management — a selfhood that is formed by self-management in assemblies, committees, and councils. We can never "outgrow" the Hellenic ecclesia or the American town meeting without debasing the word "growth" to mean mere change rather than development. The existence of an authentic public presupposes the most direct system of communication we can possibly achieve, notably, face-to-face communication. Again, another of Aristotle's caveats is appropriate here: "... in order to decide questions of justice and in order to distribute the offices according to merit it is necessary for the citizens to know each other's personal characters, since where this does not happen to be the case, the business of electing officials and trying law-suits is bound to go badly; haphazard decision is unjust in both matters, and this must obviously prevail in an excessively numerous community."(12) It need hardly be emphasized that Aristotle would have been appalled as much by the telecommunications of a "global village " as he would have been by the very concept of the world as a huge city or village. Human scale thus means human contact, not economic, cultural, and institutional comprehensibility alone. Not only should the things, forms and organizations that make up a community be comprehensible to the citizen, but the very individuals — their "personal characters" — who form the citizen body. The terms "citizen body," in this sense, assume more than an institutional concept; they take on a physical, existential, sensory, indeed protoplasmic, quality.

Thus far, I have been careful to stress the conditions that foster public life rather than the things that make for the "good life" materially. Decentralization and human scale have been emphasized as the bases for a new civic arena. Whether they are more "efficient" systems of social organization or more "ecological" types of association, as some writers have argued, has not been emphasized.(13) That a city, landscaped into the countryside, will promote a new land ethic and afford its citizens greater access to nature — perhaps even restore the urbanized farmer so prized by the Athenian polis and republican Rome — adds to the case for physical environment. But ultimately it is the very need for a reactivated citizenry that must be stressed over efficiency, ecological awareness, and vocational roundedness. Without that citizenry we now face the loss not only of our cities, but of civilization itself.

Finally, the recovery of a body politic and a civic community can scarcely be imagined without the commutarian sharing of the means of life — the material as well as social communizing that authentic community presupposes. In a technological world where the means of production are too powerful to be deployed any longer for means of domination, it is doubtful if society, much less the city, can survive a privately owned economy riddled by self-interest and an insatiable need for growth. More than the "good life," materially speaking, is involved in a communitarian system of production and distribution; the very existence of a coherent community interest is now at issue. Here, too, Hellenic culture has much to teach us about the future. Private interest can not be so dominant a motive in social relationships that it subverts the public interest. If private property once formed an underpinning of individualism in the corporatized cities of the past such as the guild-directed medievel towns, today, in the "free market" of giant oligopolies it has become the underpinning of naked egotism, indeed, the institutionalized expression of asocial behaviour of the most ruthless kind. If the city is to become a public body of active citizens, it must extend the public interest to the material as well as institutional and cultural elements of civic life.

Here we can part company with the Hellenic outlook and view the future as more than a recovery of the past. Modern technology — "hard," "soft," "appropriate," or as I would prefer to call it, liberatory — has finally made it possible for us to eliminate the fears which stalked Aristotle: "an overpopulous polis / of / foreigners and metics / who / will readily acquire the rights of citizens..." To these potential upstarts, one might also add slaves and women. The leisure or *schole* — the freedom from labour — that made it possible for Athenian citizens to devote their time to public life is no longer a birthright conferred by slavery on an ethnic elite but one conferred by technology on humanity as a whole. That we may feel free to reject that birthright for a "simpler," "labour intensive" way of life is a historic privilege that itself is conferred by the very existence of technology. Although a "global village" created by telecommunications would be an abominable negation of the city as a citizen body, "global citizenship" in clearly defined cities would constitute its highest actualization — the civic socialization of parochial folk into a universal humanity.

This vision of the urban future must now stand as it is — vague, perhaps, and broad but hopeful. Any additions or details would be utopian in the worst sense of the word. They would form a "blueprint" that seeks to design without discussion and impose without consent. A libertarian vision should be a venture in speculative participation. Half-finished ideas should be proferred deliberately, not because finished ones are difficult to formulate but rather because completeness to the point of details would subvert dialogue — and it is dialogue itself that is essential to civic relations, just as it is *logos* that forms the basis of society.

December 1978

FOOTNOTES

1. The ambiguity of the tendency is evident in the writings of Marx and Engels. Despite Engels's critical thrust in his well-known pamphlet "The Housing Question," he clearly shared Marx's view that the bourgeois city marked a distinct advance over rural "parochialism."

2. Notably organizations such as the Alliance for Neighborhood Government in the United States and the Montreal Citizens Movement (MCM) in Canada, The MCM, which already holds a considerable number of seats in Montreal's city council, has advanced the most radical program of all. "Nous devons instaurer notre propre démocratie afin de réaliser notre plan de réorganisation de la société," it declares in its latest program. And further: "Le conseil de quartier (which the MCM seeks to substitute for the existing "districts électoraux") ne devra donc jamais devenir un autre palier de gouvernement à l'intérieur de la société capitaliste" (Montreal Citizens Movement, 1976).

3. There is, in fact, no offical "sweat equity program" in New York City. The "program" is the legal and funding nexus which youthful activists on the East 11 Street project and "U-Hab," a New York homesteading group, created when early attempts were made to rebuild abandoned structures in the city. For the most recent survey of "sweat equity" projects in New York, see the Third Annual Progress Report of the Urban Homesteading Assistance Board.

4. Milton Kotler (1975), for example, has emphasized the efficiency of decentralization and F.S. Schumacher (1973), its capacity to promote ecological awareness. In the latter case, I must share some responsability for this emphasis in as much as Dr. Schumacher, quoting me by earlier pseudonym, Lewis Herber, accepts my assertion that "reconciliation of man with the natural world is no longer merely desirable, it has become necessary" (p. 107).

REFERENCES

ARENDT, H. (1954). Between past and future. New York: Viking.
ARISTOTLE (1943). Politics (B. Jowett, trans.). New York: Modern Library.
BOOKCHIN, M. (1973). The limits of the city. New York: Harper and Row.
—(forthcoming). Urbanization without cities. San Francisco: Sierra Club.
CARO, R.A. (1974). The power broker. New York: Knopf.

DOXIADES, C.A., and DOUGLAS, T.B. (1965). The new world of urban man. Philadelphia: University of Pennsylvania Press.

JENSEN, M. (1950). The new nation: A history of the United States during the confederation, 1781-1789. New York: Knopf.

KOTLER, M. (1969). Neighborhood government. New York: Bobbs-Merrill.
—(1975). "Neighborhood government." Liberation, 19 (8 and 9): 119-125.

Le CORBUSIER (1971). The city of tomorrow. Cambridge: M.I.T. Press.

McLUHAN, M., and FIORE, Q. (1968). War and peace in the global village. New York: Bantam.

New York Times (1976). March 26.

SCHUMACHER, F.S. (1973). Small is beautiful. London: Blond and Briggs.

WRIGHT, F.L. (1964). "The city as a machine." Pp. 91-94 in C.E. Elias, Jr. et al. (eds.), Metropolis: Values in conflict, Belmont, Calif.: Wadsworth.

"Toward a Vision of the Urban Future" by Murray Bookchin is reprinted from *The Rise of the Sunbelt Cities* (URBAN AFFAIRS ANNUAL REVIEWS, Vol. 14) David C. Perry and Alfred J. Watkins, Editors, copyright 1977 pp. 259-276 by permission of the Publisher, Sage Publications (Beverly Hills/London)

Marxism as
Bourgeois Sociology

Marx's work, perhaps the most remarkable project to demystify bourgeois social relations, has itself become the most subtle mystification of capitalism in our era. I refer not to any latent "positivism" in the Marxian corpus or to any retrospective recognition of its "historical limits." A serious critique of Marxism must begin with its innermost nature as the most advanced product — indeed, the culmination — of the bourgeois Enlightenment. It will no longer suffice to see Marx's work as the point of departure for a new social critique, to accept its "method" as valid despite the limited content it yielded in its day, to extol its goals as liberatory apart from its means, to view the project as tainted by its dubious heirs or adherents.

Indeed, Marx's "failure" to develop a radical critique of capitalism and a revolutionary practice emerges not even as a failure in the sense of an enterprise that remains inadequate to its goals. Quite to the contrary. At its best, Marx's work is an inherent self-deception that inadvertently absorbs the most questionable tenets of Enlightenment thought into its very sensibility and remains surprisingly vulnerable to their bourgeois implications. At its worst, it provides the most subtle apologia for a new historic era that has witnessed the melding of the "free market" with economic planning, private property with nationalized property, competition with the oligopolistic manipulation of production and consumption, the economy with the state — in short, the modern epoch of state capitalism. The surprising congruence of Marx's "scientific socialism" — a socialism which reared the goals of economic rationalization, planned production, and a "proletarian state" as essential elements of the revolutionary project — with the inherent development of capitalism toward monopoly, political control, and a seemingly "welfare state" has already brought institutionalized Marxian tendencies such as Social Democracy and Euro-Communism into open complicity with the stabilization of a highly rationalized era of capitalism. Indeed, by a slight shift of perspective, we can easily use Marxian ideology to describe this state capitalist era as "Socialist."

Can such a shift of perspective be shrugged off as a "vulgarization" or "betrayal" of the Marxian project? Or does it comprise the very realization of Marxism's most fundamental assumptions — a logic that may have even been hidden to Marx himself? When Lenin describes socialism as "nothing but state capitalist monopoly made to benefit the whole people," does he violate the integrity of the Marxian project with his own "vulgarizations"? Or does he reveal underlying premises of Marxian theory that render it historically into the most sophisticated ideology of advanced capitalism? What is basically at stake in asking these questions is whether there are shared assumptions between all Marxists that provide real premises for Social-Democratic and Euro-Communist practice and Lenin's futuristics. A theory that is so readily "vulgarized," "betrayed," or, more sinisterly, institutionalized into bureaucratic power forms by nearly all of its adherents may well be one that lends itself to such "vulgarizations," "betrayals," and bureaucratic forms *as a normal condition of its existence.* What may seem to be "vulgarizations," "betrayals," and bureaucratic manifestations of its tenets in the heated light of doctrinal disputes may prove to be the fulfillment of its tenets in the cold light of historical development. In any case, all the historical roles, today, seem to have been totally miscast. Rather than refurbishing Marxism so that it can catch up with the many advanced phases of modern capitalism, it may well be that many advanced phases of modern capitalism in the more traditional bourgeois countries have yet to catch up with Marxism as the most sophisticated *ideological* anticipation of the capitalist development.

Let there be no mistake that I am engaged in an academic play of words. Reality exhibits even more compelling paradoxes than theory. The Red Flag flies over a world of Socialist countries that stand at mutual war with each other, while Marxian parties outside their perimeter form indispensable props for an increasingly state capitalist world that, ironically enough, arbitrates between — or aligns itself with — its contending Socialist neighbors. The proletariat, like its plebian counterpart in the ancient world, shares actively in a system that sees its greatest threat from a diffuse populace of intellectuals, urban dwellers, feminists, gays, environmentalists — in short, a trans-class "people" that still expresses the utopian ideals of democratic revolutions long passed. To say that Marxism merely takes no account, today, of this utterly unMarxian constellation is to be excessively generous toward an ideology that has become the "revolutionary" persona of state capitalist reaction. Marxism is exquisitely constructed to *obscure* these new relationships, to distort their meaning, and, where all else fails, to reduce them to its economistic categories.

The Socialist countries and movements, in turn, are no less "socialist" for their "distortions" than for their professed "achievements." Indeed, their "distortions" acquire greater significance than their "achievements" because they reveal in compelling fashion the ideological apparatus that serves to mystify state capitalism. Hence, more than ever, it is necessary that this apparatus be explored, its roots unearthed, its logic revealed, and its spirit exorcised from the modern revolutionary project. Once drawn into the clear light of critique, it will be seen for what it truly is — not as "incomplete," "vulgarized" or "betrayed" but rather as the historic essence of counter-revolution, indeed, of counterrevolution that has more effectively used every liberatory vision against liberation than any historic ideology since Christianity.

MARXISM AND DOMINATION

Marxism converges with Enlightenment bourgeois ideology at a point where both seem to share a scientistic conception of reality. What usually eludes many critics of Marx's scientism, however, is the *extent* to which "scientific socialism" objectifies the revolutionary project and thereby necessarily divests it of all ethical content and goals. Recent attempts by neo-Marxists to infuse a psychological, cultural, and linguistic meaning into Marxism challenge it on its own terms without candidly dealing with its innermost nature. Whether consciously or not, they share in the mystifying role of Marxism, however useful their work may be in strictly theoretical terms. In fact, as to the matter of scientific methodology, Marx can be read in many ways. His famous comparison in the "Preface" to *Capital* of the physicist who experimentally reproduces natural phenomena in their "pure state" and his own choice of England as the "*locus classicus*" of industrial capitalism in his own day obviously reveals a scientistic bias that is only reinforced by his claim that *Capital* reveals the "natural laws" of "economic movement" in capitalism; indeed, that the work treats "the economic formation of society (not only capitalism — M.B.)... as a process of natural history..." On the other hand, such formulations can be counterbalanced by the dialectical character of the *Grundrisse* and of *Capital* itself, a dialectic that probes the internal transformations of capitalist society from an organic and immanent standpoint that hardly accords with the physicist's conception of reality.

What decisively unites both the scientism of physics and the Marxian dialectic, however, is the concept of "lawfulness" itself — the preconception that social reality and its trajectory can be explained in terms that remove human visions, cultural influences, and most significantly, ethical goals from the social process. Indeed, Marxism elucidates the function of these cultural, psychological, and ethical "forces" in terms that make them contingent on "laws" which act behind human wills. Human wills, by their mutual interaction and obstruction, "cancel" each other out and leave the "economic factor" free to determine human affairs. Or to use Engels's monumental formulation, these wills comprise "innumerable intersecting forces, an infinite series of parallelograms of forces which give rise to one resultant — the historic event." Hence, in the long run, "the economic ones are ultimately decisive." (Letter to J. Bloch) It is by no means clear that Marx, who adduces the physicist's laboratory as a paradigm, would have disagreed with Engels's social geometry. In any case, whether social "laws" are dialectical or not is beside the point. The fact is that they constitute a consistently *objective* basis for social development that is uniquely characteristic of the Enlightenment's approach to reality.

We must pause to weigh the full implications of this turn in what could be called Marx's "theory of knowledge." Greek thought also had a notion of law, but one that was guided more by a concept of "destiny" or *Moira* than "necessity" in the modern sense of the term. *Moira* embodied the concept of "necessity" governed by *meaning*, by an ethically conditioned goal fixed by "destiny." The actual realization of "destiny" was governed by justice or *Dike* which preserved the world order by keeping each of the cosmic elements within their appointed bounds. The mythic nature of this conception of "law" should not close our eyes to its highly ethical content. "Necessity" was not merely compulsion but *moral* compulsion that had *meaning* and *purpose*. Insofar as human knowledge has a right to assume that the world is an orderly one — an assumption that modern science shares with mythic cosmologies if only to make knowledge possible — it has a right to assume that this order has intelligibility or meaning. It can be translated by human thought into a purposive constellation of relations. From the implicit concept of goal that is inherent in any notion of an orderly universe, Greek philosophy could claim the right to speak of "justice" and "strife" in the cosmic order, of "attraction" and "repulsion," of "injustice" and "retribution." Given the eventual need for a nature philosophy that will guide us toward a deeper sense of ecological insight into our warped relationship with the natural world, we are by no means free of a less mythic need to restore this Hellenic sensibility.

The Enlightenment, by divesting law of all ethical content, produced an objective cosmos that had order without meaning. Laplace, its greatest astronomer, removed not only god from his description of the cosmos in his famous reply to Napoleon, but also the classical ethos that guided the universe. But the Elightenment left one arena open to this ethos — the social arena, one in which order still had meaning and change still had purpose. Enlightenment thought retained the ethical vision of a moral humanity that could be educated to live in a moral society. This vision, with its generous commitment to freedom, equality, and rationality was to be the well-spring of utopian socialism and anarchism in the century to follow.

Ironically, Marx completed Enlightenment thought by bringing the Laplacian cosmos into society — not, to be sure, as a crude mechanist but certainly as a scientist in harsh opposition to any form of social utopianism. Far more significant than Marx's belief that he had rooted socialism in science is the fact that he had rooted the "destiny" of society in science. Henceforth, "men" were to be seen (to use Marx's own words in the "Preface" to

Capital) as the "personification of economic categories, the bearer of particular class interest," not as individuals possessed of volition and of ethical purpose. They were turned into the objects of social law, a law as divested of moral meaning as Laplace's cosmic law. Science had not merely become a means for describing society but had become its fate.

What is significant in this subversion of the ethical content of law — indeed, this subversion of dialectic — is the way in which domination is elevated to the status of a natural fact. Domination is annexed to liberation as a precondition for social emancipation. Marx, while he may have joined Hegel in a commitment to consciousness and freedom as the realization of humanity's potentialities, has no *inherent* moral or spiritual criterion for affirming this destiny. The entire theory is captive to its own reduction of ethics to law, subjectivity to objectivity, freedom to necessity. Domination now becomes admissible as a "precondition" for liberation, capitalism as a "precondition" for socialism, centralization as a "precondition" for decentralization, the state as a "precondition" for communism. It would have been enough to say that material and technical development are preconditions for freedom, but Marx, as we shall see, says considerably more and in ways that have sinister implications for the realization of freedom. The constraints, which utopian thought at its best placed on any transgression of the moral boundaries of action are dismissed as "ideology." Not that Marx would have accepted a totalitarian society as anything but a vicious affront to his outlook, but there are no *inherent* ethical considerations in his theoretical apparatus to exclude domination from his social analysis. Within a Marxian framework, such an exclusion would have to be the result of objective social law — the process of "natural history" — and that law is morally neutral. Hence, domination can be challenged not in terms of an ethics that has an inherent claim to justice and freedom; it can be challenged — or validated — only by objective laws that have a validity of their own, that exist behind the backs of "men" and beyond the reach of "ideology." This flaw, which goes beyond the question of Marx's "scientism," is a fatal one, for it opens the door to domination as the hidden incubus of the Marxian project in all its forms and later developments.

THE CONQUEST OF NATURE

The impact of this flaw becomes evident once we examine the premises of the Marxian project at their most basic level, for at this level we find that domination literally "orders" the project and gives it intelligibility. Far more important than Marx's concept of social development as the "history of class struggle" is his drama of the extrication of humanity from animality into society, the "disembeddedness" of humanity from the cyclic "eternality" of nature into the linear temporality of history. To Marx, humanity is socialized only to the degree that "men" acquire the technical equipment and institutional structures to achieve the "conquest" of nature, a "conquest" that involves the substitution of "universal" mankind for the parochial tribe, economic relations for kinship relations, abstract labour for concrete labour, social history for natural history. Herein lies the "revolutionary" role of capitalism as a social era. "The bourgeois period of history has to create the material basis of the new world — on the one hand the universal intercourse founded upon the mutual dependency of mankind, and the means of that intercourse; on the other hand the development of the productive powers of man and the transformation of material production into a scientific domination of natural agencies," Marx writes in *The Future Results of British Rule in India* (July, 1853). "Bourgeois industry and commerce create these material conditions of a new world in the same way as geological revolutions have created the surface of the earth. When a great social revolution shall have mastered the results of the bourgeois epoch, the market of the world and the modern powers of production, and subjected them to the common control of the most advanced peoples, then only will human progress cease to resemble that hideous pagan idol, who would not drink the nectar but from the skulls of the slain."

The compelling nature of Marx's formulations — their evolutionary schema, their use of geological analogies to explain historical development, their crassly scientistic treatment of social phenomena, their objectivization of human action as a sphere beyond ethical evaluation and the exercise of human will — are all the more striking because of the period in which the lines were written (Marx's *Grundrisse* "period"). They are also striking because of the historic "mission" Marx imparted to English rule in India: the "destruction" of ancient Indian lifeways ("the annihilation of old Asiatic society") and the "regeneration" of India as a bourgeois nation ("the laying of the material foundations of Western society in Asia"). Marx's consistency in all of these areas deserves respect, not a tasteless refurbishing of classic ideas with eclectical exegesis and a theoretical adorning or "updating" of Marx with patchwork conclusions that are borrowed from utterly alien bodies of ideas. Marx is more rigorous in his notion of historic progress as the conquest of nature than his later acolytes and, more recently, neo-Marxians. Nearly five years later, in the *Grundrisse*, he was to depict the "great civilizing influence of capital" in a manner that accords completely with his notion of the British "mission" in India: "the production (by capital) of a stage of society compared with which all earlier stages appear to be merely *local progress* and idolatry of nature. Nature becomes for the first time simply an object for mankind, purely a matter of utility; it ceases to be recognized as a power in its own right; and the theoretical knowledge of its independent laws appears only as a stratagem designed to subdue it to human requirements, whether as the object of consumption or as the means of production. Pursuing this tendency, capital has pushed beyond national boundaries and prejudices, beyond the deification of nature and the inherited, self-sufficient satisfaction of existing needs confined within well-defined bounds, and the reproduction of the traditional way of life. It is destructive of all this, and permanently revolutionary, tearing down all obstacles that impede the development of productive forces, the expansion of needs, the diversity of production and the exploitation and exchange of natural and intellectual forces."

These words could be drawn almost directly from D'Holbach's vision of nature as an "immense laboratory," from D'Alembert's paeans to a new science that sweeps "everything before it... like a river which has burst its dam," from Diderot's hypostasization of technics in human progress, from Montesqieu's approving image of a ravished nature — an image that, judiciously mixed with William Petty's metaphor of nature as the "mother" and labour as the "father" of all commodities, clearly reveal the Enlightenment matrix of Marx's outlook. As Ernst Cassirer was to conclude in

an assessment of the Enlightenment mind: "The whole eigh-
teenth century is permeated by this conviction, namely, that in
the history of humanity the time had come to deprive nature of its
carefully guarded secrets, to leave it no longer in the dark to be
marveled at as an incomprehensible mystery but to bring it under
the bright light of reason and analyze it with all its fundamental
forces." *(The Philosophy of the Enlightenment)*

The Enlightenment roots of Marxism aside, the notion that
nature is "object" to be used by "man" leads not only to the total
despiritization of nature but the total despiritization of "man."
Indeed, to a greater extent than Marx was prepared to admit,
historic processes move as blindly as natural ones in the sense
that they lack consciousness. The social order develops under
the compulsion of laws that are as suprahuman as the natural
order. Marxian theory sees "man" as the embodiment of two
aspects of material reality: firstly, as a producer who defines
himself by labour; secondly, as a social being whose functions are
primarily economic. When Marx declares that "Men may be
distinguished from animals by consciousness, by religion or
anything else you like (but they) begin to distinguish themselves
from animals as soon as they begin to produce their means of
subsistence," *(The German Ideology)*, he essentially deals with
humanity as a "force" in the productive process that differs from
other material "forces" only to the degree that "man" can
conceptualize productive operations that animals perform in-
stinctively. It is difficult to realize how decisively this notion of
humanity breaks with the classical concept. To Aristotle, "men"
fulfilled their humanity to the degree that they could live in a *polis*
and achieve the "good life." Hellenic thought as a whole
distinguished "men" from animals by virtue of their rational
capacities. If a "mode of production" is not simply to be regarded
as a means of survival but a "definite *mode of life*" such that
"men" are *"what* they produce and *how* they produce" *(The
German Ideology)*, humanity, in effect, can be regarded as an
instrument of production. The "domination of man by man" is
primarily a *technical* phenomenon rather than an *ethical* one.
Within this incredibly reductionist framework, whether it is valid
for "man" to dominate "man" is to be judged mainly in terms of
technical needs and possibilities, however distasteful such a

criterion may seem to Marx himself had he faced it in all its brute clarity. Domination, too, as we shall see with Engels' essay "On Authority," becomes a technical phenomenon that underpins the realm of freedom.

Society, in turn, becomes a mode of labour that is to be judged by its capacity to meet material needs. Class society remains unavoidable as long as the "mode of production" fails to provide the free time and material abundance for human emancipation. Until the appropriate technical level is achieved, "man's" evolutionary development remains incomplete. Indeed, popular communistic visions of earlier eras are mere ideology because "only *want* is made general" by premature attempts to achieve an egalitarian society, "and with want the struggle for necessities and all the old shit would necessarily be reproduced." *(The German Ideology).*

Finally, even where technics reaches a relatively high level of development, "the realm of freedom does not commence until the point is passed where labour under the compulsion of necessity and of external utility is required. In the very nature of things it lies beyond the sphere of material production in the strict meaning of the term. Just as the savage must wrestle with nature, in order to satisfy his wants, in order to maintain his life and reproduce it, so civilized man has to do it, and he must do it in all forms of society and under all possible modes of production. With his development the realm of natural necessity expands, because his wants increase; but at the same time the forces of production increase, by which these wants are satisfied. The freedom in this field cannot consist of anything else but of the fact that socialized man, the associated producers, regulate their interchange with nature rationally, bring it under their common control, instead of being ruled by it as by some blind power; that they accomplish their task with the least expenditure of energy and under conditions most adequate to their human nature and most worthy of it. But it always remains a realm of necessity. Beyond it begins that development of human power, which is its own end, the true realm of freedom, which, however, can flourish only upon that realm of necessity as its basis. The shortening of the working day is its fundamental premise." *(Capital,* Vol. III) The bourgeois conceptual framework reaches its apogee, here in images of the "savage who must wrestle with nature," the unlimited expansion of needs that stands opposed to "ideological" limits to need (i.e., the Hellenic concepts of measure, balance, and self-sufficiency), the rationalization of production and labour as desiderata in themselves of a strictly technical nature, the sharp dichotomy between freedom and necessity, and the conflict with nature as a condition of social life in all its forms — class or classless, propertied or communistic.

Accordingly, socialism now moves within an orbit in which, to use Max Horkheimer's formulation, "Domination of nature involves domination of man" — not only "the subjugation of external nature, human and nonhuman" but human nature. *(The Eclipse of Reason)* Following his split from the natural world, "man" can hope for no redemption from class society and exploitation until he, as a technical force among the technics created by his own ingenuity, can transcend his objectification. The precondition for this transcendence is quantitatively measurable: the "shortening of the working day is its fundamental premise." Until these preconditions are achieved, "man" remains under the tyranny of social law, the compulsion of need and survival. The proletariat, no less than any other class in history, is captive to the impersonal processes of history. Indeed, as the class that is most completely dehumanized by bourgeois conditions, it can only transcend its objectified status through "urgent, no longer disguisable, absolutely imperative need..." For Marx, "The question is not what this or that proletarian, or even the whole proletariat at the moment, *considers* as its aim. The question is *what the proletariat is*, and what, consequent on that *being*, it will be compelled to do." *(The Holy Family)* Its "being," here, is that of object and social law functions as *compulsion*, not as "destiny." The subjectivity of the proletariat remains a product of its objectivity — ironically, a notion that finds a certain degree of truth in the fact that any radical appeal merely to the objective factors that enter into the forming of a "proletarian consciousness" or class consciousness strike back like a whiplash against Socialism in the form of a working class that has "bought into capitalism," that seeks its share in the affluence provided by the system. Thus where reaction is the real basis of action and need is the basis of motivation, the bourgeois spirit becomes the "world spirit" of Marxism.

The disenchantment of nature yields the disenchantment of humanity. "Man" appears as a complex of interests and class consciousness as the generalization of these interests to the level of consciousness. To the degree that the classical view of self-realization through the polis recedes before the Marxian view of self-preservation through Socialism, the bourgeois spirit acquires a degree of sophistication that makes its earlier spokesmen (Hobbes, Locke) seem naive. The incubus of domination now fully reveals its authoritarian logic. Just as necessity becomes the basis of freedom, authority becomes the basis of rational coordination. This notion, already implicit in Marx's harsh separation of the realms of necessity and freedom — a separation Fourier was to sharply challenge — is made explicit in Engels's essay "On Authority." To Engels, the factory is a natural fact of technics, not a specifically bourgeois mode of rationalizing labour; hence it will exist under communism as well as capitalism. It will persist "independently of all social organization." To coordinate a factory's operations requires "imperious obedience," in which factory hands lack all "autonomy." Class society or classless, the realm of necessity is also a realm of command and obedience, of ruler and ruled. In a fashion totally congruent with all class ideologists from the inception of class society, Engels weds Socialism to command and rule as a natural fact. Domination is reworked from a social attribute into a precondition for self-preservation in a technically advanced society.

HIERARCHY AND DOMINATION

To structure a revolutionary project around "social law" that lacks ethical content, order that lacks meaning, a harsh opposition between "man" and nature, compulsion rather than consciousness — all of these, taken together with domination as a precondition for freedom, debase the concept of freedom and assimilate it to its opposite, coercion. Consciousness becomes the recognition of its lack of autonomy just as freedom becomes the recognition of necessity. A politics of "liberation" emerges that reflects the development of advanced capitalist society into nationalized production, planning, centralization, the rationalized control of nature — and the rationalized control of "men." If the proletariat cannot comprehend its own "destiny" by itself, a party that speaks in its name becomes justified as the authentic expression of that consciousness, even if it stands opposed to the proletariat itself. If capitalism is the historic means whereby humanity achieves the conquest of nature, the techniques of bourgeois industry need merely be reorganized to serve the goals of Socialism. If ethics are merely ideology, Socialist goals are the product of history rather than reflection and it is by criteria mandated by history that we are to determine the problems of ends and means, not by reason and disputation.

There seem to be fragments in Marx's writings that could be counterposed to this grim picture of Marxian Socialism. Marx's "Speech at the Anniversary of the *People's Paper*" (April, 1856), for example, describes the enslavement of "man" by "man" in the attempt to master nature as an "infamy." The "pure light of science seems unable to shine but on a dark background of ignorance" and our technical achievements "seem to result in endowing material forces with intellectual life, and in stultifying human life into a material force." This moral evaluation recurs in Marx's writings more as explanations of historic development than justifications that give it meaning. But Alfred Schmidt, who quotes them at length in *Marx's Concept of Nature*, neglects to tell us that Marx often viewed such moral evaluations as evidence of immature sentimentality. The "speech" mocks those who "wail" over the misery that technical and scientific advances yield. "On our part," Marx declares, "we do not mistake the shape of the shrewd spirit (one may justifiably translate "shrewd spirit" to read "cunning of reason" — M.B.) that continues to mark all these contradictions. We know that to work well the new-fangled forces of society, they only want to be mastered by new-fangled men — and such are the working men." The speech, in fact, ends with a tribute to modern industry and particularly to the English proletariat as the "first born sons of modern industry."

Even if one views Marx's ethical proclivities as authentic, they are marginal to the core of his writings. The attempts to redeem Marx and fragments of his writings from the logic of his thought and work becomes ideological because it obfuscates a thorough exploration of the meaning of Marxism as a practice and the extent to which a "class analysis" can reveal the sources of human oppression. We come, here, to a fundamental split within Socialism as a whole: the limits of a class analysis, the ability of a theory based on class relations and property relations to explain history and the modern crisis.

Basic to anti-authoritarian Socialism — specifically, to Anarchist Communism — is the notion that hierarchy and domination cannot be subsumed by class rule and economic exploitation, indeed, that they are more fundamental to an understanding of the modern revolutionary project. Before "man" began to exploit "man," he began to dominate woman; even earlier — if we are to accept Paul Radin's view — the old began to dominate the young through a hierarchy of age-groups, gerontocracies, and ancestor-worship. Power of human over human long antedates *the very formation of classes and economic modes of social oppression.* If "The history of all hitherto existing society is the history of class struggles," this order of history is preceded by an earlier, more fundamental conflict: social domination by gerontocracies, patriarchy, and even bureaucracy. To explore the emergence of hierarchy and domination is obviously beyond the scope of this work. I have dealt with it in considerable detail in my forthcoming book, *The Ecology of Freedom.* Such an exploration would carry us beyond political economy into the realm of the domestic economy, the civil realm into the family realm, the class realm into the sexual realm. It would provide us with an entirely new psychosocial set of foundations from which to read the nature of human oppression and open an entirely new horizon from which to gauge the true meaning of human freedom. We would certainly have to shed the function Marx imparts to interest and technics as social determinants — which is not to deny their role historically, but to search into the claims of non-economic factors such as status, order, recognition, indeed, into rights and duties which may even be materially burdensome to commanding strata of society. This much is clear: it will no longer do to insist that a classless society, freed of material exploitation, will necessarily be a liberated society. There is nothing in the social future to suggest that bureaucracy is incompatible with a classless society, the domination of women, the young, ethnic groups or even professional strata.

These notions reveal the limits of Marx's own work, his inability to grasp a realm of history that is vital to understanding freedom itself. So blind is Marx to authority as such that it becomes a mere technical feature of production, a "natural fact" in "man's" metabolism with nature. Woman, too, becomes an exploited being not because she is rendered docile by man (or "weak" to use a term that Marx regarded as her most endearing trait) but because her labour is enslaved to man. Children remain merely "childish," the expression of untamed and undisciplined "human nature." Nature, needless to say, remains mere object of utility, its laws to be mastered and commanded in an enterprise of conquest. There can be no Marxian theory of the family, of feminism, or of ecology because Marx negates the issues they raise or worse, transmutes them into economic ones. Hence, attempts to formulate a Marxian feminism tend to degenerate into "wages for housewives," a Marxian psychology into a Marcusan reading of Freud, and a Marxian ecology into "pollution is profitable." Far from clarifying the issues that may help define the revolutionary project, these efforts at hybridization conceal them by making it difficult to see that "ruling class" women are ruled by "ruling class" men, that Freud is merely the alter ego of Marx, that ecological balance presupposes a new sensibility and ethics that are not only different from Marxism but in flat opposition to it.

Marx's work is not only the most sophisticated ideology of state capitalism but it impedes a truly revolutionary conception of freedom. It alters our perception of social issues in such a way that we cannot relevantly anchor the revolutionary project in sexual relations, the family, community, education, and the fostering of a truly revolutionary sensibility and ethics. At every point in this enterprise, we are impeded by economistic categories that claim a more fundamental priority and thereby invalidate the enterprise at its outset. Merely to amend these economistic categories or to modify them is to acknowledge their sovereignty over revolutionary consciousness in altered form, not to question their relationship to more fundamental ones. It is to build obscurantism into the enterprise from the outset of our investigation. The development of a revolutionary project must *begin* by shedding the Marxian categories from the very beginning, to fix on more basic categories created by hierarchical society from its inception all the more to place the economic ones in their proper context. It is no longer simply capitalism we wish to demolish; it is an older and more archaic world that lives on in the present one — the domination of human by human, the rationale of hierarchy as such.

February, 1979

On Neo-Marxism,
Bureaucracy,
and the
Body Politic

The historic failure of proletarian socialism, particularly its Marxian form, to provide a revolutionary theory and practice for our time has been followed by a highly abstract form of socialist theoretics that stands sharply at odds with the very notion of a revolutionary project — notably, a theory that is meant to yield a viable revolutionary practice.

If this judgment seems harsh, it hardly conveys the extent to which this theoretics has become a considerable culture industry in its own right. The retreat of socialism from the factory to the academy — an astonishing phenomenon that cannot be justified by viewing "knowledge" as a technical force in society — has denied socialism the right to a decent internment by perpetuating it as a professionalized ideology. An enfeebled theory, long drained of its sweeping liberatory claims, socialism has been turned from a social phenomenon into an academic discipline, from a historic reality into a mere specimen of intellectual history that is cultured exotically all the more to obscure the need for an entirely new conception of theory and practice.

Indeed, to the degree that the academy itself has become increasingly disengaged from society, it has used socialist theoretics to indulge its worst intellectual habits. The remains of a once-insurgent movement have provided the intellectual nutrients for academic conceptual frameworks that are utterly alien to it — a level of discourse, a range of perceptions, a terminology, and a body of intellectual pretensions that mutually reinforce the reduction of academic ideology to socialism and of socialism to ideology. One must leave it to the conscience of the socialist academics to ask themselves if Marx's account of social development as a history of class struggle can be translated into a history of "distorted communication," [1] his critique of political economy into a specific "paradigm" of "intersubjectivity," and his relations of production into "symbolically mediated forms of social interaction." An earlier generation of Marxian theorists, however serious their shortcomings, would have banished the very term "sociology" from the vocabulary of radical ideas, not to speak of its desiccated categories and its odious pretensions to exactitude. Today, this vocabulary has been replaced by a more ennervated one in which socially neutral terms and concepts, denuded of the flesh and blood of experience, pirouette around each other in an intellectual ballet that imparts to them an almost dream-like transcendental quality. The most technically convoluted strategies for stating the obvious — Marx's scientism, economism, and his roots in the Enlightenment — are cultivated to create a dichotomy between theoretics and reality that effectively immunizes concepts to the test of experience.

Partly in reaction to this trend, experience itself has been hypostasized at the expense of theoretical coherence — to a point, at times, when the refreshing immediacy of reality fosters a reverence for raw facts of "perception," indeed, for the authority of the episodic and anecdotal. It remains to be seen if Habermas's highly formalized theoretics can be given real social substance by the research of his colleagues at Starnberg or if various phenomenological and structural tendencies that have been drifting through Marxism can bring socialism into a meaningful confrontation with contemporary industrial capitalism. But in all of these cases, theoretical critique has been notable for its absence of radical reconstruction. Neither the later generation of "critical theorists" nor their opponents as reflected by newer formalizations of Marxism have given substance to their visions of freedom and practice. Shaped by academic templates like speech situations, systems theory, *Verstehen*, and research guided by the technical criteria of sociology, the harsh fact remains that socialism has been converted from a once viable social reality into the "idea" of socialism in much the same sense that Collingwood dealt with the "idea" of nature. Theoretical coherence has not been spared the revenge of a lack of experience any more than experience has been spared the revenge of a lack of theoretical coherence. Both have become equally abstract in their one-sidedness and partiality.

What is most disturbing about the self-absorption of so many of these theoretical and empirical tendencies — tendencies which may be broadly designated as "neo-Marxian" — is the promiscuity with which they meld utterly antithetical radical goals and traditions. Libertarian concepts and authoritarian ones, individualistic and collectivistic, economistic and cultural, scientistic and ethical — all have been funded together into an ecumenical "radicalism" that lacks the consistency required by a serious revolutionary practice. Classical Marxian tendencies, functioning under the imperatives of organized political movements, were compelled to press the logic of their premises to the point of a combative social engagement with bourgeois reality. Neo-Marxism enjoys the luxury of theoretical reveries in which basically incompatible visions of freedom intermingle and become diffuse and obscure.

Let me state this problem concretely. Are the differences between decentralization and centralization merely differences of degree or of kind? Should we seek to strike some enigmatic "balance" between them or are they fundamentally incompatible with each other? Is direct democracy in a "mass society" (to use Marcuse's fascinating expression in his discussion of this issue) impossible without the delegation of power to representatives or must it literally be direct, face-to-face, of the kind that prevailed in the Athenian polis, the French revolutionary sections of 1793, and the New England town meetings? Can direct democracy be equated with workers' councils, soviets, the German *Räte*, an equation that is made not only by neo-Marxists, council communists, but also many anarchosyndicalists? Or do these essentially executive forms stand at odds with the communes and popular assemblies emphasized by anarcho-communists? Can bureaucracy of any kind coexist with libertarian institutions or are they inexorably opposed to each other?

Doubtless, these questions raise many problems of terminology that can easily obscure points of agreement between seemingly contrasting views. To some neo-Marxists who see centralization and decentralization merely as difference of degree, the word "centralization" may merely be an awkward way of denoting means for *coordinating* the decisions made by decentralized bodies. Marx it is worth noting, greatly confused this distinction when he praised the Paris Commune as a "working, not a parliamentary body, executive and legislative at the same time.(2) In point of fact, the consolidation of "executive and legislative" functions in a single body was regressive. It simply identified the process of policy-making, a function that rightly should belong to the people in assembly, with the technical execution of these policies, a function that could be left to strictly administrative bodies subject to rotation, recall, limitations of tenure, wherever possible, selected by sortition. Accordingly, the melding of policy formation with administration placed the institutional emphasis of classical socialism on centralized bodies, indeed, by an ironical twist of historical events, bestowing the privilege of formulating policy on the "higher bodies" of socialist hierarchies and their execution precisely on the more popular "revolutionary committees" below.

Similarly, the concept of "representation" intermingled with "direct democracy" serves to obscure the distinction between popular institutions which should decide policy and the "representative" institutions which should merely execute them. In this connection, Rousseau's famous passage on the constitutive nature of a "people" in *The Social Contract* applies even more to the "mass society" of our times than the institutionally articulated one of his era. "Sovereignty, for the same reason that makes it inalienable, cannot be represented" Rousseau declares; "it lies essentially in the general will and will does not admit of representation: it is either the same or other; there is no intermediate possibility. The deputies of the people, therefore, are not and cannot be its representatives: they are merely its stewards, and can carry through no definitive acts. Every law the people has not ratified *in person* is null and void — is, in fact, not a law. The people of England regards itself as free: but it is grossly mistaken: it is free only during the election of members of parliament. As soon as they are elected, slavery overtakes it, and it is nothing." However problematical Rousseau's concept of "general will" may be, quite aside from his archaic concept of "law," the premises that underly it cannot be evaded: "... the moment a people allows itself to be represented, it is no longer free: *it no longer exists.*"(3) (My emphasis — M.B.)

It is precisely in terms of a "general will" more libertarian and individuated than any conceived by Rousseau that reveals the workers' councils, soviets, and the *Räte* to be socially one-sided and potentially hierarchical. Councils may be popularly constituted, but they are not *constitutive* of a "public sphere." As the locus of the decision-making process in society, they absorb within executive bodies the liberties that more appropriately belong to a clearly delineable body politic and thereby subvert institutions such as communes, cooperatives, and popular assemblies that indeed constitute a people and express a popular will. Councils, in effect, usurp the political subjectivity that should be shared by all in social forms that express the individual's claim to social sovereignty. That Bolshevism recognized this possibility and later cynically exploited it is revealed by the emphasis Lenin placed on the factory as the social basis of the soviets. Here, indeed, a "proletarian public sphere," to use Oscar Neckt's phrase, was acknowledged and hypostasized—not as a truly democratic arena, but as the locus for a "proletarian public" that could be strategically deployed against the great mass of "unreliable" peasants whose villages comprised the authentic "public sphere" of revolutionary Russia.

But the factory, far from being the strongest aspect of the "proletarian public sphere" is, in fact, its most vulnerable.* However much its social weight is reinforced by revolutionary shop committees and the most democratic forms of self-management, the factory is in no sense an autonomous social organism. Quite to the contrary, it is a particularly dependent one that can only function—indeed, exist—in conjunction with other factories and sources of raw materials. The Bolsheviks were to astutely use this very limitation of the factory to centralize the "proletarian public sphere" to a point where they were to remove the last vestigial remains of proletarian democracy: first, by employing the soviets to isolate the factory from its place in the local community; then, by shifting power from the community to the nation in the form of national congresses of soviets. The use of soviets to interlink the proletariat from factory to factory across the entire breadth of Russia, literally amputating it as a social

---

* I say this provocatively because the myth still persists among council communists, many neo-Marxists, and particularly anarchosyndicalists (who, owing to the resurgence of the CNT in Spain, represent a very vocal constituency in the European libertarian Left) that "workers control" of the economy is equivalent to worker's control of society. All theoretical considerations aside, the ease with which the CNT was out-maneuvered by the bourgeois state, despite its massive control of the Catalan economy in 1936-37, should have dispelled such simple economistic notions of power a generation ago.

stratum from any comprehensible roots in specific localities where it could function effectively, served to hopelessly delimit its powers and to rigorously centralize it. In the immense, national congresses of soviets staged annually during the revolutionary years, the Russian proletariat had lost all power over the soviets even before the authority of the congresses had been completely usurped by the Bolshevik party.[4]

Quite likely, the centralization of the proletariat could have been achieved by the Bolsheviks in any case, without manipulating the soviet hierarchy. The very *class* nature of the proletariat, its existence as a creature of a national division of labour and its highly particularistic interests that rarely rise to the level of a general interest, belie Marx's claims for its universality and its historic role as a revolutionary agent. These attributes, which hindsight clearly reveals today, explain the failure of all classical "proletarian revolutions" in the past. Neither the Paris Commune, which was really fought out by the last remnants of the traditional French *sans culottes*, nor the Spanish revolution, which was fought out by workers with rural roots, are exceptions. Indeed, Social Democracy and Leninism in all its varieties used this particularistic interest with great effect against broader revolutionary tendencies in society as witness Ebert's shrewd manipulation of the German *Räte*, Stalin's infamous "Lenin Levy," and more recently, the commanding influence of European Communist and Socialist parties over the working class today.

Space does not make it possible to deal with the hierarchical nature of the factory structure and its impact on the formation of proletarian consciousness. If labour is the "steeling school" of the proletariat, as the young Marx was to emphasize, its locus, the factory, is a "school" based on "imperious obedience," as Engels was to add in later years — indeed, a "school" marked by the complete absence of "autonomy."[5] I have explored this issue elsewhere, in a work written more than a decade ago, and more recently, in my forthcoming *Ecology of Freedom*, where I question the existence of the factory as a natural fact of technics that must persist "independently of all social organization" (Engels).[6]

What is significant in all of these issues is the way they are *integrated* by neo-Marxism into the very problematical premises of classical Marxism, thereby neutralizing them as the bases for a thoroughly new radical theory and practice. Perhaps the most striking examples of these incongruities can be culled from Marcuse's sixties writings, a literature which juxtaposes traditional, shopworn interpretations of political reality with philosophical, esthetic, and psychoanalytic insights that, in themselves, clearly pave new theoretical ground. These incongruities cannot be dismissed as the blind-spots of an otherwise far-ranging mind. I must reluctantly insist that they impugn the integrity of the larger vision Marcuse was to advance, the extent to which it was fully thought out, and the political conclusions that followed from it.

It is not trivial to ask why a work like *An Essay on Liberation* that contrasted the need for a "moral radicalism" with the scientistic radicalism of Marxian orthodoxy; that called for a "passing from Marx to Fourier" and "from realism to surrealism"; that celebrated the "new sensibility" of the sixties counter-culture for its sensuousness, playfulness, and the challenge it posed to the "*esprit de sérieux* in the socialist camp"; that singled out the "aesthetic dimension" as "a sort of gauge for a free society" — indeed, that with all of this buoyant utopianism, could have casually included the observation that the "global dominion of corporate capitalism... keeps the socialist orbit on the defensive, all too costly not only in terms of military expenditures but also in the perpetuation of a repressive bureaucracy." Or claim that in Vietnam, Cuba, and China, "a revolution is being defended and driven forward which struggles (!) to eschew the bureaucratic administration of socialism." Or, still further, deals with the "Third World" as an "external proletariat" and its insurgent peasantry as a "rural proletariat" with the inevitable implication (stated more explicitly by Marcuse during a lecture at New York University a year earlier) that the apparent docility of the "internal proletariat" of the Euro-American "orbit" did not negate Marx's traditional theory of class struggle when capitalism is viewd as a global phenomenon.(7)

One cannot afford to merely grimace at such distasteful Bolshevik apologetics for the "socialist orbit" as a society "deformed" by a "repressive bureaucracy" because of capitalist encirclement. Nor can one regard it as an expression of the *geist* of the time that Marcuse, a man thoroughly schooled in the history of the interwar Left, could mystify the Vietnamese, Cuban, and Chinese "revolutions" as anti-bureaucratic — certainly not without deliberately ignoring the Bolshevik legacy claimed by their leaders, the Stalinist structure of their parties, and the specious nature of the "revolutions" themselves. For nearly two generations, Marxists had debated the question of whether "repressive bureaucracies" within the "socialist orbit" (which certainly includes Vietnam, Cuba, and China) were merely "deformations" produced by capitalist encirclement or whether the "socialist orbit" itself constituted a historically new typology that required critique in its own right. The schizophrenic nature of Marcuse's vision was to find its most striking expression in *Counter-Revolution and Revolt* where, incredibly, the "mass" Communist parties of Europe and their unions were placed on the "Left of Social Democracy" and, as a result of this meaningless "constellation," were described as "still a potentially revolutionary force."(8) Such observations are not episodic errors in judgement; they reflect a preformed social outlook that is more basic than encomiums to "moral radicalism," "Fourier," "surrealism," and the "aesthetic dimension" as "a sort of gauge for a free society."

Characteristically, when the chips are down, Marcuse like many neo-Marxists, falls on the side of centralization, delegated power, councils, and authority, as against decentralization, direct democracy, popular assemblies, and spontaneity. Again, like his melding of "moral radicalism" with Bolshevik apologetics, he does not explore the conflicting logic of these concepts, but mystifies them with a libertarian rhetoric that conceals his orthodox Marxist foundations. Occasionally, this rhetoric does violence to historical fact. For one who has lived through the Spanish Civil War era, for example, it is astonishing to read that the "international brigades" — a force Stalinist movements crassly employed for counterrevolutionary as well as military purposes — symbolized the "union of young intellectuals and workers."(9) Not only was the formulation maladroit thirty years after the war, but it grossly misled the ill-informed radical youth who revered Marcuse as their elder statesman.* We are reaping the harvest of such historical sloppiness, today, with an effluvium of romantic eulogies to the Rosenbergs and the Stalinist hacks of the 1930s — this, quite aside from a revival of Stalinism by young sectarians who have been schooled in the writings of Ho, Mao, and Fidel. Doubtless, to impute these trends to Marcuse's political sloppiness would be ridiculous. But that he contributed even passingly to the making of such myths rather than their ruthless demystification is not to be shrugged off as accidental and raises even larger issues about the premises of neo-Marxism as such.

Accordingly, even as Marcuse exultantly praises the "rebels" of May-June 1968 for using "direct action" to transform the "indirect democracy of corporate capitalism into a direct democracy," his libertarian fervor is increasingly dispelled by the formulations which follow. "Direct action," and more pointedly, "direct democracy," vaporize into "elections and representation (that) no longer serve as institutions of domination." This hopelessly feckless formula is groomed with such traditionally Marxian rhetoric as "genuinely free selection and election of candidates, revocability at the discretion of constituencies, and uncensored education and information." Even Lenin in *State and Revolution* dispensed more generous liberties that Marcuse. What links Lenin and Marcuse in a common belief is their shared view that "in a modern mass society," to use Marcuse's words, "democracy, no matter in what form, is not conceivable without a system of representation." To reduce this formula to its molecular constituents, Marcuse cannot envision socialism without a "mass society" anymore than Engels can envision socialism without factories.(10)

Not surprisingly, Marcuse is more at home with the "seminal achievements of... the 'councils' ('soviets,' *Räte*) as organizations of self-determination, self-government (or rather preparation for self-government) in local popular assemblies." That

---

* For my own part, I could cite many personal experiences where young people who read this passage in Marcuse's essay and viewed such repellent "documentaries" as *To Die in Madrid* had to be educated into the real facts about Spain, not to speak of such myths as the "libertarian" proclivities of Maoism and theory of an "external proletariat," a position that was later to become the keystone of Weatherman propaganda.

Räte and "local popular assemblies" stand in historic contradiction to each other is not posed as an issue because the contradiction lacks intelligibility if one thinks of a free society in largely institutional or structural terms — which are the terms with which Marcuse operates on a political level. If his Freudo-Marxism reclaims the sovereignty of the ego, of play and the "aesthetic dimension" in daily life, it lacks any viable life-line to his notion of socialism as a "mass society." This dualism that divides Marcuse's anarchism on the personal plane from his Marxian pragmatics on the social must inevitably lead to the absorption of the personal by the social, of the "black flag" (to use his own metaphors) by the "red flag."[11] When he advances the slogan, "Spontaneity does not contradict authority," is it necessary to ask what he means by the word "authority." Self-discipline, education, and wisdom, as I have argued elsewhere in advancing the notion of "informed spontaneity" — or obedience, submission, and surrogation of will? It is by no means clear that one can infer from Marcuse's Freudo-Marxism that the rights he acknowledges for the individual can be translated into social and institutional terms. The two are loosely bonded precisely because Marcuse sees no contradiction between his anarchism on the personal level and his Marxism on the social. Theory may permit this dichotomy to exist indefinitely as an exotic flower with a prickly stem, hence the success neo-Marxism enjoys as an academic project. Practice must bring the two into bitter contradiction with each other once neo-Marxism removes itself from the campus — and where it has done so, it exercises virtually no influence.

It would be a grave error to view my remarks on Marcuse as a critique of Marcuse as an *individual* thinker. Inasmuch as his theoretics have dealt more directly with social problems than that of any other neo-Marxist body of theory, they more clearly reveal the limits of the neo-Marxian project. Habermas is veiled by a formalism so abstract and a jargon so equivocal and dense that he is almost beyond the reach of pointed criticism. Castoriadis has abandoned Marxism completely. More importantly, the seeming schizophrenia of Marcuse's theoretics is not a personal trait but a *generic* one. Owing to Marcuse's own courage in venturing into social issues that neo-Marxists usually avoid — direct democracy, decentralization, representation, spontaneity, and liberatory social structures — he clearly reveals the extent to which these issues are intrinsically alien to Marxism as such, indeed to socialism. To this list of issues, one may reasonably add ecology, urbanism, and more fundamentally, hierarchy, domination, and a liberatory rationality.

What neo-Marxists have not candidly faced is the extent to which Marxism in all its forms is organically structured to respond to social changes that lend themselves to analyses of class relations, economic exploitation, industrial rationalization, political institutions, and mass constituences. To the degree social changes raise broader issues of hierarchy, domination, ecological dislocations, liberatory technologies, social forms based on face-to-face relations, and individual sovereignty, these issues must be "hydrolyzed" (if I may be permitted to use a biological analogy) into simpler, more "soluble" ingredients that render them accessible to Marxian categories, indeed, to a Marxian outlook. That such monumental social issues must be degraded so that they can be absorbed by Marxism raises the basic question of whether the theory can be perpetuated in its wholeness or whether it should not be fragmented and its more viable components absorbed into a much broader theory and practice that will eschew the very use of terms like "Marxism" and "socialism."*

Ultimately, a line will have to be drawn that, by definition, excludes any project that can tip decentralization to the side of centralization, direct democracy to the side of delegated power, libertarian institutions to the side of bureaucracy, and sponta-

---

* I cannot help but note that Freudo-Marxism itself is an unstable hybridization of subjective categories with the value-free "social science" Marx sought to bestow on socialism. Women's liberation, like ecology, urbanism, even "workers' control" and neighborhood sovereignty, must be grafted on to the Marxian corpus like alien theoretical transplants. Alas, the sutures barely hold the grafts to the main body. A veritable industry, maintained by a number of well-known "neo-Marxist" hacks, has been established to provide the necessary cosmetics for the disfiguring effects of this bizarre surgery. But behind it all, one invariably encounters the same Marxian outlook with its fixation on the proletariat ("external" or "internal," "old" or "new"), on economic data and power constellations. Important as these areas surely are, they are not the last word in social analyses and as mere subjects of analyses do not provide the fundamental bases for theoretical reconstruction and a new radical practice.

neity to the side of authority. Such a line, like a physical barrier, must irrevocably separate a libertarian zone of theory and practice from the hybridized socialisms that tend to denature it. This zone must build its anti-authoritarian, utopian, and revolutionary commitments into the very recognition it has of itself, in short, into the very way it defines itself. Given the intellectual opportunism that marks our era, there is no way that a libertarian zone can retain its integrity and *transparency* without describing its parameters in terms that reveal every conceivable form of treachery to its ideals, at which point it must cease to *be* what it professes to be. I would hold that such a zone can only be denoted by the term "anarcho-communism," a term that denies the validity of all claims of domination by definition. Accordingly, to admit of domination is to cross the line that separates the libertarian zone from the socialist. Whosoever eschews the term in the name of a revolutionary project that is theoretically more delectable and socially more popular remains unreliable in his or her commitment to libertarian goals as such — goals that must remain tentative insofar as they are not rooted in the fixidity of consistently anti-authoritarian premises. Perhaps such a fixidity of premises may be intellectually distasteful or socially impractical. These are legitimate questions that must be decided by discussion or personal conscience. But the very fixidity of premises that define anarcho-communism as a consistently libertarian zone is the sole guarantee that a revolutionary project will not slither back to forms of theory and practice that inherently lend themselves to opportunistic compromises.

Traditions and personalities must not be permitted to stand in the way of our self-understanding of the issues involved. One may look askance at a Proudhon for his philistinism, at Bakunin for his naievete, at Kropotkin for his didacticism, at Durruti for his terrorism — and anarchist theoretics generally for its simplicity. Even if each such assessment were true, which I do not believe to be the case it would merely be episodic in the face of a social crisis so massive and a social response so opportunistic that we can no longer retain any revolutionary project without the most compelling moral imperatives. Existentially, our era allows for no commitment that falls short of the anarcho-communist project for liberation, certainly not without leading to the betrayal of humanity's potentiality for freedom.

In any case, neo-Marxism and "libertarian socialism" fail us in the content they impart to a liberated society. To mingle direct democracy with delegated power, to build a free society on the concept of a "mass society," to reduce hierarchy to class relations and domination to economic exploitation reveal a gross failure to understand the meaning of *society* — of human consociation — as a realm of freedom. With the politicization of society by state institutions, the substitution of bureaucratic ties for human relations, the homogenization of social forms and personal relations, socialist theoretics too has lost its very sense of society as more than a vague "public sphere" subject to rational, albeit "humanistic," controls. In this wasteland of social forms, we are obliged to ask questions that would have been taken for granted in an earlier era. What constitutes a human community and a society based on self-management? What constitutes that classical self-acting agent we denote by the term "citizen"? To the extent that these questions are not adequately answered, concepts like direct democracy and self-management remain formal abstractions that can be hybridized and distorted without regard to any abiding criteria of social freedom. Ultimately, the answers we give to these questions determine the authenticity of our commitment to a free society.

We have used words like "modernity" and "industrial" society to conceal a basic difference between capitalism and precapitalist societies, a difference that is highly relevant to the questions I have raised above. In whatever ways precapitalist societies differed from each other, they differed from capitalism in the fact that they were basically *organic*, richly articulated in forms and structures that were to be ultimately challenged and destroyed by bourgeois market relations. Even where the eye moves beyond the egalitarian world of the early human bands and clans, underlying all the bureaucratic and political formations that were to layer the surface of tribal, village, and guild-like societies were the extended families, tribal relationships, village structures, guilds, and even neighborhood associations that retained a subterranean autonomy of their own. Marx was to address himself to the tenacity of these "subpolitical" formations in his observations on the "small and extremely ancient" communities in India "that are based on the possession of land in common, on the blending of agriculture and handicrafts and on an unalterable division of labour, which serves as a fixed plan and basis for action whenever a new community is started."

The organic nature of these communities, which Marx was to emphasize even more strongly in the *Grundrisse*, is described in primarily economic terms, in economic categories that subtly degrade the human content of their associative implications and absorb them into the framework of historical economism that vitiates Marxian anthropology. But their inner social power, their vitality as human impulses toward sociation, seeps through Marx's remarks nevertheless. "The law that regulates the division of labour in the community acts with the irresistibile authority of a law of nature, while each individual craftsman, the smith, the carpenter and so on, conducts in his workshop all the operations of his handicraft in the traditional way, but independently, and without recognizing any authority. The simplicity of the productive organism in these self-sufficing communities which constantly reproduce themselves in the same form and, when accidentally destroyed, spring up again on the same spot and with the same name — this simplicity supplies the key to the riddle of the unchangeability of Asiatic societies, which is in such striking contrast with the constant dissolution and refounding of Asiatic states, and their never-ceasing changes of dynasty. The structure of the fundamental economic elements of society remain untouched by the storms which blow up in the cloudy regions of politics."(12)

One could wish for a discussion of this "riddle" in less reductionist economic categories, although the entire passage, taken word for word, is a fascinating guide to Marx's methodology even when he moves beyond the sphere of bourgeois society. Whether Marx had a "social philosophy" or not, his treatment of history is intellectually unified by an economism that itself could pass for a social philosophy. Kropotkin, whose associationist sensibility is much stronger than Marx's, points out that the early medieval city "could hardly be named a State as regard its interior organization, because the middle ages knew no more of the present centralization of functions than of the present territorial centralization. Each group had its share of sovereignty. The city was usually divided into four quarters, or into five to seven sections radiating from a centre, each quarter or section roughly corresponding to a certain trade or profession which prevailed in it, but nevertheless containing inhabitants of different social positions and occupations — nobles, merchants, artisans, or even half-serfs; and each section or quarter constituted a quite independent agglomeration. In Venice, each island was an independent political community. It had its own organized trades, its own commerce in salt, its own jurisdiction and administration, its own forum; the nomination of a doge by the city changed nothing in the inner independence of the units. In Cologne, we see the inhabitants divided into... neighborhood guilds, which dated from the Franconian period," each of which had its own judge, jury, and local militia commander. Kropotlin quotes J.R. Green to the effect that in London, before the Conquest, social life was based on "a number of little groups scattered here and there over the area within the walls, each growing up with its own life and institutions, guilds, sokes, religious houses and the like, and only drawing together into a municipal union." "The mediaeval city thus appears as a double federation," Kropotkin concludes: "of all householders united into small territorial unions — the street, the parish, the section — and of individuals united by oaths into guilds according to their professions; the former being a product of the village-community origin of the city, while the second is a subsequent growth called to life by new conditions." (13)*

---

* The patronizing attitude of many Marxist theorists toward Kropotkin's work in this area and the cultivated oblivion they exhibit toward historical disputes that were waged between Marxists and anarchists over such widely ranging issues as the general strike and the importance of popular control of revolutionary institutions is evidence of an odious "partyness" that must be directly confronted wherever it exists. Are we to forget that Rose Luxemburg in the *Mass Strike, the Political Party and Trade Unions* grossly misrepresented the anarchist emphasis on the general strike after the 1905 revolution in Russia in order to make it acceptable to Social Democracy? That Lenin was to engage in the same misrepresentation on the issue of popular control in *State and Revolution?* That in recent years Marxist writers, who have adduced the factory as a "school" for conditioning the proletariat into submission to union and party hierarchies have yet to acknowledge the anarchist literature that originally pointed to this problem? Much the same can be said around such issues as ecology, utopianism, and even gay and women's liberation. As long as neo-Marxists stake out a claim to concepts that are historically alien to their traditions in Marxism, they not only perpetuate the mystification of radical history, but exhibit a moral probity that is hardly better than that of the society they profess to oppose.

The most striking feature of the capitalist market is its ability to unravel this highly textured social structure, to invade and divest earlier social forms of their complexity of human relations. Even as capitalism seems to amplify the autonomy and claims of the individual, it does so by attenuating the content and structure of society. As *Gemeinschaft* theorists like Buber have pointed out: "When we examine the capitalist society which has given birth to socialism, *as a society*, we see that it is a society inherently poor in structure and growing visibly poorer every day. By the structure of a society is to be understood its social content or community content: a society can be called structurally rich to the extent that it is build up of genuine societies, that is, local communes and trade communes and their step by step association. What Gierke says of the Co-operative Movement in the Middle Ages is true of every structurally rich society: it is 'marked by a tendency to expand and extend the unions, to produce larger associations over and above the smaller associations, confederations over and above individual unions, all-embracing confederations over and above particular confederations.' At whatever point we examine the structure of such a society we find the cell-tissue 'Society' everywhere, i.e. a living and life-giving collaboration, an essentially autonomous consociation of human beings, shaping and re-shaping itself from within. Society is naturally composed not of disparate individuals but of associative units and the associations between them."

The capitalist economy and the centralized state "peculiar to it" begin to hollow out this highly articulated social structure until the modern "individualizing process" ends up as an atomizing process, a process that divests the individual of the social substance indispensable to individuality itself. Although the old organic forms retain "their outer stability, for the most part," they become "hollow in sense and in spirit — a tissue of decay. Not merely what we call the 'masses" but the whole of society is in essence amorphous, unarticulated, poor in structure. Neither do those associations help which spring from the meeting of economic or spiritual interests — the strongest of which is the party: what there is of human intercourse in them is no longer a living thing, and the compensations for the lost community-forms we seek in them can be found in none. In the face of all this, which makes 'society' a contradiction in terms, the 'utopian' socialists have aspired more and more to a restructuring of society; not, as the Marxist critic thinks, in any romantic attempt to revive the stages of development that are over and done with, but rather in alliance with the decentralized counter-tendencies which can be perceived underlying all economic and social evolution, and in alliance with something that is slowly evolving in the human soul: the most intimate of all resistances — resistance to mass or collective loneliness."(14)

There are observations I have brought into Buber's remarks — partly directly, partly by selective quotation — that are not properly integral to his outlook. Buber does not oppose state forms as such, a difference that mars his admiration for Kropotkin — only state forms "peculiar" to capitalism. Nor does he oppose a market economy as such — only a bourgeois one. His discussion of "utopian" socialism is highly selective; it ignores "utopian" socialists like Saint-Simon who stand on a level below his own and others, like Fourier, who go far beyond him. Like a good Proudhonian, he seems oblivious to the possibility that "all-embracing confederations over and above particular confederations" could easily yield social hierarchies as domineering as ruling classes. But his emphasis on the "cell tissue 'Society'" provides a much-needed correction of social theories that focus primarily on the skeletal infrastructure of society, be it economic or institutional. By denuding society of virtually all its molecular substance, Marxian theory and modern sociology generally have been able to formulate many broad principles of social development; indeed, analyses of production relations, social relations, and historical "stages" of society lend themselves to more seductively elegant logical constructs than analyses of concrete, often highly particularized local associations. But these generalizations, valuable as they may be, are all too often achieved by defining social life in highly formalized and abstract terms. The "laws" and categories derived by creating formal typologies are often gained at the expense of insights that the molecular structures provide and the challenging conclusions they imply. Indeed, the attempt to cast society in essentially generic terms can easily provide ideological support for the "hollowing out" of associative units by capitalism and the state.* By rendering social thought blind to the significance of these units — villages, neighborhoods, cooperatives, and the like — Marxian and bourgeois sociology take for granted and even participate in the preemption of community by bureaucracy, associated individuals by privatized egos, the society by the state.

To state the issue more broadly, the buyer-seller relationship of the market place, carried by the logic of the commodity relationship to the point of a market society, literally simplifies social life to the level of the inorganic. I have pointed out elsewhere that ecologically, the most significant problem we face today is not merely environmental pollution but environmental simplification.(15) Capitalism is literally undoing the work of organic evolution. By creating vast urban agglomerations of concrete, metal, and glass, by turning soil into sand, by overriding and undermining highly complex ecosystems that yield local differences in the natural world — in short, by replacing a complex organic environment with a simplified inorganic one — market society is literally disassembling a biosphere that has supported humanity for countless millenia. In the course of replacing the complex ecological relationships, on which all complex living things depend, for more elementary ones, capitalism is restoring the biosphere to a stage where it will be able to

---

* Historically, one of the most striking examples of this support must be placed directly at the doorstep of Marx himself. For Marx to have described capital as a "great civilizing influence" that not only reduces nature purely to an "object for man (Menschen — "mankind" in the McLellan translation, "humankind" in the Nicolaus!), purely as an object of utility," but also as a force that drives beyond "all traditional, confined, complacent, encrusted satisfactions of present needs, and reproductions of old ways of life" must now be viewed as more closely akin to this ideological process than a form of naive nineteenth-century evolutionism. (*Grundrise*, Random House, pg. 410; the Nicolaus translation has been corrected to remove the fiction that Marx was a committed feminist in his terminology) These remarks by Marx must not be dismissed as a mere theoretical matter. Bitter conflicts within the Russian and Spanish revolutionary movements over opponents and supporters of the more desirable features of village society were to reflect conflicting attitudes toward Marx's encomiums to the "historically progressive" role of capitalism, particularly in its destruction of precapitalist formations. Isaiah Berlin, in his excellent introduction to Franco Venturi's *Roots of Revolution* (Grosset & Dunlap, 1960), has discussed this cleavage in the Russian revolutionary movements with great sympathy for the anarchistic Populists. I have dealt with the same issue in the Spanish revolutionary movements in my *Spanish Anarchists* (Free Life Editions, 1977), a work that is also available as a Harper & Row paperback.

support only simpler forms of life. If his great reversal of the evolutionary process continues, it is by no means fanciful to suppose that the preconditions for more complex forms of life will be irreparably destroyed and the earth will become incapable of supporting humanity itself.

This process of simplification, however, is by no means confined to ecology; it is also a social phenomenon, as sweeping in its implications for human history as it is for natural history. If the competitive nexus of market society, based on the maxim "grow or die" must literally simplify the organic world, so too must the reduction of all social relations to exchange relations literally simplify the social world. Divested of any content but the brute relationships of buying and selling, of homogenized, mass-produced objects that are created and consumed for their own sake, social form itself undergoes the attenuation of institutions based on mutual aid, solidarity, vocational affiliations, creative endeavour, even love and friendship. The "cell tissue 'Society'" is thus reduced to the monadic ego; the extended family to the nuclear family and finally to disassociated sexual partners who enjoy neither the responsabilities of commitment nor emotional affinities but live in the vaccum of estranged intercourse and the insecurities of passionless indifference.

Indeed, the logic of market society is the market *qua* society: the emergence of objects, of commodities, as the materialization of *all* social relationships.* No longer are we simply confronted

---

* I have emphasized the word "all" because a market *society* is no longer a market *economy*. The colonization of every aspect of life by capitalism — personal as well as social, domestic as well as industrial, retail as well as productive — is a relatively recent phenomenon that really came into its own after World War II. Until the 1950s, the individual could still find a refuge from the workaday world of the capitalist economy in the private world of home and neighborhoods. Not until the postwar years did capitalism fully colonize the realm of consumption; its prewar triumphs were largely limited to the realm of production. Neighborhoods, structured around a viable domestic world, small retail shops, and a dazzling variety of cultural societies, existed up to the early 1950s. The dissolution of neighborhoods by suburbs, of retail shops by shopping malls, and cultural societies by television, not to speak of domestic life by the nuclear family, finally ended the neighborhood as a form of village life within the city. Capitalist consumption, now triumphant, has ended even the most externalized notions of a "public space." The nearest thing to such a "space" is literally the shopping mall, where consumers engage in a ballet with commodities and adolescents wander amidst deserted lobbies to meet for sexual assignations and, of course, smoke marijuana.

with the "fetishization" of commodities or the alienation of labour, but rather with the erosion of consociation as such, the reduction of people to the very isolated objects they produce and consume. Capitalism, in dissolving virtually every viable form of community association, installs the isolated ego as its nuclear social form, just as clans, families, *polis*, guilds, and neighborhoods once comprised the nuclear social forms of precapitalist society.

Social regression on this scale imparts a new function to bureaucracy. Under capitalism, today, bureaucratic institutions are not merely systems of social control; they are literally institutional substitutes for social form. They comprise the skeletal framework of a society that, as Greek social thought would have emphasized, edges on inherent disorder.(16) However much market society may advance productive forces, it takes its historic revenge not only in the rationalization it inflicts on society, but the destruction it inflicts on the highly articulated social relations that once provided the springboard for a viable social opposition. The most disturbing feature of modern bureaucracy is not merely the coercion regimentation, and control it imposes on society, but the extent to which it is literally *constitutive* of modern society: the extent to which it validates itself as the realm of "order" against the chaos of social dissolution. Just as the ancient city — its temples, gardens, political institutions, and well-cultivated environs — represented human order as against the ever-menacing encroachment of natural "disorder," so bureaucracy emerges as the structural sinews and bones that sustain the dissolving, decaying flesh of market society. Precapitalist societies have resisted or simply side-stepped bureaucratic formations that were imposed upon them with the highly articulated internal life they developed on their own or inherited from the past. Capitality society becomes *bureaucratized* to its very marrow precisely because the market can never provide society with an internal life of its own.

This fact expresses both the possibilities of bureaucracy as a social infrastructure and its historical limits. The very anonymity of bureaucracy reveals the authority of the system over personality, of the social framework over its "personnel." The ease with which Stalinism reproduced itself structurally as a grotesque persistence of bureaus amidst a chronic execution of bureaucrats is testimony to a total depersonalization of social control today — the appalling *asociality* that bourgeois society finally achieves in its mythic "socialization" of humanity. Together with the "denaturing" of humanity, capitalism creates a synthetic society so completely divested of organic attributes that its social relations are literally mineralized into objects. The bureaucrat is truly faceless because he or she has no protoplasmic existence; the depraved notion that administrative decision-making can be taken over by computers and public expression by electronic media — a notion seriously considered as a step in the direction of "direct democracy" by theoretically sophisticated radical groups like the French Situationists, not only zany science-fiction "utopians" — increasingly renders the flesh-and-blood bureaucrat and citizen an anachronism. As in Platonic metaphysics, the immediate world of perception becomes the imperfect, transient "copy" of an *eidos* that transcends the uncertain and chaotic materiality of life itself. If bureaucracy represents the culmination of social order, capitalism totally belies the historic destiny Marx imputed to it as the means for universalizing humanity and providing it with the means for controlling its own destiny. Bureaucracy, as a system perfected to the point of voiceless depersonalization, now represents a *mute society* even more divested of self-articulation than "mute nature." In the structureless void to which capitalism has reduced society, the public realm literally becomes a public *space*, public only in the sense that it is occupied by interlinking bureaus. Flow diagrams and systems theory become the language of corporate entities that, lacking even the presence of the lusty "robber barons," consist of objects moving through depersonalized agencies. The homeostasis of these corporate entities depends not upon personal judgements but the corrective power of deviations. Contemporary language unerringly calls this "feedback," "input," and "output," not discourse, dialogue or judgement.

There is a moral that must be drawn from this massive regression to the inorganic: capitalism has not performed the historic function of "disembedding" humanity from nature. Over and beyond the haunting power of archaic tradition over the present is an "embeddedness in nature" itself — a *Naturwüchsigkeit* — that found expression in the organic consociation of human beings: initially, a consociation expressed in clannic ties, a sexual division of labour, the eminence of the elders, and a "nature idolatry" that slowly cemented human ties into ever-expansive forms of association. Doubtless, these were primarily biological facts, not social; organic, not synthetic. But the price humanity has paid for its socialization — for the "denatural-ization" of blood groups into territorial units, tribes into towns, and the stranger into citizenship — has taken the form of capitalism, a rapacious society that has carried through human socialization by "tearing down all the barriers which hem in the development of the forces of production, the expansion of needs, the all-sided development of production, and the exploitation and exchange of natural and material forces."[17]

If it is true, as Jeremy Shapiro has argued, that for Marx capitalism creates the conditions for removing human beings from their "immersion" in archaic traditions and in nature by "(1) setting abstract labour free as a force of production through the process in which labour creates its own conditions, and (2) freeing individuals from their identification with particular social roles allotted to them by the social division of labour...," it is no less true that capitalism removes them from organic nature only to "reembed" them in *inorganic* nature.[18] It removes them from a "concrete labour" that knows nature in all its wealth of forms and immerses them in an abstract labour that knows only abstract matter; it removes them from their personal identification with a social division of labour by divesting them of the very subjective apparatus required for personality. Although capitalism may seem to free labour as a force of production in the organic sphere, it enslaves it to the inorganic, transporting it from the world of living materiality to the world of dead materiality. Capitalism may have freed humanity from the archaic "idolatry of nature," but it did so only by committing humanity to the modern idolatry of quantity. In Marxism itself, it may well be that the present releases the hold of the archaic past on itself, but the present holds the past captive to fictive conceptions of history that divest human consociation of all human attributes but "interest," "productive power," domination, and the values of the bourgeois Enlight-enment conceived as a project of rationalization and control.

If the "dialectic of history," as Shapiro tells us, is to be "resolved through completion of the self-transcendence of nature that occurs when embeddedness in nature is overcome and human beings bring the historical process under control," then this "control" must involve the re-absorption of nature into society as a "retribalized" humanity in which the archaic solidarity based on kinship is replaced by free choice of association, shared concerns, and love.(18) Communes, cooperatives, and assemblies — in fact, new *poleis*— must replace the poverty of social forms created by the void we call "capitalism." Let there be no mistake about the fact that we are never "disembedded" from nature. Indeed, it has never been a question of whether we were "embedded" in nature or not, but rather the *kind* of nature we have always been "embedded" in — organic or inorganic, ecoligical or physical, real or mythic, whole or one-sided, subjectivized or "mindless." Only the absence of a nature philosophy that reveals the natural history of mind from the very inception of the organic world to the present, a philosophy that can reveal the changing gradations of a natural dialectic into a social, that can relate the realm of "instrumental action" to "communicative," and ultimately human society with nature as the voice of a "mute nature" resubjectivized by human consciousness — only by virtue of this lacuna in the interface between nature and society is it possible to speak of "disembeddedness" in disregard of the meaning of a truly organic society.

Today, any meaningful project for the reconstruction of a revolutionary theory and practice must take its point of departure from three basic premises: the reconstitution of the "cell tissue 'Society'" in the *physical* sense of the term, as a body politic, that is bereft of the institutions of delegated authority; the abolition of domination in all its forms — not merely economic exploitation; and the obvious precondition for the latter achievement, the abolition of hierarchy in all its forms — not merely social classes. The reductionist attitude of Marxism that defines a body politic in the ambiguous terms of a "public sphere," of domination in terms of economic exploitation, and hierarchy in terms of economic classes, masks and dissolves the differences between these concepts. That we could easily achieve a "public sphere" that professes to be free of class rule and economic exploitation, yet is riddled by patriarchy, bureaucracy, and a system of ruled and ruler based on professional, ethnic, and age differences, is painfully evident if we are to judge from the experiences of the "socialist orbit." To speak to the needs of an organic society — the formation of an authentic body politic and a socially active citizenry — is to restore society as genuine "cell tissue." Society, in effect, must become a body politic in the literal sense that the citizen must be *physically* in control of the social process, a living *presence* in the formation and execution of social policy.

Rousseau is only too accurate in recognizing that a body politic, divested of *embodiment* as a citizen assembly, is the negation of a people. The term "people" has no meaning if it lacks the institutional structure for exhibiting its physical presence and imparting to that presence a decisive social meaning — if it cannot assemble to debate, formulate, and decide the policies that shape social life. To the degree that the formulation of these policies is removed by mediated and delegated institutions, from the face-to-face decision-making process of the people in assembly, to that degree is the people subverted as the only authentic constitutive force of social life and society, vested in the sovereignty of the few, reduced to an abstraction, an unpeopled "public sphere" or a mere "public space." Underlying every enterprise for the dissolution of the body politic into the faceless sovereignty of delegated authority is the hidden belief in an "elect" that is alone endowed with the capacity to rule and command. Ultimately, this view amounts to a denial of the human potentiality for self-management, to the spark within *every* individual to achieve the powers of social wisdom that a privileged few claim for themselves. That circumstances, be they resolved into the denial of education, free time, access to culture, and even an enlightened familial background, not to speak of material and occupational circumstances, have concealed this spark to the "masses" themselves is no argument for the fact that social life, particularly as it concerns the individual, could be otherwise.

Delegated authority, in effect, not only negates a people but the claims of selfhood that are underlying to the notion of popular self-management. As I have emphasized elsewhere, a society that professes to be based on self-management is inconceivable without self-activity.(19) Indeed, revolution can be defined as the most advanced form of self-activity, as direct action raised to a level where the land, the factories, indeed the very streets, are directly taken over by the autonomous people. In the absence of this level of activity, social consciousness remains mere *mass* consciousness that can easily be manipulated by hierarchies. Delegated authority vitiates the individuation of the "masses" into self-conscious beings who can take direct, unmediated control of society into their own hands. It denies not only the constitution of a "public sphere" into a body politic, but the individual into a social agent — into a "citizen" in the Athenian sense of the term.

We live today under the tyranny of a present that is often more oppressive than the past, Sartre's imagery of the "slime" of the past notwithstanding to the contrary. Our social "models" for freedom have been the Russian Revolution and the so-called "revolutions" of the Third Word, of the councils, soviets, and shop committees that are so seductive to many neo-Marxists as forms of social administration. I would join M.I. Finley in seriously asking if we should not try to recover the more fascinating example of the Athenian polis which, despite its many shortcomings, provides more expansive *institutional* examples for a liberated society than any we are familiar with today. That Athenian democracy was based on a "sovereign Assembly... open to every citizen" and convened at least forty times a year; that it was consciously "amateurish" and antibureaucratic, managed by a rotating council of 500 whose chairmen were selected by lot for only a single day, a council itself constituted by sortition as well as election — these features together with its astonishing court system, militia, and extensive use of the lot hardly require elaboration.[20] Athenian amateurism rested on a regard for selfhood that Platonistic readings of the *polis* tend to de-emphasize. To the degree that the Hellenic democratic theory found written expression, it may well have been in the concepts of Protagoras that are handed down to us through the patently biased dialogue of Plato's. Free men possess *politike techne*, the "art of political judgement," as Finley translates the phrase, a judgement that uniquely defines humanity as a cooperative species, possessed of *philia* (shall we say "solidarity" rather than the more conventional translation of the word as "friendship"?) and *dike* (justice). But beyond these traits they possess a sense of community that by *nature* destines them to live in a polis. These traits of a free citizen, taken together, constitute a controlled *selfhood*, what we call "self-control," that renders community life or *koinonia* possible. "Neither the sovereign Assembly, with its unlimited right of participation, nor the popular jury-courts (dicastery — M.B.) nor the selection of officials by lot nor ostracism could have prevented either chaos on the one hand or tyranny on the other had there not been self-control among enough of the citizen-body to contain its behaviour within bounds," observes Finley. Moreover, this self-control was an active form of selfhood, not the *apathia* or absence of feeling we so often associate with contemporary citizenship within a depersonalized formal system of "rights" and "duties." "There was a tradition (Aristotle, *Constitution of Athens*, 8.5) that in his legislation early in the sixth century B.C. Solon passed the following law, specifically aimed against apathy: 'When there is civil war in the city, anyone who does not take up arms on one side or the other shall be deprived of civil rights and of all share in the affairs of government.' The authenticity of the law is doubtful, but not the sentiment. Pericles expressed it, in the same Funeral Oration in which he noted that poverty is no bar, by saying (Thucydides, 2.40.3): 'Any man may at the same time look after his own affairs and those of the state... We consider anyone who does not share in the life of the citizen not as minding his own business but as useless."[21]

It is ironical that we must turn to John Stuart Mill, rather than his socialist contemporaries, for an insightful evaluation of how direct participation in social life and the development of selfhood mutually reinforce each other to form the civic virtues and commitments of the citizen — that make active citizenship the highest expression of selfhood. The defects of Athenian democracy notwithstanding, the practices of the dicastery and popular assemblages, Mill was to observe, "raised the intellectual standard of an average Athenian citizen far beyond anything of which there is yet an example in any other mass of men, ancient or modern." The Athenian citizen was obliged "to weigh interests not his own; to be guided, in case of conflicting claims, by another rule than his private partialities; to apply, at every turn, principles and maxims which have for their reason of existence the common good..." He accordingly found himself associated "in the same work with minds more familiarized than his own with these ideas and operations" which supplied "reason to his understanding and stimulation to his feeling for the general interest."(22)

Hannah Arendt was to formulate this educative process — an integral feature of what the Greeks called *paideia*, the spiritual *forming* of the individual — as an "enlarged mentality" that renders authentic judgement possible.(23) The *polis* was not only an end but a means that made political practice ("participation" is a feeble terms) a mode of self-formation. At this level, a people not merely arrives at a "general interest" but begins to transcend "interest" as such. "Interest," a term nourished by the bourgeois enlightenment that surfaces throughout the Marxian literature as "class interest" and in neo-Marxism as "knowledge interest," is replaced by the possibility of mutuality and consociation based on the Hellenic concept of *philia* or, in the Christian tradition, by *agape*.

The young Hegel, despite his scorn for a Christian equality that saw the slave as "the brother of his owner," was deeply rooted in the millenarian ideal of a new human union and the Joachimite vision of an era of fulfillment. In this trinitarian vision, love, as embodied in the Holy Spirit, transcends the faith that marked the era of the Son and the law that marked the era of the Father. For the young Hegel, "True love, or love proper, exists only between living beings *who are alike in power* and thus in one another's eyes living beings from every point of view" — and, by the same token, to achieve this penultimate recognition of the "living beings" who are loved, they must be alike in power. (My emphasis — M.B.) *Agape*, as conceived in Hegel's eschatological vision, no longer knows the drive of "interest"; indeed, it "deprives man's opposite of all foreign character, and discovers life itself without any further defect." This is not a world in which gray is painted on gray. "In love the separate does still remain, but as something united and no longer as something separate; life (in the subject) senses life (in the object)." Indeed, love supplants law and one may justifiably ask if, in this era when all living beings are alike in power, there is any need for mediation and the state.(24)*

Assemblage attains its fullness in a world where "interest" yields to *philia* and *agape*, where judgement emerges from the self-formative intercourse and spiritual education of an "enlarged mentality." Endowed with this mentality, "even when I shun all company or am completely isolated while forming an opinion, I am not simply together only with myself in the solitude of philosophic though" Arendt observes; "I remain in this world of mutual interdependence where I can make myself the representative of everyone else. To be sure, I can refuse to do this and form an opinion that takes only my own interest, or the interests of the group to which I belong, into account... But the very quality of an opinion as of a judgement depends upon its degree of impartiality."(25) "Impartiality" must be taken literally if Arendt's point is to have meaning — as a condition that rises above the "partial," or one-sided, and the "partiality" of a predetermined commitment. The emergence of a "general interest" is, in effect, the abolition of the "partiality" of a self rooted in "interest" and in a one-sided society.

It is a truism that "opinion" and judgement so formed have material preconditions and a historical background that has received sufficient emphasis not to require discussion here. Arendt's "enlarged mentality" must emerge from a terrain that is materially incompatible with the formation of "class interest" and its ideological expression as "class consciousness". But once these material preconditions are emphasized, we must add that a "proletarian public sphere" is an anachronism because the proletariat *as* a proletariat, as the fictive expression of a *public* sphere, is an "interest" that opposes the universalization and abolition of "interest" and the formation of a public. It is not accidental that Marx follows in the wake of bourgeois reality by denuding the proletariat of the social and personal forms without which it cannot develop its public existence as part of a universalized humanity. Marx's writings "hollow out" the prole-

---

* To my knowledge, this implicit anarchism in the young Hegel has been ignored by neo-Marxists and its Joachimite roots examined only casually, if at all. The considerable attention which has been given to labour and language in Hegel's early writings has often slighted their utopian dimension and has turned Hegel not merely into a "precursor" of Marxism but also one of its victims.

tariat as ruthlessly as capitalism hollows out the "cell tissue 'Society'". Just as abstract labour confronts abstract matter, so abstract classes confront each other in a conflict of "interests" that exists beyond their will or even their clear comprehension. That Marx conceives the proletariat as a category of political economy — as the "owner" of labour power, the object of exploitation by the bourgeoisie, and a creature of the factory system — reflects and *ideologizes* its actual one-sided condition under capitalism as a "productive force," not as a *revolutionary* force. Marx leaves us in no doubt about this conception. As the class that is most completely dehumanized, the proletariat transcends its dehumanized condition and comes to embody the human totality "through urgent, no longer disguisable, absolutely imperative *need*..." Accordingly: "The question is not what this or that proletarian, or even the whole proletariat at the moment *considers* as its aim. The question is *what the proletariat is,* and what, consequent on that *being,* it will be compelled to do."[26] (The emphasis throughout is Marx's and provides a telling commentary on his de-subjectivization of the proletariat.) I will leave aside the rationale that this formula provides for an elitist organization. For the present, it is important to note that Marx, following the tradition of classical bourgeois political economy, totally objectifies the proletariat and removes it as a true subject. The revolt of the proletariat, even its humanization, ceases to be a *human* phenomenon; rather, it becomes a function of inexorable economic laws and "imperative need." The essence of the proletariat *as* proletariat is its non-humanity, its creature nature as the product of "absolutely imperative need" — of brute "interest." Its subjectivity falls within the category of harsh necessity, explicable in terms of economic law. The psychology of the proletariat, in effect, is political economy.

The real proletariat resists this reduction of its subjectivity to the product of need and lives increasingly within the realm of *desire,* of the *possibility* to become other than it is. Concretely, the worker resists the work ethic because it has become irrational in view of the possibilities for a non-hierarchical society. The worker, in this sense, transcends her or his creature nature and increasingly becomes a subject, not an object; a non-proletarian, not a proletarian. *Desire,* not merely need, *possibility,* not merely necessity, enter into her or his self-formation and self-activity. The worker begins to shed her or his status of *workerness*, her or his existence as a mere *class* being, as an object of economic forces, as mere "being," and becomes increasingly available to the development of an "enlarged mentality."

As the *human* essence of the proletariat begins to replace its factory essence, the worker can now be reached as easily outside the factory as in it. Concretely, the worker's aspect as a woman or man, as a parent, as an urban dweller, as a youth or elderly person, as a victim of environmental decay, as a dreamer (the list is nearly endless), comes increasingly to the foreground. The factory walls become permeable to the development of an "enlarged mentality" to the degree that personal and broadly social concerns *begin to compete with the worker's "proletarian" concerns and values*. No "workers group" can become truly revolutionary unless it deals with the individual worker's human aspirations, unless it helps to de-alienate the worker's personal milieu and begins to transcend the worker's factory milieu. It is indeed doubtful if, in the event of truly revolutionary change, that workers will *want* to control production and bask in the glories of an economy based on "worker's control." They will probably want to alter production, indeed sever society's technical commitment to the factory as such. This kind of working class will become revolutionary not *in spite* of itself but *because* of itself, literally as a result of its awakening selfhood.*

For Aristotle, "man is by nature a political animal; and so even

---

* Most of my observations about the proletariat were made at the *Telos* Conference on Organization at Buffalo, New York, in November, 1971, and were developed in my article "On Spontaneity and Organization". These observations can be traced back to my "Listen, Marxist!" of April, 1969. They have since been appropriated by many Neo-Marxists to add a legitimation precisely to a "proletarian consciousness" an interest that my remarks were meant to challenge. I adduce this type of distortion primarily to guard the reader against "neo-Marxist" tendencies that attach basically alien ideas to the withering conceptual framework of Marxism — not to say something new but to preserve something old with ideological formal-dehyde — to the detriment of any intellectual growth that the distinctions are designed to foster. This is mystification at its worst, for it not only corrupts ideas but the very capacity of the mind to deal with them. If Marx's work can be rescued for our time, it will be by dealing with it as an invaluable part of the development of ideas, not as pastiche that is legitimated as a "method" or continually "updated" by concepts that come from an alien zone of ideas.

when men have no need of assistance from each other they nonetheless desire to live together." For although they share a "common interest" in a good life, "they also come together and maintain the political partnership (actually *politiken koinonian* — M.B.) for the sake of life merely..."[27] For Marx, "Men can be distinguished from animals by consciousness, by religion or anything else you like. They themselves begin to distinguish themselves from animals as soon as they begin to *produce* their means of subsistence, a step which is conditioned by their physical organization. By producing their means of subsistence men are indirectly producing their actual material conditions."[28]

Between these two definitions of "man" lie more than two thousand years not only of human "progress" in mastery over nature, but social regression in the denuding of society. The degradation of *koinonia* into the division of labour and of *philia* into class solidarity, finally of the self into an endless fount of egotism and needs, is a historical *fact* that cannot be ignored. But it is also an *ideology* that cannot be hypostasized and mystified as "revolutionary." To deal with capitalism alone as a myth of "praxis" that incorporates precisely what should be exorcised from "civilization" as a whole in Freud, Adorno, Horkheimer, and frankly, Fourier's meaning of the term, is a betrayal of the larger revolutionary project that awaits the critique and practice of an "enlarged mentality." If we are not merely at the end of capitalism but at the end of "civilization" as Fourier might have observed — of hierarchy and domination — it is not enough to speak any longer of class and exploitation but rather of *rank as such* at the most molecular levels of human consociation. Critical theory, too, was to challenge "civilization" as a sphere of domination and a rationality of domination, but it did not deal with hierarchy, with a sensibility that organizes *difference* into a sphere of command and obedience. Hence, it too became victim to the hidden hierarchical dimension that perpetuates domination, the proclivity to stand above the flux of life and ultimately the test of experience. For the "emancipatory interest" to ferret out its tradition of emancipation in the academy, to build its moral imperatives within the boughs of its own intellectual Eden, is to replace revolutionary history and its far-reaching lessons by intellectual history with its diet of pale gruel. Not that theory has no imperatives of its own, but rather that it cannot be defined as a "praxis" that is guarded from life by ivy-covered walls.

It was the young Hegel, again, who most clearly formulated the place of wisdom as *paideia*, specifically in the fruitful interchange of teacher and taught rather than leader and led — a *paideia* that informs the development of a revolutionary culture or "movement" as much as it does a revolutionary sensibility. That age, experience, and personal talents may confer wisdom is no reason that they should confer power. Hegel's distinction between Jesus and Socrates draws this point out unerringly on its authentic social terrain. The Christian apostles were mere acolytes. "Lacking any store of spiritual energy of their own," Hegel observes, "they had found the basis of their conviction about the teachings of Jesus principally in their friendship with him and dependence on him. They had not attained truth and freedom by their own exertions; only by laborious learning had they acquired a dim sense of them and certain formulas about them. Their ambition was to keep this doctrine faithfully and to transmit it faithfully to others without any addition, without letting it acquire any variations in detail by working on it themselves."

By contrast, Socrates's friends from "their youth up... had developed their powers in many directions. They had absorbed that democratic spirit which gives an individual a greater measure of independence and makes it impossible for any tolerably good head to depend wholly and absolutely on one person. In their state it was worth while to have a political interest, and an interest of that kind can never be sacrificed. Most of them had already been pupils of other philosophers and other teachers. They loved Socrates because of his virtue and his philosophy, not virtue and his philosophy because of him. Just as Socrates had fought for his native land, had fulfilled all the duties of a free citizen as a brave soldier in war and a just judge in peace, so too all his friends were something more than mere inactive philosophers, than mere pupils of Socrates."(28)

The *polis*, with its emphasis on freedom and activity, stands opposed to the congregation with its emphasis on reverence and quietism. Hegel touches precisely on the differing social contexts that produce pupils in Greece and disciples in Judea, teachers and leaders, the democratic *koinonia* of the *polis* and the hierarchical infrastructure of the Church. In the tension between these two extremes, different senses of selfhood emerge: the controlled self formed by the light of spirit, reason and solidarity and the controlled self formed by the whip-lash of a rationalized society, dogma, and fragmentation. In reality, there is no longer room for an intermediate ground, whether in the revolutionary movement or in society. The history of this century has been poisoned by the endless "gains" and "mediations" that threaten to become the bonfires of society itself — the "improvements" that have been brought into the service of a domination so ubiquitous that it brings the self into complicity with its own enslavement. Nearly forty years ago, Horkheimer could have written that *"The revolutionary movement negatively reflects the situation which it is attacking."*(29) Today these words seem tame. The "revolutionary" movement — as the Left calls itself — *positively supports the situation it professes to attack*. The mass party is the precondition for the existence of a mass society, the political face of its institutional bureaucracy. The entire future of the Left diverges on whether it seeks to recover a body politic — the *koinonia* of a face-to-face citizenry — or whether, in the name of the "pragmatic," the "expedient," and the appropriate "mediations" it will foster the ever-greater rationalization of the society with the rhetoric of progress, planning, reform — and even "revolution."

Beyond the intramural disputes of the Left lie the larger social issues of historic recovery and social advance. The municipal tradition, however faint, persists in western society today as an American tradition that may well speak to an American revolutionary movement with greater meaning than the European emphasis on centralization. "The continued growth of the New England town by division of the central nucleus into new cells, having an independent life of their own, recalled the earlier pattern of Greece," Lewis Mumford has observed. "But the New England towns added a new feature that has never been sufficiently appreciated nor as widely copied as it deserved: the township. The township is a political organization which encloses a group of towns, villages, hamlets, along with the open country area that surrounds them: it performs the functions of local government, including the provision of schools and the care of local roads, without accepting the long-established division between town and country."

Mumford's lament that the failure of "both the Federal and the State Constitutions" to incorporate the township as the basic unit of American democracy "was one of the tragic oversights of post-revolutionary political development" is an understatement. The "post-revolutionary political development" of the early republic was largely counterrevolutionary and the township, particularly its town meetings, were deliberately excluded precisely because they gave "concrete organs" to an "abstract political system of democracy..."(30) As Merril Jensen has pointed out in a fascinating account of that very period, "the nature of city government came in for heated discussion." Town meetings, whether legal or informal, "had been a focal point of revolutionary activity." The anti-democratic reaction that set in after the American Revolution was marked by efforts to do away with town meeting governments that had spread well beyond New England to the mid-Atlantic and Southern states. Attempts by conservative elements were made to establish a "corporate form (of municipal government) whereby the towns could be governed by mayors and councils" elected from urban wards. Judging from New Jersey, the merchants "backed incorporation consistently in the efforts to escape town meetings." Such efforts were successful not only in cities and towns of that state but also in Charleston, New Haven, and eventually even Boston. Jensen, addressing himself to the incorporated form of municipal government and restricted suffrage that replaced the more democratic assembly form of the revolutionaries of 1776 in Philadelphia, expresses a judgement that could apply to all the successful efforts in behalf of municipal incorporation following the revolution: "The counter-revolution in Philadelphia was complete."(31)

Here, then, lies a history and a liberatory tradition that awaits full and conscious expression as a demand for human scale, local popular control, decentralization, and face-to-face democracy both within the revolutionary movement and within society. In turning the notion of the "people" against its bourgeois utopian origins, this liberatory tradition recovers and transcends a vision for which the material premises were established by bourgeois society itself. A new "revolutionary subject" exists in the social vacuum left by society and the centralized power at its summits.(32) The system turns everyone against it — be it the conservationist or the small struggling entrepreneur, the worker or the intellectual, women, blacks, aged, or the seemingly privileged suburbanite. The denuding of the individual from "brothers" and "sisters" into "citizens" and finally "taxpayers" expresses the common lot of every individual who is burdened by a terrifying sense of powerlessness that is so easily mistaken for apathy. Bureaucracy can never blanket this open, unoccupied social domain. This domain can eventually be filled by neighborhood assemblies, cooperatives, popular societies, and affinity groups that are spawned by an endless array of social ills — above all, *decentralized* groups that form a counterweight and a radicalizing potential to the massive centralization and concentration of social power in an era of state capitalism.

Socialism, inspired by the imagery of the Robespierrist Committee of Public Safety, offers no promise of affecting (indeed, of comprehending) this new social development, so congenial to the American social tradition. The simplification of the "social problem" into issues like the restoration of local power, the increasing hatred of bureaucratic control, the silent resistance to manipulation on the everyday level of life holds the only promise of a new "revolutionary subject" on which resistance and eventually revolution can be based. It is to these issues that revolutionary theory must address itself, and it is to a re-institutionalization of a conscious body politic that revolutionary practice must direct its efforts.

April 1978

FOOTNOTES

1. See Albrecht Wellmer: "Communications and Emancipation: Reflections on the Linguistic Turn in Critical Theory" in *On Critical Theory*, ed. John O'Neill (Seabury Pres, 1976), p. 254.

2. Karl Marx: "The Civil War in France," *Selected Works*, Vol. II (Progress Publishers, 1969), p. 220.

3. Jean-Jacques Rousseau: *The Social Contract* (Everyman Edition, 1959), pp. 94, 96. Rousseau's influence on Hannah Arendt is almost as great as Aristotle's. Compare these remarks with Arendt's in *On Revolution* (Viking Press, 1965), pp. 239-40.

4. See my *Post-Scarcity Anarchism* (Black Rose Books, 1977), pp. 150-53.

5. Karl Marx and Frederick Engels: *The Holy Family* (Progress Publishers, 1956), pp. 52-53; Frederick Engels: "On Authority" in Marx, Engels, Lenin: *Anarchism and Anarcho-Syndicalism* (International Publishers, 1972), p. 102.

6. Ibid., p. 102.

7. Herbert Marcuse: *An Essay on Liberation* (Beacon Press, 1969), pp. VII, VIII, 22, 57, 64, 80,85.

8. Herbert Marcuse: *Counter-Revolution and Revolt* (Beacon Press, 1972), p. 41.

9. Marcuse: *An Essay on Liberation*, op. cit., p. 14.

10. Marcuse, ibid., p. 69 and fn. on same page.

11. Ibid., p. VIII.

12. Karl Marx: *Capital*, vol. I (Vintage, 1977), pp. 477-78, 479.

13. Peter Kropotkin: *Mutual Aid* (Extending Horizons Books, 1955), pp. 179-80, 181.

14. Martin Buber: *Paths in Utopia* (Beacon Press, 1958), op. 13-14.

15. See *Post-Scarcity Anarchism,* op. cit., p. 65.

16. Karl Marx: *Grundrisse* (Random House, 1973), p. 410.

17. Jeremy J. Shapiro: "The Slime of History" in *On Critical Theory,* op. cit., pp. 147-48.

18. Ibid., p. 149.

19. See my "On Spontaneity and Organization, *Liberation,* March, 1972, pp. 6-7. (See pp. 249-274 below)

20. M.I. Finley: *Democracy: Ancient and Modern* (Rutgers University Press, 1973), p. 18.

21. Ibid., pp. 29-30.

22. John Stuart Mill: *Considerations on Representative Government* (World Classics Edition, 1948), pp. 196-98.

23. Hannah Arendt: "Truth and Politics" in *Philosophy, Politics and Society* (edited by Peter Laslett and W.G. Runciman (Blackwell & Co., 1967), p. 115.

24. G.W.F. Hegel: *The Early Theological Writings* (University of Chicago Press, 1948), pp. 304-5.

25. Hannah Arendt, "Truth and Politics," Op. cit., p. 115.

26. Karl Marx and Frederick Engels: *The Holy Family,* op. cit., pp. 52-53.

27. Aristotle: *Politics* (Loeb Classical Library, 1932), 1278b15-30 and Karl Marx and Frederick Engels: *The German Ideology* (International Publishers, 1947), p. 7.

28. G.W.F. Hegel: *The Early Theological Writings,* op. cit., p. 81, 82.

29. Max Horkheimer: "The Authoritarian State," *Telos,* Spring, 1973, p. 6.

30. Lewis Mumford: *The City in History* (Harcourt, Bacee & World, 1961), p. 332.

31. Merril Jensen: *American in the Era of the Articles of Confederation*

32. See my "Toward a Vision of the Urban Future" in *Urban Affairs Annual Review* (Sage Publications, 1978) in press. (See pp. 171-191 above)

On spontaneity
and
organisation

It is supremely ironical that the socialist movement, far from being in the "vanguard" of current social and cultural developments, lingers behind them in almost every detail. This movement's shallow comprehension of the counterculture, its anemic interpretation of women's liberation, its indifference to ecology, and its ignorance even of new currents that are drifting through the factories (particularly among young workers) seems all the more grotesque when juxtaposed with its simplistic "class analysis," its proclivity for hierarchical organization, and its ritualistic invocation of "strategies" and "tactics" that were already inadequate a generation ago.

Contemporary socialism has shown only the most limited awareness that people by the millions are slowly redefining the very meaning of freedom. They are constitutively enlarging their image of human liberation to dimensions that would have seemed hopelessly visionary in past eras. In ever-growing numbers they sense that society has developed a technology that could completely abolish material scarcity and reduce toil to a near vanishing point. Faced with the possibilities of a classless post-scarcity society and with the meaninglessness of hierarchical relations, they are intuitively trying to deal with the problems of communism, not socialism.* They are intuitively trying to eliminate domination in *all* its forms and nuances, not merely material exploitation. Hence the widespread erosion of authority

---

* "Communism" has come to mean a stateless society, based on the maxim, "From each according to his ability and to each according to his needs." Society's affairs are managed directly from "below" and the means of production are communally "owned." Both Marxists and anarchists (or, at least, anarcho-communists) view this form of society as a common goal. Where they disagree is primarily on the character and role of the organized revolutionary movement in the revolutionary process and the intermediate "stages" (most Marxists see the need for a centralized "proletarian dictatorship," followed by a "socialist" state — a view anarchists emphatically deny) required to achieve a communist society. In the matter of these differences, it will be obvious that I hold to an anarchist viewpoint.

as such—in the family, in the schools, in vocational and professional arenas, in the church, in the army, indeed, in virtually every institution that supports hierarchical power and every nuclear relationship that is marked by domination. Hence, too, the intensely *personal* nature of the rebellion that is percolating through society, its highly subjective, existential, and cultural qualities. The rebellion affects *everyday life* even before it visibly affects the broader aspects of social life and it undermines the *concrete* loyalties of the individual to the system even before it vitiates the system's abstract political and moral verities.

To these deep-seated liberatory currents, so rich in existential content, the socialist movement continues to oppose the constrictive formulas of a particularistic "working class" interest, the archaic notion of a "proletarian dictatorship," and the sinister concept of a centralized hierarchical party. If the socialist movement is lifeless today, this is because it has lost all contact with life.

We are travelling the full circle of history. We are taking up again the problems of a new organic society on a new level of history and technological development—an organic society in which the splits within society, between society and nature, and within the human psyche that were created by thousands of years of hierarchical development can be healed and transcended. Hierarchical society performed the baneful "miracle" of turning human beings into mere instruments of production, into objects on a par with tools and machines, thereby defining their very humanity by their usufruct in a universal system of scarcity, of domination, and, under capitalism, of commodity exchange. Even earlier, before the domination of man by man, hierarchical society brought woman into universal subjugation to man, opening a realm of domination that reached beyond exploitation—a realm of domination for its own sake, of domination in its most reified form. Domination, carried into the very depths of personality, has turned us into the bearers of an archaic, millenia-long legacy that fashions the language, the gestures, indeed, the very posture we employ in everyday life. All the past revolutions have been too "olympian" to affect these intimate and ostensibly mundane aspects of life, hence the ideological nature of their professed goals of freedom and the narrowness of their liberatory vision.

By contrast, the goal of the new development toward communism is the achievement of a society based on self-management in which each individual participates fully, directly, and in complete equality in the unmediated management of the collectivity. Viewed from the aspects of its concrete human side, such a collectivity can *be* nothing less than the fulfillment of the liberated self, of the free subject divested of all its "thingifications," of the self that can concretize the management of the collectivity as an authentic mode of *self*-management. The enormous advance scored by the counter-cultural movement over the socialist movement is attested precisely by a personalism that sees in impersonal goals, even in the proprieties of language, gesture, behaviour and dress, the perpetuation of domination in its most insidious unconscious forms. However marred it may be by the general unfreedom that surrounds it, the countercultural movement has thus *concretely* redefined the now innocuous word "revolution" in a truly revolutionary manner, as a *practice* that subverts apocryphal abstractions and theories.

To identify the claims of the emerging self with "bourgeois individualism" is a grotesque distortion of the most fundamental existential goals of liberation. Capitalism does not produce individuals; it produces atomized egotists. To distort the claims of the emerging self for a society based on self-management and to reduce the claims of the revolutionary subject to an economistic notion of "freedom" is to seek the "crude communism" that the young Marx so correctly scorned in the 1844 Manuscripts. The claim of the libertarian communists to a society based on self-management asserts the right of each individual to acquire control over her or his everyday life, to make each day as joyous and marvelous as possible. The abrogation of this claim by the socialist movement in the abstract interests of "Society," of "History," of the "Proletariat," and more typically of the "Party," assimilates and fosters the *bourgeois* antithesis between the individual and the collectivity in the interests of bureaucratic manipulation, the renunciation of desire, and the subservience of the individual and the collectivity to the interests of the State.

There can be no society based on self-management without self-activity. Indeed, revolution *is* self-activity in its most advanced form: direct action carried to the point where the streets, the land, and the factories are appropriated by the autonomous people. Until this order of consciousness is attained, consciousness at least on the social level remains *mass* consciousness, the object of manipulation by elites. If for this reason alone, authentic revolutionaries must affirm that the most advanced form of class consciousness is self-consciousness: the individuation of the "masses" into conscious beings who can take direct, unmediated control of society and of their own lives. If only for this reason, too, authentic revolutionaries must affirm that the only real "seizure of power" by the "masses" is the *dissolution* of power: the power of human over human, of town over country, of state over community, and of mind over sensuousness.

It is in the light of these demands for a society based on self-management, achieved through self-activity and nourished by self-consciousness, that we must examine the relationship of spontaneity to organization. Implicit in every claim that the "masses" require the "leadership" of "vanguards" is the conviction that revolution is more a problem of "strategy" and "tactics" than a social process;* that the "masses" cannot create their own liberatory institutions but must rely on a state power — a "proletarian dictatorship" — to organize society and uproot counterrevolution. Every one of these notions is belied by history, even by the particularistic revolutions that replaced the rule of one class by another. Whether one turns to the Great French Revolution of two centuries ago, to the uprisings of 1848, to the Paris Commune, to the Russian revolutions of 1905 and March, 1917, to the German Revolution of 1918, to the Spanish Revolution of 1934 and 1936 or the Hungarian Revolution of 1956, one finds a social process, sometimes highly protracted, that culminated in the overthrow of established institutions without the guidance of "vanguard" parties (indeed, where these parties

---

* The use of military or quasi-military language — "vanguard," "strategy," "tactics" — betrays this conception fully. While denouncing students as "petty bourgeois" and "shit," the "professional revolutionary" has always had a grudging admiration and respect for that most inhuman of all hierarchical institutions, the military. Compare this with the counterculture's inherent antipathy for "soldierly virtues" and demeanour.

existed they usually lagged behind the events). One finds that the "masses" formed their own liberatory institutions, be these the Parisian sections of 1793-1794, the clubs and militias of 1848 and 1871, or the factory committees, workers' councils, popular assemblies, and action committees of later upheavals.

It would be a crude simplification of these events to claim that counterrevolution reared its head and triumphed where it did merely because the "masses" were incapable of self-coordination and lacked the "leadership" of a well-disciplined centralized party. We come here to one of the most vexing problems in the revolutionary process, a problem that has never been adequately understood by the socialist movement. That coordination was either absent or failed — indeed, that effective counterrevolution was even *possible* — raises a more fundamental issue than the mere problem of "technical administration." Where advanced, essentially premature revolutions failed, this was primarily because the revolutions had no material basis for consolidating the *general* interest of society to which the most radical elements staked out an historic claim. Be the cry of this general interest "Liberty, Equality, Fraternity" or "Life, Liberty, and the Pursuit of Happiness," the harsh fact remains that the technological premises did not exist for the consolidation of this general interest in the form of a harmonized society. That the general interest divided again during the revolutionary process into antagonistic particular interests — that it led from the euphoria of "reconciliation" (as witness the great national fetes that followed the fall of the Bastille) to the nightmare of class war, terror, and counterrevolution — must be explained primarily by the *material limits* of the social development, not by technical problems of political coordination.

The great bourgeois revolutions succeeded socially even where they seemed to fail "technically" (i.e., to lose power to the radical "day-dreaming terrorists") *because they were fully adequate to their time.* Neither the army nor the institutions of absolutist society could withstand their blows. In their beginnings, at least, these revolutions appeared as the expression of the "general will," uniting virtually all social classes against the aristocracies and monarchies of their day, and even dividing the aristocracy against itself. By contrast, all "proletarian revolutions" have failed because the technological premises were inadequate for the *material* consolidation of a "general will," *the only basis on which the dominated can finally eliminate domination.* Thus the October Revolution failed socially even though it seemed to succeed "technically" — all Leninist, Trotskyist, and Stalinist myths to the contrary notwithstanding — and the same is true for the "socialist revolutions" of Asia and Latin America. When the "proletarian revolution" and its time are adequate to each other — and precisely *because* they are adequate to each other — the revolution will no longer be "proletarian," the work of the particularized creatures of bourgeois society, of its work ethic, its factory discipline, its industrial hierarchy, and its values. The revolution will be a *people's* revolution in the authentic sense of the word.*

It is not for want of organization that the past revolutions of radical elements ultimately failed but rather because all prior societies were organized systems of want. In our own time, in the era of the final, generalized revolution, the general interest of society can be tangibly and *immediately* consolidated by a post-scarcity technology into material abundance for *all*, even by the disappearance of toil as an underlying feature of the human condition. With the lever of an unprecedented material abundance, the revolution can remove the most fundamental premises of counterrevolution — the scarcity that nourishes privilege and the rationale for domination. No longer need *any* sector of society "tremble" at the prospect of a communist revolution, and this should be made evident to *all* who are in the least prepared to listen.*

In time, the framework opened by these qualitatively new

---

* The word "people" (*le peuple* of the Great French Revolution) will no longer be the Jacobin (or, more recently, the Stalinist and Maoist) fiction that conceals antagonistic class interests within the popular movement. The word will reflect the general interests of a truly human movement, a general interest that expresses the material possibilities for achieving a classless society.
* The utter stupidity of the American "left" during the late Sixties in projecting a mindless "politics of polarization" and thereby wantonly humiliating so many middle-class — and, yes, let it be said: *bourgeois* — elements who were prepared to listen and to learn, can hardly be criticized too strongly. Insensible to the *unique* constellation of possibilities that stared it in the face, the "left" simply fed its guilt and insecurities about itself and followed a politics of systematic alienation from all the authentic radicalizing forces in American society. This insane politics, coupled

possibilities will lead to a remarkable simplification of the historic "social question." As Josef Weber observed in *The Great Utopia*, this revolution — the most universal and totalistic to occur — will appear as the "next *practical* step," as the immediate praxis involved in social reconstruction. And, in fact, step by step the counter-culture has been taking up, not only subjectively, but also in their most *concrete and practical forms*, an immense host of issues that bear directly on the utopian future of humanity, issues that just a generation ago could be posed (if they were posed at all) only as the most esoteric problems of theory. To review these issues and to reflect upon the dizzying rapidity with which they emerged in less than a decade is simply staggering, indeed, unprecedented in history. Only the principal ones need be cited: the autonomy of the self and the right to self-realization; the evocation of love, sensuality, and the unfettered expression of the body; the spontaneous expression of feeling; the de-alienation of relations between people; the formation of communities and communes; the free access of all to the means of life; the rejection of the plastic commodity world and its careers; the practice of mutual aid; the acquisition of skills and counter-technologies; a new reverence for life and for the balance of nature; the replacement of the work ethic by meaningful work and the claims of pleasure; indeed, a *practical* redefinition of freedom that a Fourier, a Marx, or a Bakunin rarely approximated in the realm of thought.

The point to be stressed is that *we are witnessing a new Enlightenment* (more sweeping even than the half-century of enlightenment that preceded the Great French Revolution) that is slowly challenging not only the authority of established institutions and values but authority as such. Percolating down-

---

with a mindless mimicry of the "third world," a dehumanizing verbiage (the police as "pigs," opponents as "fascists"), and a totally dehumanizing body of values, vitiated all its claims as a "liberation movement." The student strike that followed the Kent murders revealed to the "left" and the students alike that they had succeeded only too well in polarizing American society, but that *they*, and not the country's rulers, were in the minority. It is remarkable testimony to the inner resources of the counter-culture that the debacle of SDS led not to a sizeable Marxist-Leninist party but to the well-earned disintegration of the "Movement" and a solemn retreat back to the more humanistic cultural premises that appeared in the early Sixties — humanistic premises that the "left" so cruelly ravaged in the closing years of that decade.

ward from the intelligentsia, the middle classes, and youth generally to all strata of society, this Enlightenment is slowly undermining the patriarchal family, the school as an organized system of repressive socialization, the institutions of the state, and the factory hierarchy. It is eroding the work ethic, the sanctity of property, and the fabric of guilt and renunciation that internally denies to each individual the right to the full realization of her or his potentialities and pleasures. Indeed, no longer is it merely capitalism that stands in the dock of history, but the cumulative legacy of domination that has policed the individual from within for thousands of years, the "archetypes" of domination, as it were, that comprise the State within our *unconscious* lives.

The enormous difficulty that arises in understanding this Enlightenment is its invisibility to conventional analyses. The new Enlightenment is not simply changing consciousness, a change that is often quite superficial in the absence of other changes. The usual changes of consciousness that marked earlier periods of radicalization could be carried quite lightly, as mere theories, opinions, or a cerebral punditry that was often comfortably discharged outside the flow of everyday life. The significance of the new Enlightenment, however, is that it is altering the *unconscious apparatus of the individual* even before it can be articulated consciously as a social theory or a commitment to political convictions.

Viewed from the standpoint of a typically socialist analysis — an analysis that focuses almost exclusively on "consciousness" and is almost completely lacking in psychological insights — the new Enlightenment seems to yield only the most meagre "political" results. Evidently, the counter-culture has produced no "mass" radical party and no visible "political" change. Viewed from the standpoint of a communist analysis, however — an analysis that deals with the unconscious legacy of domination — the new Enlightenment is slowly dissolving the individual's obedience to institutions, authorities, and values that have vitiated every struggle for freedom. These profound changes tend to occur almost unknowingly, as for example among workers who, in the *concrete* domain of *everyday life*, engage in sabotage, work indifferently, practice almost systematic absenteeism, resist authority in almost every form, use drugs, and acquire various freak traits — and yet, in the *abstract* domain of *politics* and *social philosophy*, acclaim the most conventional homilies of the system. The explosive character of revolution, its suddenness and utter unpredictability, can be explained only as the eruption of these unconscious changes into consciousness, as a release of the tension between unconscious desires and consciously held views in the form of an outright confrontation with the existing social order. The erosion of the unconscious restrictions on these desires and the full expression of the desires that lie in the individual unconscious is a precondition for the establishment of a liberatory society. There is a sense in which we can say that the attempt to change consciousness is a struggle for the unconscious, both in terms of the fetters that restrain desire and the desires that are fettered.

Today, it is not a question of whether spontaneity is "good" or "bad," "desirable" or "undesirable." Spontaneity is integrally part of the very dialectic of self-consciousness and self-dealienation that removes the subjective fetters established by the present order. To deny the validity of spontaneity is to deny the most liberatory dialectic that is occuring today; as such, for us it must be a given that exists in its own right.

The term should be defined lest its content disappear in semantic quibbling. Spontaneity is not mere impulse, certainly not in its most advanced and truly human form, and this is the only form that is worth discussing. Nor does spontaneity imply undeliberated behaviour and feeling. Spontaneity is behaviour, feeling and *thought* that is free of *external* constraint, of *imposed* restriction. It is self-controlled, *internally* controlled, behaviour, feeling, and thought, not an uncontrolled effluvium of passion and action. From the libertarian communist viewpoint, spontaneity implies a capacity in the individual to impose self-discipline and to formulate sound guidelines for social action. Insofar as the individual removes the fetters of domination that have stifled her or his self-activity, she or he is acting, feeling, and thinking spontaneously. We might just as well eliminate the word "self" from "self-consciousness," "self-activity," and "self-management" as remove the concept of spontaneity from our comprehension of the new Enlightenment, revolution, and communism. If there is an imperative need for a communist consciousness in the revolutionary movement today, we can never hope to attain it without spontaneity.

Spontaneity does not preclude organization and structure. To the contrary, spontaneity ordinarily yields non-hierarchical forms of organization, forms that are truly organic, self-created, and based on voluntarism. The only serious question that is raised in connection with spontaneity is whether it is *informed* or not. As I have argued elsewhere, the spontaneity of a child in a liberatory society will not be of the same order as the spontaneity of a youth, or that of a youth of the same order as that of an adult; each will simply be more informed, more knowledgeable, and more experienced than its junior.* Revolutionaries may seek today to promote this informative process, but if they try to contain or destroy it by forming hierarchical movements, they will vitiate the very process of self-realization that will yield self-activity and a society based on self-management.

No less serious for any revolutionary movement is the fact that only if a revolution is spontaneous can we be reasonably certain that the "necessary condition" for revolution has matured, as it were, into the "sufficient condition." An uprising planned by an elite and predicated on a confrontation of power with power is almost certain today to lead to disaster. The state power we face is too formidable, its armamentarium is too destructive, and, if its structure is still intact, its efficiency is too compelling to be removed by a contest in which weaponry is the determining factor. The system must fall, not fight; and it will fall only when its institutions have been so hollowed out by the new Enlightenment, and its power so undermined physically and morally, that an insurrectionary confrontation will be more symbolic than real. Exactly when or how this "magic moment," so characteristic of revolution, will occur is unpredictable. But, for example, when a local strike, ordinarily ignored under "normal" circumstances, can ignite a revolutionary general strike, then we will know that the conditions have ripened — and this can occur only when the

---

* Obviously I do not believe that adults today are "more informed, more knowledgeable, and more experienced" than young people in any sense that imparts to their greater experience any revolutionary significance. To the contrary, most adults in the existing society are mentally cluttered with preposterous falsehoods and if they are to achieve any real learning, they will have to undergo a considerable unlearning process.

revolutionary process has been permitted to find its own level of revolutionary confrontation.*

If it is true that revolution today is an act of consciousness in the *broadest* sense and entails a demystification of reality that removes all its ideological trappings, it is not enough to say that "consciousness follows being." To deal with the development of consciousness merely as the reflection in subjectivity of the development of material production, to say as the older Marx does that morality, religion, and philosophy are the "ideological reflexes and echoes" of actuality and "have no history and no development" of their own, is to place the formation of a communist consciousness on a par with the formation of ideology and thereby to deny this consciousness any authentic basis for transcending the world as it is given.* Here, communist consciousness itself become an "echo" of actuality. The "why" in the explanation of this consciousness is reduced to the "how," in typical instrumentalist fashion; the subjective elements involved in the transformation of consciousness become completely objectified. Subjectivity ceases to be a domain for itself, hence the failure of Marxism to formulate a revolutionary psychology of its own and the inability of the Marxists to comprehend the new

---

* This is a vitally important point and should be followed through with an example. Had the famous Sud-Aviation strike in Nantes of May 13, 1968, a strike that ignited the massive general strike in France of May-June, occurred only a week earlier, it probably would have had only local significance and almost certainly would have been ignored by the country at large. Coming when it did, however, after the student uprising, the Sud-Aviation strike initiated a sweeping social movement. Obviously, the tinder for this movement had accumulated slowly and imperceptibly. The Sud-Aviation strike did not "create" this movement; it *revealed* it, which is precisely the point that cannot be emphasized too strongly. What I am saying is that a militant action, presumably by a minority — an action unknowingly radical even to itself — had revealed the fact that it was the action of a *majority* in the only way it could reveal itself. The social material for the general strike lay at hand and *any* strike, however trivial in the normal course of events (and perhaps unavoidable), might have brought the general strike into being. Owing to the unconscious nature of the processes involved, there is no way of foretelling when a movement of this kind will emerge — and it will emerge only when it is left to do so on its own. Nor is this to say that will does not play an active role in social processes, but merely that the will of the individual revolutionary must become a *social* will, the will of the great majority in society, if it is to culminate in revolution.

* The young Marx in *Toward the Critique of Hegel's Philosophy of Law* held a quite different view: "It is not enough that thought should seek its actualization; actuality must itself strive toward thought."

Enlightenment that is transforming subjectivity in all its dimensions.

Revolutionaries have the responsibility of helping others become revolutionaries, not of "making" revolutions. And this activity only begins when the individual revolutionary undertakes to remake herself or himself. Obviously, such a task cannot be undertaken in a personal vacuum; it presupposes existential relations with others of a like kind who are loving and mutually supportive. This conception of revolutionary organization forms the basis of the anarchist affinity group. Members of an affinity group conceive of themselves as sisters and brothers whose activities and structures are, in Josef Weber's words, "transparent to all." Such groups function as catalysts in social situations, not as elites; they seek to advance the consciousness and struggles of the larger communities in which they function, not assume positions of command.

Traditionally, revolutionary activity has been permeated by the motifs of "suffering," "denial," and "sacrifice," motifs that largely reflected the guilt of the revolutionary movement's intellectual cadres. Ironically, to the extent that these motifs still exist, they reflect the very anti-human aspects of the established order that the "masses" seek to abolish. The revolutionary movement (if such it can be called, today) thus tends, even more than ideology, to "echo" the prevailing actuality — worse, to condition the "masses" to suffering, sacrifice, and denial at its own hands and in the aftermath of the revolution. As against this latter-day version of "republican virtue," the anarchist affinity groups affirm not only the rational but the joyous, the sensuous, and the aesthetic side of revolution. They affirm that revolution is not only an assault on the established order but also a festival in the streets. The revolution is desire carried into the social terrain and universalized. It is not without grave risks, tragedies, and pain, but these are the risks, tragedies, and pain of birth and new life, not of contrition and dealth. The affinity groups affirm that only a revolutionary movement that holds this outlook can create the so-called "revolutionary propaganda" to which the new popular sensibility can respond — a "propaganda" that is art in the sense of a Daumier, a John Milton, and a John Lennon. Indeed, truth today can exist only as art and art only as truth.*

The development of a revolutionary movement involves the seeding of America with such affinity groups, with communes and collectives — in cities, in the countryside, in schools, and in factories. These groups would be intimate, decentralized bodies that would deal with all facets of life and experience. Each group would be highly experimental, innovative, and oriented toward changes in life-style as well as consciousness; each would be so constituted that it could readily dissolve into the revolutionary institutions created by the people and disappear as a separate social interest. Finally, each would try to reflect as best it could the liberated forms of the future, not the given world that is reflected by the traditional "left." Each, in effect, would constitute itself as an energy center for transforming society and for colonizing the present by the future.

Such groups could interlink, federate, and establish communication on a regional and national level as the need arises without surrendering their autonomy or uniqueness. They would be organic groups that emerged out of living problems and desires, not artificial groups that are foisted on social situations by elites. Nor would they tolerate an organization of cadres whose sole nexus is "programmatic agreement" and obedience to functionaries and higher bodies.

We may well ask if a "mass organization" can be a revolutionary organization in a period that is not yet ripe for a communist revolution? The contradiction becomes self-evident once we couple the word "mass" with "communist revolution."* To be sure, mass movements have been built in the name of socialism and communism during non-revolutionary periods, but they have achieved mass proportions only by denaturing the concepts of socialism, communism, and revolution. Worse, they not only betray their professed ideals by denaturing them, but they also

---

* As the decline of fictional literature attests. Life is far more interesting than fiction, not only as social life but as personal experience and autobiography.

* I would argue that we are not in a "revolutionary period" or even a "pre-revolutionary period," to use the terminology of the Leninists, but rather in a revolutionary epoch. By this term I mean a *protracted* period of social disintegration, a period marked precisely by the Enlightenment discussed in the previous sections.

become obstacles in the way of the revolution. Far from shaping the destiny of society, they become the creatures of the very society they profess to oppose.

The temptation to bridge the gap between the given society and the future is inherently treacherous. Revolution is a rupture not only with the established social order but with the psyche and mentality it breeds. Workers, students, farmers, intellectuals, indeed all potentially revolutionary strata, literally *break with themselves* when they enter into revolutionary motion, not only with the abstract ideology of the society. And until they make this break, they are not revolutionaries. A self-styled "revolutionary" movement that attempts to assimilate these strata with "transitional programs" and the like will acquire their support and participation for the wrong reasons. The movement, in turn, will be shaped by the people it has vainly tried to assimilate, not the people by the movement. Granted that the number of people who are revolutionary today is miniscule; granted, furthermore, that the great majority of the people today is occupied with the problems of survival, not of life. But it is precisely this *preoccupation* with the problems of survival, and the values as well as needs that promote it, that *prevents* them from turning to the problems of life — and then to revolutionary action. The rupture with the existing order will be made only when the problems of life infiltrate and assimilate the problems of survival — when life is understood as a precondition for survival today — not by rejecting the problems of life in order to take up the problems of survival, i.e., to achieve a "mass" organization made up only of "masses."

Revolution is a magic moment not only because it is unpredictable; it is a magic moment because it can also precipitate into consciousness within weeks, even days, a disloyalty that lies deeply hidden in the unconscious. But revolution must be seen as more than just a "moment"; it is a complex dialectic even within its own framework. A majoritarian revolution does not mean that the great majority of the population must necessarily go into revolutionary motion all at the same time. Initially, the people in motion may be a minority of the population — a substantial, popular, spontaneous minority, to be sure, not a small, "well-disciplined," centralized, and mobilized elite. The consent of the majority may reveal itself simply in the fact that it will no longer *defend* the established order. It may "act" by *refusing* to act in support of the ruling institutions — a "wait and see" attitude to determine if, by denying the ruling class its loyalty, the ruling class is rendered powerless. Only after testing the situation by its passivity may it pass into overt activity — and then with a rapidity and on a scale that removes in an incredibly brief period institutions, relations, attitudes, and values that have been centuries in the making.

In America, any organized "revolutionary" movement that functions with distorted goals would be infinitely worse than no movement at all. Already the "left" has inflicted an appalling amount of damage on the counter-culture, the women's liberation movement, and the student movement. With its overblown pretensions, its dehumanizing behaviour, and its manipulatory practices, the "left" has contributed enormously to the demoralization that exists today. Indeed, it may well be that in any future revolutionary situation, the "left" (particularly its authoritarian forms) will raise problems that are more formidable than those of the bourgeoisie, that is, if the revolutionary process fails to transform the "revolutionaries."

And there is much that requires transforming — not only in social views and personal attitudes, but in the very way "revolutionaries" (especially male "revolutionaries") interpret experience. The "revolutionary," no less than the "masses," embodies attitudes that reflect an inherently domineering outlook toward the external world. The western mode of perception traditionally defines selfhood in antagonistic terms, in a matrix of opposition between the objects and subjects that lie outside the "I." The self is not merely an ego that is distinguishable from the external "others"; it is an ego that seeks to master these others and to bring them into subjugation. The subject/object relation defines subjectivity as a function of domination, the domination of objects and the reduction of other subjects to objects. Western selfhood, certainly in its male forms, is a selfhood of appropriation and manipulation in its very self-definition and definition of relationships. This self- and relational definition may be active in some individuals, passive in others, or reveal itself precisely in the mutual assignment of roles based on a domineering and dominated self, but domination permeates almost universally the prevailing mode of experiencing reality.

Virtually every strain in western culture reinforces this mode of experiencing—not only its bourgeois and Judeo-Christian strains, but also its Marxian one. Marx's definition of the labour process as *the* mode of self-definition, a notion he borrows from Hegel, is explicitly appropriative and latently exploitative. Man forms himself by changing the world: he appropriates it, re-fashions it according to his "needs," and thereby projects, materializes, and verifies himself in the objects of his own labour. This conception of man's self-definition forms the point of departure for Marx's entire theory of historical materialism. "Men can be distinguished from animals by consciousness, by religion or anything else you like," observes Marx in a famous passage from *The German Ideology*. "They begin to distinguish themselves from animals as soon as they begin to *produce* their means of subsistence... As individuals express their life, so they are. What they are, therefore, coincides with their production, both with *what* they produce and with *how* they produce. The nature of individuals thus depends on the material conditions determining their production."

In Hegel's *Phenomenology of the Spirit*, the theme of labour is taken up within the context of the master/slave relationship. Here, the subject becomes an object in the dual sense that another self (the slave) is objectified and concomitantly reduced to an instrument of production. The slave's labour, however, becomes the basis for an autonomous consciousness and selfhood. Through work and labour the "consciousness of the slave comes to itself...," Hegel observes. "Labour is desire restrained and checked, evanescence delayed and postponed; in other words, labour shapes and fashions the thing." The activity of "giving shape and form" is the "pure self-existence of (the slave's) consciousness, which now in the work it does is externalized and passes into the condition of permanence. The consciousness that toils and serves accordingly attains by this means the direct apprehension of that independent being as its self."

Hegel transcends the imprisonment of labour in the master/slave relationship—i.e., in the framework of domination—with the dialectic that follows this "moment." Eventually, the split between subject and object as an antagonism is healed, although as reason fulfilled in the wholeness of truth, in the Absolute Idea. Marx does not advance beyond the moment of the master/slave relationship. The moment is transfixed and deepened into the Marxian theory of class struggle — in my view a grave shortcoming that denies consciousness the history of an *emergent* dialectic — and the split between subject and object is never wholly reconciled. All interpretations of the young Marx's "Feuerbachian naturalism" notwithstanding, humanity, in Marx's view, transcends domination ambivalently, by dominating nature. Nature is reduced to the "slave," as it were, of a harmonized society, and the self does not annul its Promethean content.* Thus, the theme of domination is still latent in Marx's interpretation of communism; nature is still the object of human domination. So conceived, the Marxian concept of nature — quite aside from the young Marx's more ambivalent notions — vitiates the reconciliation of subject and object that is to be achieved by a harmonized society.

That "objects" *exist* and *must* be "manipulated" is an obvious precondition for human survival that no society, however harmonized, can transcend. But whether "objects" exist *merely* as objects or whether their "manipulation" remains *merely* manipulation — or indeed, whether labour, as distinguished from art and play, constitutes the primary mode of self-definition — is quite another matter. The key issue around which these distinctions turn is domination — an appropriative relation that is defined by an egotistical conception of need.* Insofar as the self's need exists exclusively for itself, without regard to the integrity (or what Hegel might well call the "subjectivity") of the other, the

---

* One sees this in Marx's restless concept of practice and especially of material "need," which expands almost indefinitely. It is also clearly seen in the exegetical views of Marxian theorists, whose concepts of an unending, willful, power-asserting practice, assumes almost Dionysian proportions.

* And "need," here, in the sense of psychic as well as material manifestations of egotism. Indeed, domination need not be exploitative in the material sense alone, as merely the appropriation of surplus labour. Psychic exploitation, notably of children and women, may well have preceded material exploitation and even established its cultural and attitudinal framework. And unless exploitation of this kind is totally uprooted, humanity will have made no advance into humanness.

other remains *mere* object for the self and the handling of this object becomes *mere* appropriation. But insofar as the other is seen as an end in itself and need is defined in terms of mutual support, the self and the other enter into a *complementary* relationship. This complementary relationship reaches its most harmonized form in true art, just as will reaches its most harmonized form in authentic play.* Complementarity as distinguished from domination — even from the more benign forms of contractual relationships and mutual aid designated as "reciprocity" — presupposes a new animism that respects the other for its own sake and responds *actively* in the form of a creative, loving, and supportive symbiosis.

Dependence *always* exists. *How* it exists and *why* it exists, however, remain critical toward an understanding of any distinction between domination and complementarity. Infants will always be dependent upon adults for satisfying their most elemental physiological needs, and younger people will always require the assistance of older ones for knowledge and the assurances of experience. Similarly, older generations will be dependent upon the younger for the reproduction of society and for the stimulation that comes from inquiry and fresh views toward experience. In hierarchical society, dependence ordinarily yields subjugation and the denial of the other's selfhood. Differences in age, in sex, in modes of work, in levels of knowledge, in intellectual, artistic, and emotional proclivities, in physical appearance — a vast array of diversity that could result in a nourishing constellation of interrelationships and interdependencies — are all reassembled objectively in terms of command and obedience, superiority and inferiority, rights and duties, privileges and denials. This hierarchical organization of appearances occurs not only in the social world; it finds its counterpart in the way phenomena, whether social, natural, or personal, are internally experienced. The self in hierarchical

---

* Music is the most striking example where art can exist for itself and even combine with play for itself. The competitive sports, on the other hand, are forms of play that are virtually degraded to marketplace relations, notably in the frenzy for scoring over rivals and the egocentric antagonisms that the games so often engender. The reader should note that a dialectic exists within art and play, hence my use of the words "true art" and "authentic play," i.e., art and play as ends in themselves.

society not only lives, acts, and communicates hierarchically; it thinks and feels hierarchically by organizing the vast diversity of sense data, memory, values, passions, and thoughts along hierarchical lines. Differences between things, people, and relations do not exist as ends in themselves; they are organized hierarchically in the mind itself and pitted against each other antagonistically in varying degrees of dominance and obedience even when they could be complementary to each other in the prevailing reality.

The outlook of the early organic human community, at least in its most harmonized form, remained essentially free of hierarchical modes of perception; indeed, it is questionable if humanity could have emerged from animality without a system of social reciprocities that compensated for the physical limitations of a puny, savannah-dwelling primate. To a large extent, this early non-hierarchical outlook was mystified; not only plants and animals, but wind and stones were seen as animate. Each was seen, however, as the spiritualized element of a whole in which humans participated as one among many, neither above nor below the others. Ideally, this outlook was fundamentally egalitarian and reflected the egalitarian nature of the community. If we are to accept Dorothy Lee's analysis of Wintu Indian syntax, domination in any form was absent even from the language; thus a Wintu mother did not "take" her infant into the shade, she "went" with her child into the shade. No hierarchies were imputed to the natural world, at least not until the human community began to become hierarchical. Thereafter, experience itself became increasingly hierarchical, reflecting the splits that undermined the unity of the early organic human community. The emergence of patriarchalism, of social classes, of the towns and the ensuing antagonism between town and countryside, of the state and finally of the distinctions between mental and physical labour that divided the individual internally undermined this outlook completely.

Bourgeois society, by degrading all social ties to a commodity nexus and by reducing all productive activity to "production for its own sake," carried the hierarchical outlook into an absolute antagonism with the natural world. Although it is surely correct to say that this outlook and the various modes of labour that produced it also produced incredible advances in technology, the fact remains that these advances were achieved by bringing the conflict between humanity and nature to a point where the natural fundament for life hangs precariously in the balance. The institutions that emerged with hierarchical society, moreover, have now reached their historical limits. Although once the social agencies that promoted technological advance, they have now become the most compelling forces for ecological disequilibrium The patriarchal family, the class system, the city, and the state are breaking down on their own terms; worse, they are becoming the sources of massive social disintegration and conflict. As I've indicated elsewhere, the means of production have become too formidable to be used as means of domination. It is domination itself that has to go, and with domination the historical legacy that perpetuates the hierarchical outlook toward experience.

The emergence of ecology as a social issue reminds us of the extent to which we are returning again to the problems of an organic society, a society in which the splits within society and between society and nature are healed. It is by no means accidental that the counter-culture turns for inspiration to Indian and Asian outlooks toward experience. The archaic myths, philosophies, and religions of a more unified, organic world become alive again only because the issues they faced are alive again. The two ends of the historic development are united by the word "communism": the first, a technologically primitive society that still lived in awe and fear of nature; the second, a technologically sophisticated utopia that could live in reverence for nature and bring its consciousness to the service of life. Moreover, the first lived in a social network of rigidly defined reciprocities based on custom and compelling need; the second could live in a free constellation of complementary relations based on reason and desire. Both are separated by the enormous development of technology, a development that opens the possibility of a transcendence of the domain of necessity.

That the socialist movement has failed utterly to see the implications of the communist issues that are now emerging is attested by its attitude toward ecology: an attitude that, when it is not marked by patronizing irony, rarely rises above petty muckraking. I speak, here, of *ecology*, not environmentalism.

Environmentalism deals with the serviceability of the human habitat, a passive habitat that people *use*, in short, an assemblage of things called "natural resources" and "urban resources." Taken by themselves, environmental issues require the use of no greater wisdom than the instrumentalist modes of thought and methods that are used by city planners, engineers, physicians, lawyers — and socialists. Ecology, by contrast, is an artful science or scientific art, and at its best, a form of poetry that combines science and art in a unique synthesis.* Above all, it is an outlook that interprets all interdependencies (social and psychological as well as natural) non-hierarchically. Ecology denies that nature can be interpreted from a hierarchical viewpoint. Moreover, it affirms that diversity and spontaneous development are ends in themselves, to be respected in their own right. Formulated in terms of ecology's "ecosystem approach," this means that each form of life has a unique place in the balance of nature and its removal from the ecosystem could imperil the stability of the whole. The natural world, left largely to itself, evolves by colonizing the planet with ever more diversified life forms and increasingly complex interrelationships between species in the form of food chains and food webs. Ecology knows no "king of beasts"; all life forms have their place in a biosphere that becomes more and more diversified in the course of biological evolution. Each ecosystem must be seen as a unique totality of diversified life forms in its own right. Humans, too, belong to the whole, but only as one part of the whole. They can intervene in this totality, even try to manage it consciously, provided they do so in its own behalf as well as society's; but if they try to "dominate" it, i.e., plunder it, they risk the possibility of undermining it and the natural fundament for social life.

The dialectical nature of the ecological outlook, an outlook that

---

* "Art" in the sense that ecology demands continual improvisation. This demand stems from the variety of its subject matter, the ecosystem: the living community and its environment that form the basic unit of ecological research. No one ecosystem is entirely like another, and ecologists are continually obliged to take the uniqueness of each ecosystem into account in their research. Although there is a regressive attempt to reduce ecology to little more than systems analysis, the subject matter continually gets in the way, and it often happens that the most pedestrian writers are obliged to use the most poetic metaphors to deal with their material.

stresses differentiation, inner development, and unity in diversity should be obvious to anyone who is familiar with Hegel's writings. Even the language of ecology and dialectical philosophy overlap to a remarkable degree. Ironically, ecology more closely realizes Marx's vision of science as dialectics than any other science today, including his own cherished realm of political economy. Ecology could be said to enjoy this unique eminence because it provides the basis, both socially and biologically, for a devastating critique of hierarchical society as a whole, while also providing the guidelines for a viable, harmonized future utopia. For it is precisely ecology that validates on scientific grounds the need for social decentralization based on new forms of technology and new modes of community, both tailored artistically to the ecosystem in which they are located. In fact, it is perfectly valid to say that the affinity-group form and even the traditional ideal of the rounded individual could be regarded as ecological concepts. Whatever the area to which it is applied, the ecological outlook sees unity in diversity as a holistic dynamic totality that tends to harmoniously integrate its diverse parts, not as an aggregate of neutrally co-existing elements.

It is not fatuity alone that blocks the socialist movement's comprehension of the ecological outlook. To speak bluntly, Marxism is no longer adequate to comprehend the communist vision that is now emerging. The socialist movement, in turn, has acquired and exaggerated the most limiting features of Marx's works without understanding the rich insights they contain. What constitutes the *modus operandi* of this movement is not Marx's vision of a humanity integrated internally and with nature, but the particularistic notions and the ambivalences that marred his vision and the latent instrumentalism that vitiated it.

History has played its own cunning game with us. It has turned yesterday's verities into today's falsehood, not by generating new refutations but by creating a new level of social possibility. We are beginning to see that there is a realm of domination that is broader than the realm of material exploitation. The tragedy of the socialist movement is that, steeped in the past, it uses the methods of domination to try to "liberate" us from material exploitation.

We are beginning to see that the most advanced form of class consciousness is self-consciousness. The tragedy of the socialist movement is that it opposes class consciousness to self-consciousness and denies the emergence of the self as "individualism"—a self that could yield the most advanced form of collectivity, a collectivity based on self-management.

We are beginning to see that spontaneity yields its own liberated forms of social organization. The tragedy of the socialist movement is that it opposes organization to spontaneity and tries to assimilate the social process to political and organizational instrumentalism.

We are beginning to see that the general interest can now be sustained after a revolution by a post-scarcity technology. The tragedy of the socialist movement is that it sustains the particular interest of the proletariat against the emerging general interest of the dominated as a whole—of all dominated strata, sexes, ages, and ethnic groups.

We must begin to break away from the given, from the social constellation that stands immediately before our eyes, and try to see that we are somewhere in a process that has a long history behind it and a long future before it. In little more than half a decade, we have seen established verities and values disintegrate on a scale and with a rapidity that would have seemed utterly inconceivable to the people of a decade ago. And yet, perhaps, we are only at the beginning of a disintegrating process whose most telling effects still lie ahead. This is a revolutionary epoch, an immense historical tide that builds up, often unseen, in the deepest recesses of the unconscious and whose goals continually expand with the development itself. More than ever, we now know a fact from lived experience that no theoretical tomes could establish: consciousness can change rapidly, indeed, with a rapidity that is dazzling to the beholder. In a revolutionary epoch, a year or even a few months can yield changes in popular consciousness and mood that would normally take decades to achieve.

And we must know what we want, lest we turn to means that totally vitiate our goals. Communism stands on the agenda of society today, not a socialist patchwork of "stages" and "transitions" that will simply mire us in a world we are trying to overcome. A non-hierarchical society, self-managed and free of domination in all its forms, stands on the agenda of society today, not a hierarchical system draped in a red flag. The dialectic we seek is neither a Promethean will that posits the "other" antagonistically nor a passivity that receives phenomena in repose. Nor is it the happiness and pacification of an eternal status quo. Life begins when we are prepared to accept all the forbidden experiences that do not impede survival. Desire is the sense of human possibility that emerges with life, and pleasure the fulfillment of this possibility. Thus, the dialectic we seek is an unceasing but gentle transcendence that finds its most human expression in art and play. Our self-definition will come from the humanized "other" of art and play, not the bestialized "other" of toil and domination.

We must always be on a quest for the new, for the *potentialities* that ripen with the development of the world and the new visions that unfold with them. An outlook that ceases to look for what is new and potential in the name of "realism" has already lost contact with the present, for the present is always conditioned by the future. True development is cumulative, not sequential; it is growth, not succession. The new always embodies the present and past, but it does so in new ways and more adequately as the parts of a greater whole.

November 1971

To the memory of our martyred dead, Nicolo Sacco and Bartolomeo Vanzetti — let time never allow us to forget...

Conclusion: Utopianism and Futurism

To build the future from the rich potentialities of humanity, not from paralyzing limitations created by presentday social barbarism; to seek what is fresh, new, and emergent in the human condition, not what is stagnant, given, and regressive; to work within the realm of what *should* be, not what is — these alternatives separate two entirely antagonistic ways about thinking about the world. Truth, conceived as an evolving process of thought and reality, always appears on the margins of experience and practice, even as the center seems triumphant and almost all-pervasive. To be in the minority is not necessarily testimony to the futility of an ideal or a vision; it is often a token of what is yet to come in the fulfillment of human and social potentialities. Indeed, nothing is more insidious than the myth that rapid success and popularity are evidence of truth. Success and popularity, in the sense of a massive human commitment to an ideal, are matters of growth, painstaking education, development, and the ripening of conditions that render the actualization of human and social potentialities the real epochal changes in the individual and society.

To build the future from the social limitations of society, from the stagnant, the given, and the regressive is to see the "future" merely as an extrapolation of the present. It is the "future" as present quantified, whether by expansion or attrition. Vulgarians like the Alvin Tofflers have made futurism into a matter of "shock"; the Paul Ehrlichs into a matter of demographic catastrophe; the Marshall MacLuhans into a matter of media; the Herman Kahns and Anthony Weiners into a matter of technocratic "scenarios"; the Buckminster Fullers into a matter of mechanistic design; the Garrett Hardins into a matter of ecofascistic ethics. Whatever claims these futurists may make for their "visions" or "dreams," their scenarios are notable for one compelling fact: they offer no challenge to the bases of the status quo. What exists in nearly all futuristic "scenarios" and "visions" is the extension of the present — be it into the year "2000," into space, into the oceans or under the earth. The status quo, in effect, is enlarged rather than challenged, even by futurists who profess to favour "miniaturization" and "decentralization." It is presupposed that the existing political, economic, property, and value systems, often the existing cities, media networks, bureaucracy, multinational corporations, market structure, monetary relations, and even military and police machinery—all, will *continue to exist* in one form or another. Futurists rarely examine their highly conventional presuppositions. Like the customs of archaic societies, the premises of the prevailing society are not merely assumed but rather so completely introjected into futuristic thought that its hierarchical, domineering, and property structure do not even lie on the surface of consciousness. These structures are extended to the future *as such*, hence the future merely becomes the present writ large (or small) with the verbal veneer of a utopian vocabulary. It is interesting to note that Kubrick's cult movie, "2001," retains the military cadres, the scientistic banalities, the cold-war ambience, even the fast-food emporia and svelte airline hostesses of the period in which it was produced. The "light show" that explodes toward the end of the movie, a product of the thirties dance floor, is Kubrick's principal concession to the counterculture of the sixties—a culture that has since become a caricature of itself.

Futurism, in fact, is the specious "utopianism" of environmentalism as distinguished from the unsettling logic of ecology. It can afford to be schizoid and contradictory because the society from which it projects its "visions" is itself schizoid and contradictory. That Buckminister Fuller can describe man as "a self-balancing, 28-jointed adapter-base biped, an electrochemical reduction plant, integral with the segregated stowages of special energy extracts in storage batteries," the human nervous system as a "universally distributed telephone system needing no service for 70 years if well-managed," and the human mind as a "turret in which are located telescopic and microscopic self-registering and recording range-finders, a spectroscope, *et cetera*"—and still be described by his dazzled acolytes as an "ecologist," a "citizen of the world" (one may justly ask: which one?), and as a "utopian visionary" should come as no surprise. It would be trite merely to examine the extent to which Fuller's "ecology" parallels La

Mettrie's treatment of man as a machine. What counts is that his constituency often fail to exhibit even a glimmer of insight into his analytically mechanistic outlook and the serious challenge it poses to an organically ecological sensibility. Ultimately, it is not the schizophrenia of Fuller that is startling and the extent to which his acolytes meld his mechanistic contradictions with ecology but, even more fundamentally, the schizophrenia and contradictions that riddle present-day society. If holism implies, at the very least, a unity and coherence of relations, the present-day society is the most fragmented in history.

A society that has substituted means for ends, consistency for truth, technique for virtue, efficiency for the human good, quantity for quality, and object for subject is a society that is literally designed for no other purpose but survival on any terms. To continue to "exist" — whether or not that existence is meaningful, satisfying, creative, and realizes the potentialities of the human spirit — leads to adaptation as an end in itself. Insofar as survival is the only principle or end that guides the behaviour of the present-day society, *any* means that can promote that end is socially acceptable. Hence solar power can co-exist with nuclear power, "appropriate" technology with high technology, "voluntary simplicity" with media-orchestrated opulence, decentralization, with centralization, "limits to growth" with unlimited accumulation, communes with multinational corporations, hedonism with austerity, and mutual aid with competition.

But beneath this goal of survival is not mere existence as such. The present-day society has a definite character. It is a propertied society that concentrates economic power in corporate elites. It is a militaristic society that concentrates the means of violence in professional soldiers. It is a bureaucratic society that concentrates political power in centralized state institutions. It is a patriarchal society that allocates authority to men in varying degrees. And it is a racist society that places a minority of whites in a self-deceptive sovereignty over a vast worldwide majority of peoples of colour. Taken together, the prevailing society retains assumptions about the economy, politics, sex roles, and ethnic heritage of humanity that are prudently hidden from consciousness. Hence its concern with survival and adaptation is guided by distinct institutions, values, prejudices, and traditions that must always be open to critical examination. Survival and adaptation keep these assumptions hidden by providing a technique for masking them with the rhetoric of "tolerance" and "co-existence." The society will "co-exist" with anything or any vision that does not follow its logic of critique and fulfillment. To "play the game" with a cordial smile, to mingle the most odious contradictions with courtesy, to seek the lowest common denominator in ideas and constituencies with stylish "sensitivity," to ignore coherence and consistency by appealing to "consensus" and "unity" — all of this makes "coexistence" the device *par excellence* for adaptation, survival, and above all, the domination and sovereignty of the status quo.

The essence of futurism and, for that matter, of environmentalism and Marxism is that the society's institutions, values, and prejudices are not examined in a truly fundamental sense. Where futurism does more than merely extend the present into the future, it often denatures alternatives that are designed to radically replace the present by a qualitatively new society. When Le Corbusier and his traditional opponent, Frank Lloyd Wright, both described the city as a "machine," their disputes over urban gigantism and centralization became meaningless. Their shared notion that human communities can be described in mechanistic terms effaced the real significance of their differences. When Fuller can now describe the earth as a "spaceship," his claims to an ecological sensibility become a travesty of ecology. When MacLuhan can impart to media a capacity to produce a "global village," the contradictory nature of the term itself renders his "utopianism" into a mockery of utopia. Unless we study this society with a third eye that is not born of its institutions, relations, and values, we become ideologically and morally entrapped in presuppositions that have been built into our normal thinking as unconsciously as breathing.

The power of utopian thinking, properly conceived as a vision of a new society that questions *all* the presuppositions of the present-day society, is its inherent ability to see the future in terms of radically new forms and values. By "new," I do not merely mean "change" — "change" that can merely be quantitative, inertial, and physical. I mean "new" in terms of *development* and *process* rather than "motion" and "displacement." The latter are merely logistical phenomena; they are changes of place and quantity as distinguished from a development that is qualitative. Hence, under the rubric of "utopia" I place only consistently revolutionary visions of a future that are *emergent*, the results of deep-seated processes that involve the radical reconstruction of personality, sensibility, sexuality, social management, technics, human relations, and humanity's relationship with nature. The time lapse that turns present into future is not merely quantitative; it is a change in development, form, and quality.

Utopian thinking has its own history as well as the historically specific visions utopias unconsciously absorb from the society they wish to replace. That More's utopia tolerated slavery, that Andrea's was modelled on the monastaries of his time, that Mably and Morelly based their codes of "nature" on Sparta, and that Rabelais's Abbey of Theleme partly anticipated the court life of Versailles are obvious. Utopias have been modelled on long-gone recollections of tribal society, the Athenian polis, modern "primitive" communities, or, as in Bacon's case, the laboratory, in Sade's the boudoir, and in the contemporary cinema, the "Saturday night" discotheque toward which the entire week converges. What crucially distinguishes utopias, be they real or specious, from each other is the extent to which they are libertarian. From this standpoint, even the remarkable man who devised the word "utopia," Thomas More, could hardly be called a utopian, not to speak of Plato, Campanella, Andrea, Bacon, Defoe, and the so-called "communists" of the Enlightenment, Mably and Morelly, later Saint-Simon, Cabet, and Bellamy.

By contrast, folk utopias like the Land of Cockaygne, visions of the future advanced by the Diggers of the English Revolution, Rabelais's Abbey of Theleme, and most notably, Charles Fourier's phalanstery and William Morris's quasi-medieval commune, remain inherently libertarian. What strikes us about these visions is their own seemingly *unconscious* counterthrust to the unstated presuppositions of "civilization" (to use this word in Fourier's sense). Even where they seem to accept the claims of property (Rabelais and Fourier), they inherently deny its authority over freedom. "Do as thou wilst!"—the explicit maxim of Rabelais's Abbey of Theleme and the implicit maxim of Fourier's phalanstery — necessarily subverts the power of property by denying the power of authority itself. To the hidden presuppositions of the present-day society, these utopians advance hidden presuppositions of their own which we shall examine below. Hence the need for the *concreteness* of utopian thinking, its specific and day-to-day character, its narrative qualities. Literally, one form of *everyday* life is opposed to another form of *everyday* life. Ironically, the theoretical paucity of utopian thinking, at least in the past, is its *raison d'être,* its hold on the mind and on behaviour. Rousseau realized the importance of that power in *Émile* just as Sade in the *Philosophy of the Bedroom.* Human beings as the embodiment of ideals deal with us without losing their credibility and concreteness. Their very humanness — one thinks here particularly of Rabelais's *Gargantua and Pantagruel,* of Diderot's *Jacques le Fataliste* and *Bougainville* dialogue, and Claude Tillier's *Mon Oncle Benjamin* — engages *our* humanness in the fullness of life and personal involvement.

The immensity of the maxim, "Do as thou wilst!", is a direct expression of freedom that goes beyond the most expansive notions of democracy, even of the direct democracy practiced by the Athenian popular assembly, the New England town meetings of the 1760s, and the revolutionary Parisian sections of 1793. Ultimately, what these utopians affirm are the claims of *personality* (not merely those of an abstractly conceived "individual") over the power of custom, tradition, and institutions. When the Spanish Anarchists of the 1930s raised the cry, "Death to institutions — not to people," they more closely approximated this fleeting Rabelaisian and Fourierist recognition of personality than any radical movement of our era. Not that institutions as such were abolished in Rabelais's and Fourier's utopias, both of which have a manorial ambience. But their institutions exist to reinforce and enrich personality, not to diminish human uniqueness and creativity. The very tension that emerges between individual and society, so marked even in the decadent phase of the *polis,* is simply removed.

The removal of this tension is the most significant feature of the libertarian utopias. Literally, it is achieved by recognizing not only the claims of freedom but of spontaneous expression. Sexuality, art, pleasure, variety, play, and unimpeded self-expression are avowed over technical rationalization, propaganda, happiness, uniformity, and mass mobilization—features that the authoritarian utopians were to share with the authoritarian socialists and, no less pointedly, many futurists of the present day. The historic demand for "happiness" had been replaced by the more liberatory demand for pleasure. The claims of unfettered sexuality, variety, creation, and a full recognition of individual proclivities and personal uniqueness become the ends that efficiency, coordination, work, and technics are meant to serve. The two major divisions of life that were to be opposed to each other by all great social theorists from Plato to Freud—the "realms" of freedom and necessity—are thus integrated.

That the libertarian utopians of the past did not provide "blueprints" for the future that we can regard as acceptable today hardly requires emphasis. "Blueprints," in any case, were vehicles for a concreteness that pitted the presuppositions of the new against the old. Their need for detail is now irrelevant to an age that requires full *consciousness* of *all* presuppositions, be they the hidden ones of the status quo or of the utopians, to attain a totally liberated ecological society. In a sense, we must now be free of history—not of its memory but its icy grasp on consciousness—to *create* history rather than to be created by it. The historical roots of the old utopians are only too clear to be acceptable to a more demanding era. The Abbey of Theleme was serviced by grooms, farmers, blacksmiths, in short, by an anonymous body of subservient people who could not practice its maxim. Nor did Fourier open his phalansteries to the destitute and the maimed, the victims of the new industrial bourgeoisie he so savagely attacked. Whether any of these utopias were possible on their own terms, within the material context of their own level of technical development, will always remain uncertain. What is important about their vision is its extraordinarily far-reaching radical nature: they had challenged and, in a faltering way, tried to remove the power of need over freedom—indeed, the tainting of the ideal of freedom by archaic notions of need. From this challenge, all else stemmed—the removal of the power of social and economic rationalization over personality, work over play, austerity over beauty, institutions over social administration, the state over society.

Utopia has now ceased to be mythic. The concern of this generation with the future, a concern that emerges from the unimaginable power hierarchy can command physically and psychically, has made utopianism a matter of foresight rather than dreamy visions. Futurism has abolished the future. It has done so by assimilating the future to a present that thereby acquires a stagnant eternality by virtue of the extent to which it permeates the eras that lie ahead. Not to form visions that break radically with the present is to deny a future that can be qualitatively different from the present. This is worse than an abolition of the wisdom of history; it is an abolition of the promise of society to advance into a more humanistic world.

Utopia redeems the future. It recovers it for the generations to come and restores it to them as a future which they can creatively form and thoroughly emancipate — not with hidden presuppositions but conscious artfulness. The greatest utopian ideals — those of Rabelais, Fourier, and Morris — must be projected beyond the limits of their time. Not only do we seek pleasure rather than the small satisfactions of "happiness," personality rather than the egotism of individuality, play rather than monotonous work, mutual aid rather than competition, beauty rather than austerity; we seek a new unity with nature, the abolition of hierarchy and domination, the fullness of spontaneity and the wealth of diversity.

To draw up a blueprint — a "scenario" — for the realization of such a utopia would be a regression to the hidden presuppositions and the concreteness that earlier utopians opposed to the hidden presuppositions and explicit realities of their own prevailing societies. We do not need the novels, diagrams, character studies, and dialogues that the traditional utopians employed to oppose one form of everyday life to another. That everyday life must be central to the revolutionary project of our times can now be stated explicitly and rooted in a wealth of consciousness and in the commitment of revolutionaries to their movements as cultures, not merely as organizations. More demanding than the "blueprints" of yesterday are the ecological imperatives of today. We must "phase out" our formless urban agglomerations into ecocommunities that are scaled to human dimensions, sensitively tailored in sized, population, needs, and architecture to the specific ecosystems in which they are to be located. We must use modern technics to replace our factories, agribusiness enterprises, and mines by new, human-scaled ecotechnologies that deploy sun, wind, streams, recycled wastes, and vegetation to create a comprehensible *people's* technology. We must replace the state institutions based on professional violence by social institutions based on mutual aid and human solidarity. We must replace centralized social forms by decentralized popular assemblies; representatives and bureaucracies by coordinating bodies of spokespersons with mandated administrative powers, each subject to rotation, sortition, and immediate recall.

All of this must be done if we are to resolve the ecological crisis that threatens the very existence of the biosphere in the decades that lie ahead. It is not a visionary "blueprint" or "scenario" that mandates these far-reaching alterations in our social structures and relations, but the dictates of nature itself. But these alterations become social desiderata because they bring the sun, wind, soil, vegetation, and animals back into our lives to achieve a new sense of renewal with nature. Without recovering an ecological relationship with the biosphere and profoundly altering our sensibilities toward the natural world, our hope of achieving an ecological society regresses to a merely futuristic "scenario."

Equally significantly, we must renew our relationship to each other in a rich nexus of solidarity and love, one that ends all hierarchical and domineering relationships in our species. To decentralize, to develop an "appropriate technology," to aspire to simplicity, all merely for reasons of logistics, technical efficiency, and conservation would be to betray the ideal of human scale, human participation, and human self-development. To compromise decentralization with centralization "where necessary" (to use Marcuse's memorable formulation), to use "appropriate technology" in conjunction with factories, to foster "voluntary simplicity" amidst mindless opulence is to taint the entire ecological project in a manner that renders the ecological crisis unresolvable. Like Gresham's Law, not only does bad money drive out good, but futuristic "scenarios" will destroy the utopian dimension of the revolutionary project. Never in the past has it been so necessary to retain the utmost clarity, coherence, and purposefulness that is required of our era. In a society that has made survival, adaptation, and co-existence a mode of domination and annihilation, there can be no compromises with contradictions — only their total resolution in a new ecological society or the inevitability of hopeless surrender.

November 1979

Andre Gorz Rides Again — or Politics as Environmentalism

Ecology and the ecological imbalances of our time open a sweeping social horizon that profoundly challenges every conventional theory in the ideological spectrum. The split between humanity and nature; the notion that man can dominate nature, a notion that derives from the domination of human by human; the role of the market economy in developing technologies that can undo the work of natural evolution in only a few generations; the absurdity of dealing with ecosystems and food webs in hierarchical terms — all of these issues and tenets raise immense possibilities for developing a radical social ecology that transcends orthodox Left ideologies at one extreme and the crudities of sociobiology at the other. A serious theorist would want to explore these issues and would want to use them reconstructively to foster the reharmonization of nature with humanity and of human with human, both as fact and sensibility.

As fact, the attempt to achieve a new harmony between humanity and nature would involve an exploration of the uses of ecotechnologies as the technical and creative means for recovering humanity's metabolism with nature in a non-Promethean way. I refer to the use of new methods of food cultivation, ecological sources of energy (solar, wind, methane, and the like), the integration of craft with "high" technologies, fulfilling forms of work or of work as play. It would involve an exploration of the decentralized, confederal, ecocommunities and forms of direct democracy that a new society would seek to create. As sensibility, the attempt to achieve a new harmony between humanity and nature would involve an exploration that opens the fascinating discussion of a nature philosophy as the basis for a new ethics, of feminism as the basis for a new sensibility, and of the commune as the new form of human interaction and the arena for self-development.

The ecological project conceived as a project of a radical social ecology would thereby provide the bases for a rich critique of prevailing ideologies — bourgeois and socialist alike — that would transcend the traditional "radical" critiques of political economy. It would open the way for a discussion of new forms of organization (for example, the affinity group), new forms of struggle (direct action, conceived as the praxis of self-management, not merely the occupation of nuclear power-plant sites), new forms of citizenship (self-activity, viewed as forms of self-realization). The ecological project, so conceived, would provide the social gymnasium for shedding the sense of powerlessness that threatens to reduce the public sphere to a bureaucratized substitute for all forms of human consociation.

Critique and practice would thus merge to form a coherent and consistently revolutionary perspective. This perspective would open a thoroughly radical critique of such crucial problems as patriarchialism, urban decay, corporate power, hierarchy, domination, pollution, technocratic manipulation — indeed, a multitude of issues that acquire meaning and authenticity in the light of a libertarian, yes, anarchist, interpretation of social ecology. Most precious of all to such a theorist would be the coherence and revolutionary consistency one would be expected to attain as a result of the theoretical and practical possibilities opened by a radical social ecology, particularly one that has a revolutionary anarchist focus.

Given these sweeping implications, Andre Gorz's *Ecology as Politics* turns out to be a very disappointing book — indeed, a highly disorienting one. Apart from the ideas Gorz pilfers quite freely from the works of anarchist theorists of the past and of the American New Left, the book contains very little that is new or interesting. It was to be hoped that French readers, at least, would have acquired a fuller knowledge of these ideas in their original form, with emendations and possibly newer interpretations by Gorz. But Gorz is content not only to repeat them (with minimal or no acknowledgement) in a cursory, often tattered fashion. He does substantially worse: he debases them and divests them of their roots, of their coherence, of their internal logic and their revolutionary thrust. *Ecology as Politics* is not only an intellectual pastiche of ideas whose theoretical pedigree is utterly alien to that of Gorz's; the book is an example of bad ecology as well as bad politics, often written in bad faith with respect to the real traditions on which Gorz leans.

What makes Gorz's book particularly distasteful is its attempt to refurbish an orthodox economistic Marxism with a new ecological anarchism. Almost every page sounds a false note. To critically review a volume of some 200 pages with the detail that it requires would yield a work two or three times the size of the original. To illustrate the magnitude of this problem, let us closely examine Gorz's "Introduction," which presumably presents the theoretical basis of the book. Although this "Introduction" is scarcely more than seven printed pages, the piece acquires particular interest when one looks beyond its pretension to sweep and scope. What lies under the carpet of Gorz's theoretical ponderosity is an appalling amount of intellectual confusion — and an interesting glimpse of Gorz's methodology, notably the sectarian Marxian orthodoxy that always subverts the author's sense of "vision" and "discovery."

From the outset, the "Introduction" begins to crumble into semantic confusion. Its purpose is to distinguish "Two Kinds of Ecology" (this is the actual subtitle of the "Introduction"). But as it actually turns out, Gorz is really concerned with two kinds of politics. To the ecologist who can use a viable politics, this might be a laudable endeavour if Gorz were intent on discussing *politics* as ecology, that is, to determine how politics can be developed in ecological terms. But actually, this is not Gorz's claim. He is trying to tell us something about ecology *itself* as it relates to social questions — to explore its special qualities and how they interface with society. And it is precisely here that the book begins to fall apart, for it becomes apparent that Andre Gorz knows very little about ecology, or, more precisely, "ecological thinking" as he puts it. There *are* in fact two different kinds of "ecology" — notably, *ecology* and *environmentalism* — but Gorz is basically oblivious to the difference. When Gorz speaks of "Two Kinds of Ecology" he is actually talking of two kinds of politics — bourgeois politics and his own. That ecology has very little to do with the distinction he means to develop becomes evident when, scarcely a few lines into the "Introduction," we are somberly advised that "Ecological *thinking* still has many opponents in the (corporate) board rooms, but *it already has enough converts in the ruling elite to ensure its eventual acceptance by major institutions of modern capitalism."* (My emphasis — M.B.)

While loose formulations of this kind might have been tolerable years ago, they become totally obfuscatory today. To describe the kind of environmentalistic thinking that goes on in corporate "board rooms" as "ecological" is to set back the clock of ecological thinking and the ecological movement historically. The attempt to rescue the term "ecology" from "board rooms" and from writers like Gorz has been long in the making. Ecology, particularly conceived as *social* ecology, contains very radical philosophical and cultural implications. These center around the non-hierarchical nature of ecosystems and the importance of diversity as a function of biotic stability. Extended to society, they suggest the need for non-hierarchical social relations and a non-hierarchical sensibility to achieve a truly harmonious balance with nature and between people. What Gorz means by "ecological thinking" in the "board rooms" is in fact what should properly be called "environmentalism," the largely *technocratic* strategems for manipulating nature. Taken as an academic discipline, "environmentalism" is essentially an instrumental body of techniques that the Massachusetts Institute of Technology once taught as "sanitary engineering." Like Barry Commoner, who consciously eschews the word "ecology" for "environmentalism," Gorz is mindful that he is advancing a *politics* that is environmentally oriented, not an ecological sensibility that is meant to yield a political orientation. To distinguish ecology from environmentalism and to explore the social thrust of ecological thinking as distinguished from the merely technical strategies of environmental thinking would actually compel Gorz to confront the serious challenges a radical social ecology raises to his *own* mode of thinking — notably, *socialist* "thinking." For the real conflict that faces the Left so far as society and the natural world is concerned *is not between a specious form of bourgeois "ecology" and socialist politics but between a libertarian form of social ecology and an economistic, technologically oriented form of socialism* — in short, Marxism. And this, as we shall see, is *not* what Andre Gorz seriously intends to do. Ecology, in effect, is reduced to environmentalism all the more to spuriously fuse Marxist "thinking" with the ecological issues of our time.

Accordingly, Gorz proceeds to underpin his own environmentalist "thinking" by asserting that capitalism, far from being faced with an ecological impasse that can tear down the entire biosphere, can actually "assimilate ecological necessities as technical constraints and adapt the conditions of exploitation to them." Ironically, this formulation is not only "sanitary engineering" with a vengenance; is is even bad Marxism. If any serious ecological conclusion is to be drawn from *Capital*, Vol. I, it is from Marx's compelling demonstration that the very law of life of capitalist competition, of the fully developed market economy, is based on the maxim, "grow or die." Translated into ecological terms, this clearly means that a fully developed market economy must unrelentingly exploit nature to a point (which even Marx could not foresee) that is literally regressive geologically and biologically. Capitalism, in effect, is not only polluting the world on a historically unprecedented scale; it is simplifying all the ecosystems of the planet, turning soil into sand, the oceans into lifeless sewers, indeed, threatening the very integrity of our sources of atmospheric oxygen. If one were to follow the logic of this tendency to its very end, capitalist — and hierarchical — society are utterly incompatible with a viable biosphere. What limits the ecological validity of Marx's view is obviously not his revelation of capitalism's "law of life" but rather the "progressive" role he imparts to capitalism's "success" in supposedly achieving the technical domination of nature. This Janus-faced aspect of Marx's writings is what throw them into conflict with an authentic ecological sensibility. Gorz, by contrast, side-steps *exactly* what we must learn in the contradictory position of Marx, namely, that the very technical achievements of capitalism, far from *assimilating* "ecological necessities as technical restraints," are governed by a "law of life" that technologically lacks *any* form of "restraint."

Having twisted himself into a pretzel, Gorz proceeds to raise a hammering demand: "Reform or revolution?" Shall we have "one" kind of "ecology," a reformist one that resolves our disequilibrium with nature by means of technology? Or shall we have another kind of "ecology" that resolves our disequilibrium with nature by means of revolution? As it turns out, these fiery demands are mere pablum. If Gorz is correct and capitalism *can* adapt to "ecological necessities" merely by developing pollution-controlling devices (and this is what Gorz means by "technical restraints"), why not have a series of nice, orderly, genteel reforms instead of a messy, possibly bloodly revolution?

It is at this point that the seemingly "semantic" distinction between ecology and environmentalism acquires considerable significance. If, as I personally suspect, Barry Commoner is really a closet Euro-Communist who, at heart, is committed to centralized economic planning, he rightly prefers to designate himself as an environmentalist rather than an ecologist. The concepts of social ecology stand at odds with his basically orthodox Marxian views. By rejecting his social theories as ecological, Commoner quite consistently can retain his refurbished Marxian views under the socially neutral term of "environmentalism."

Gorz, whether he is clearly mindful of the fact or not, does precisely the same thing. And it is not what is most viable in Marx's writing that Gorz chooses for the theoretical underpinnings of his views, but what is largely moribund or, at least, most questionable. In Gorz's view, capitalism threatens to produce a profound social crisis not as a form of *ecological* disequilibrium and breakdown but rather as a form of *economic* disequilibrium and breakdown. If one is to take Gorz's "Introduction" seriously, ecology can be regarded simply as an exacerbating factor in a much larger economic crisis that faces capitalism. If one peers behind the rich verdure of Gorzian "ecology," one finds the most dismal cobwebs of orthodox Marxism. For, when all is said and done, what Gorz really argues in his "Introduction" is that capitalism, by introducing such "technical constraints" as pollution-controlling devices increases the "organic composition of capital," that is to say, the ratio of constant capital (machinery and raw materials) to variable capital (labour). Inasmuch as labour, in Marxian economic theory, is the source of all value and hence of all profit, this changing ratio yields the horrendous result that "either the rate of profit declines or the price of products increases." Hence "price will tend to rise faster than real wages, purchasing power will be reduced, and it will be as if the cost of pollution control had been deducted from the income available to individuals for the purchase of consumer goods."* The suspicion that Gorz is concerned not with ecology or even with environmentalism but with politics, specifically with economics, not only emerges with stark clarity, but even his economics turns out to be highly dubious. Its crudity is matched only by its simplicity. To Gorz, price rises are the result not primarily of oligopolistic or monopolistic manipulations of the market, but of diminishing profits due to increasing capital costs. As it turns out, *this is precisely the argument that the bourgeoisie itself uses against environmental controls.* For Gorz to ignore the profound structural changes in modern capitalism such as price-fixing in order to rehabilitate Marx's most dubious theories in the so-called "free market" era of the last century reflects poorly not only on Gorz the environmentalist but on Gorz the economist. The essays that follow the "Introduction" in noway redeem these crudities. On the contrary, as we shall note, they echo the most preposterous shibboleths of bourgeois media propaganda.

In any case, to talk about "ecology" when one actually means environmentalism is no mere word-play. It means that one reduces ecology to environmentalism so that social ecology can be replaced by something else — in Commoner's case, by a closet form of Euro-Communism; in Gorz's case, by a very naive form of Marxian socialism that rests on economic reductionism. It is worth emphasizing that Gorz's economization of ecology is not a mere episode in his book; it is really its underlying theoretical basis and leitmotif. Scratch Gorz the ecologist and you find Gorz the environmentalist. Scratch Gorz the environmentalist and you find Gorz the vulgar Marxist. Scratch Gorz the vulgar Marxist

---

* It is interesting to note that, as far back as the 19th century, Marx's labour theory of value has been justly criticized for its schzoid nature. In *Capital,* Vol. I, the labour theory of value functions brilliantly as a *qualitative* analysis of the emergence and form of bourgeois social relations. In *Capital,* Vol. III, however, the theory functions *quantitatively* as a very dubious description of price formation, the distribution of profits between different enterprises and the so-called "tendency of the rate of profit to decline." This "tendency" has never been clearly established in terms of Marx's labour theory because it is largely unprovable. It becomes meaningless and mechanistic, in fact, when value is viewed merely in quantitative terms and it can be justly regarded as equivocal in view of the countervailing factors Marx himself invokes, factors which serve to shake the credibility of the "tendency" as an economic reality. Accordingly, this "tendency" has not only divided Marxian economists from non-Marxian, but has also led to endless quarrels among the most devout acolytes of the master for generations. For Gorz, this highly disputable "tendency" is merely adduced as given — and that is that!

and you find Gorz the reformist. To a great extent, this summarizes the basic content of the entire book.

Until Gorz concludes his "Introduction" with a survey of his "utopia," the remaining portions of the piece are largely declamations that have been stated with greater clarity and coherence in other, more original, works. That limited growth under capitalism would produce unemployment and misery, as Gorz solemnly avers, is painfully obvious. Even the bourgeoisie, in its denunciations of the environmentalist movement, has said as much. That certain goods (say, ocean liners, castles, ski slopes, and space ships — Gorz, in fact, focuses on such trivial and delectable items as Mercedes Benzs and swimming pools) must either remain scarce or be shared by everyone due to nature's cruel material limits hardly requires emphasis. Gorz's grandiose ethic — "The only things worthy of each are those which are good for all" — is so trite that it has the earmarks of a Benthamite philistine. Yes, Bentham was right: the good is the greatest happiness for the greatest number — which did not prevent Marx from viewing Bentham as a moral cretin.

Gorz's capacity to debase a subject to the level of sheer absurdity, however, finds its most telling expression in the concluding portion of the "Introduction: his "utopia." And what, pray, is Gorzutopia? With breathless ardour we learn that Gorzutopia will focus on the "production of apparently indestructible material" (hopefully, an "indestructible" Mercedes Benz, if not a solidly built swimming pool), "collective dwellings" and collectively used transport, lots of bicycles, "major industries, centrally planned," that are meant to meet basic requirements of people without regard to styles, local "public workshops" that will be well-equipped with tools and machines for every individual to use, and a salad of other proposals that are promiscuously drawn from the gardens of Peter Kropotkin, Paul Goodman, and other anarchist theorists without the slightest reference to their intellectual pedigree. None of these people are noted in terms of the broader body of ideas for which each one speaks, the tradition that each one represents, the continuity of these ideas into recent anarchist theories and reconstructive proposals. That we are saturated with Marx goes without saying, even if the brew has begun to turn sour — and, of course, with a generous amount of Gorzian eclecticism.

Is all of this possible in a market economy, cries Gorz? "No!" he resoundingly replies, "for such a 'utopia' corresponds to the most *advanced*, not the most *primitive*, form of socialism (one is prone to ask what Gorz means by this delicious contrast: hippie tribalism or the "primitive" anarchist "rebels" from whom Gorz pilfers most of his ideas for a utopia — M.B.) — to a society without bureaucracy, where the *market withers away*, where there is enough for everyone, where people are collectively and individually free to shape their lives, where people produce according to their fantasies, not only according to their needs." We will leave this explosion of "primitive" Fourieresque rhetoric aside and merely note, for the moment, that Gorzutopia acquires its appropriate seal of approval by closing with the following quotation: "in short, a society where 'the free development of each is the condition for the free development of all'" (Karl Marx, *The Communist Manifesto*, 1848)." (My emphasis — M.B.) Thus the halo of the Master is placed over an effluvium of intellectual goulash that would make even so scrupulous a theorist as the author of *The Critique of the Gotha Program*, a brilliantly unrelenting piece of criticism, disclaim his acolyte.

Now all of this may be spicey fare for certain Parisian *gauchistes* and the more naive adherents of Commoner's Citizen's Party, but it is utterly tasteless to anyone who is even minimally familiar with radical social ecology. Quality production, libertarian collectivism, and other Gorzutopian appropriations from "primitive" socialists and anarchists aside, one is stunned by the paradoxes that coexist in Gorz's "vision." How in the name of intellectual coherence can Andre Gorz dream of a "society without bureaucracy" whose "major industries" (no less!) are "centrally planned"? Note well that Gorz does not speak simply of planning or even coordination or even of regionalism — but of *centralization*. Will these "major industries" be centralized by mindless robots, by "good vibes," by stoned hippies or will they be centralized by agencies (read: bureaus) which are staffed by bureaucrats? How will this planning and centralization be executed — by mutual love, by the high moral probity so nobly exhibited by the Russian Bolsheviks, or perhaps by a harsh system of obedience and command which Engels invoked in his insidious essay "On Authority"? Gorz is at pains to tell us that we must learn to live without Mercedes Benzs and swimming pools for each family, but he tells us virtually nothing about the administrative structures around which his utopia will be organized.

If Gorz's evocation of a "society without bureaucracy" whose "major industries (are) centrally planned" seems indigestible, his image of a "market (that) withers away" produces outright heartburn. One senses that the withering away of the market is not far-removed from such ominous formulations like the "withering away of the state" — and sure enough, Gorz does not fail us: the formulation *does* appear in the book! If it should come to pass that in Gorzutopia the "market withers away," it is fair to assume that Gorzutopia will after all contain a market from its very inception. One can reasonably invoke Marx's searching analysis of the emergence of the market, its immanent capacity to undermine all forms of reciprocity and mutualism, finally its triumph over every aspect of economic life. One does not have to be a Marxist to accept the enormous catalytic role Marx imputes to the value and market relationship, any more than one has to reject anarchism to mock Proudhon's "People's Bank," patriarchal family relationships, and contractual theory of social relations.

It was to be hoped that if Gorz planned to outline the most "advanced... form of socialism," he would not do so with the most primitive theoretical equipment. Surely, he would know — we hoped — that markets in a technologically "advanced" society, burdened by a savage historical legacy of ruthless profit-seeking, parasitic exchange, and cruel egoism, would make the withering away of the market as preposterous as the withering away of the state. All of which raises the really fundamental issues of Gorz's "Introduction": is Gorz actually posing an authentic choice between reform and revolution? Or must one always look beneath Gorz's rhetoric and ask the embarrassing questions that follow from the internal logic of *Ecology as Politics*: environmentalism *or* ecology? Centralization *or* decentralization? A market economy *or* reciprocity and mutualism? State *or* society? An inextricable variant of Marxian orthodoxy *or* a consistently libertarian theory? Centralized power *or* decentralized coordination? These questions and others haunt the entire book with their contradictory alternatives, pedigree, and internal logic. Neither Gorz's intentions or rhetoric, however well-meaning their intent, can remove the intellectual confusion they are likely to foster in a reading public that is already plagued by more sinister publicists than an Andre Gorz.

Having taken up the first seven pages of *Ecology as Politics* with a modest degree of care, it should be obvious to the reader that it would be impossible to bring the same degree of detail to a critical analysis of the other essays. I shall thus confine myself to the more outstanding "idiosyncracies" that mar so much of the book. Yet for all my selectiveness, I cannot help but note that the very first paragraph of the first chapter immediately ensnares us in sheer nonsense. Thus, the chapter opens with the resounding remark: "Growth-oriented capitalism is dead"; so too, for all practical purposes, is "growth-oriented socialism." "Marxism, although irreplaceable as an instrument of analysis, has lost its prophetic value."

Now all of this is really a mouthful — and apparently it takes very little effort for Gorz to utter it. Unfortunately, "growth-oriented capitalism" (has there every been any *other* kind?) is not dead at all, not even metaphorically. To the contrary, it is alive and kicking. It is not even "dead" in the Marxian sense that it has ceased to exercise a "great civilizing influence" historically (to use Marx's formulation in the *Grundrisse*), a view that Karl Polanyi brilliantly challenged decades ago. Furthermore, since Marxism "as an instrument of analysis" has never advanced any theory of socialism but one that is also "growth-oriented" (see *Capital*, Vol. 111, *The Grundrisse*, and many smaller works by Marx), we encounter another Gorzian paradox: either Marxism is very unsatisfactory "as an instrument of analysis" or one of its most important conclusions — the historic, indeed, progressive role of growth and the expansion of "needs" — is basically unsound. Finally, in all fairness to Marx, the Master never assigned a "prophetic value" to his theories. In fact, he explicitly rejected as "utopian" any project for describing the contours of a future communist society. So Gorz's remarks begin with nonsense and they conclude with nonsense. Again, the false note that rings in virtually every page of Gorz's book is sounded at its outset. What Gorz really seems to believe, when all the rhetoric is discarded, is that Marx's "instrument of analysis" is "irreplaceable."

It may be well to pause and examine this argument since it rears itself in ghostly fashion with every defense of Marxism against its most fallacious theoretical conclusions. The Marxian corpus lies in an uncovered grave, distended by gases and festering with molds and worms. Its once rich sweep — the project of a scientific socialism, historical materialism as a base-superstructure theory of social development, the call to proletarian insurrection, the ideal of a centralized planned economy, the strategy of developing revolutionary workers' parties in industrially advanced countries of the world — all, have turned into a sickly, fetid jelly. But lest we face up to the decay of the Marxian project and draw serious lessons from its tragic destiny, we are inevitably reminded by Marxist pundits that the "instrument of analysis" survives, indeed, is "irreplaceable." Marxism, in effect, is a success as a *method* however much it is a failure as a theory.

Why such an "irreplaceable" method should yield such impoverished results remains inexplicably unclear. Indeed, the crucial relationship between methodology and reality raises far-reaching philosophical questions which can hardly be discussed at any length here. It is difficult not to note that the decline of philosophy itself from an interpretation of the world into a mere "method" of "analysis" has been the subject of brilliant critique by the theorists of the Frankfurt School, notably Max Horkheimer and Theodor Adorno. One may justifiably turn this critique against Marxism itself, which has increasingly been turned by its acolytes into an analytical instrumentalist methodology rather than a theory of actual social change. That Hegel's dialectic, too, was reduced by Marx to a "method" may very well tell us a great deal about the instrumental dimension that vitiates much of Marx's own work, but at least he clothed it in a *reality* that followed intrinsically from his use of that "method." If Marxism, too, must now be reduced to a "method" — that is, a mere *technique* of analysis deprived of its social substance or ontological content — we can fairly ask what this trend means for the corpus of its social theory.

In any case, this instrumentalist strategy for exorcising Marxism's logical theoretical results hangs like a shadow over the entire corpus, a shadow which even the most skeptical neo-Marxists have not dispelled. The orthodox Marxian sects, of course, have no problems whatever. The corpus is not seen as an irreparable failure but merely as the victim of a conspiratorial "betrayal" by "petty bourgeois" intellectuals or, to borrow from Lenin's rich political vocabularly, by "social patriots," "traitors," and "renegades" to undo the method, the theory, or both. Nevertheless, the fetishization of a "living Marxism" as a "method" persists — reinforced by intense peer pressure among radicals in the academy, a peer pressure that morally degrades its victims as well as its high priests. Indeed, utterly alien theories like syndicalism, anarchocommunism, and utopian socialism, not to speak of Freudianism and structuralism, are grafted on to Marxism in a persistent race to catch up with — rather than "lead" in — such exotic issues of our time as ecology, feminism, and neighborhood self-management.

Which still raises the question: what is this remarkable "method" that has survived a century of failure, "treachery," and misadventure? Stated quite bluntly, it is Marx's method of class analysis — a social and historical strategy for determining the conflicting material interests that have increasingly asserted humanity's "domination" of nature by means of technological growth, expanding needs, and the domination of human by human. To Marx, what makes this method so powerful is that it removes the "ideological" cloak, the "general process of social, political and intellectual life" (to use Marx's own formulations), that conceals the production relations which people enter into "independent of their will," the totality of which form the "real foundation on which arises a legal and political superstructure and to which correspond definite forms of social consciousness." ("Preface", *A Contribution to the Critique of Political Economy*)

What is decisive in any discussion of Marx's "method" — as distinguished from the Marxian corpus — is Marx's more fundamental theory of a superstructure-base interpretation of society. Without this superstructure-base theory, Marx's "method" — his "class analysis" — is simply meaningless. In short, the "method" is meaningful only if it reveals the material interests that underlie "social consciousness," that is, only if social consciousness is seen as the derivative, however broadly and indirectly, of production relations. Culture, social institutions, family relations, ideologies, and the like can only be clearly analyzed if their ultimate economic foundations and more specifically, the material and class interests they serve, are revealed. Herein lies the power and practicality of Marx's "method." As it turns out, the much-maligned Marxist sectarians, however shrill and repellent their denunciations, are very sound Marxists indeed. More so than the "neo-Marxist" critics (and presumably Gorz may be included among the latter), they insist on "revealing" the "underlying" material or class interests that ecology, feminism, and other such "ideologies" conceal—the real "base" which Marx's "method" discloses. One cannot accept the "method" without accepting the superstructure-base theory that underpins it.

Gorz's real dilemma here is that he wants to have his cake and eat it. Marx's superstructure-base theory has been the target of such powerful critical analyses, be it at the hands of Max Weber in the early part of the century or the Frankfurt School in more recent decades, that its validity is completely in question. More currently, even such "superstructural" phenomena as the State have been designated as "technologies" so that the concepts of "superstructure" and "base" have become too interchangeable to be distinguishable. Aside from the fact that modern society is clearly a capitalistic one—and we can reasonably add the "socialist" world to this category—the class analysis developed by Marx for the modern world hangs by a thread. Doubtless, Gorz would scarcely want to remove himself from the charmed circle of such superb social critics as Weber and the Institute for Social Research, but neither can he retain his prestige as an authentic Parisian *gauchiste* without the appropriate genuflections to Marx. That neither the "neo-Marxists" or Gorz have carried their analyses of Marx's "method" down to its reductionist roots as a superstructure-base theory has done nothing to remove the peer pressure that surrounds the entire issue of Marxism as a whole. That a "method" which hangs in the air without any ontological content, social reality, and intellectual validity is little more than rank instrumentalism, will hardly persuade the "neo-Marxists" to apply their own critique of bourgeois instrumentalism to Marx's.*

Gorz's *Ecology as Politics* thus incorporates problems that are not even evident to its own author. Not only is ecology confused with environmentalism, revolution with reformism, centralization with decentralization, a "withering away of the market" with a hortatory denunciation of market society (I leave aside Gorz's ability to accept a "withering away of the state"), but a resolute rejection of Marxism is completely tainted by a tacit acceptance of its theoretical core — the superstructure-base theory of society. Had Gorz confined his book to a mere journalistic account of the ecological crisis, it might be regarded as naive but well-meaning. But since *Ecology as Politics* engages in theoretical "summitry" as well as newsy chit-chat, it becomes laughable at best and grossly obfuscatory at worst.

The remainder of the book is largely journalistic. Unfortunately, as one might expect, it is no less contradictory in its treatment of facts as it is in its treatment of theory. Gorz fudges everywhere he can and rarely does he advance his views in a forthright and unequivocal manner. To be sure, one might excuse his contradictions by regarding each essay or "chapter" as a step in his development from Marxian orthodoxy toward a hybridized version of libertarian ecology. But as Hegel caustically observed of Schelling: why must he conduct his education in public? For what we witness is not how Gorz arrives at a clear libertarian outlook (one he has yet to achieve even in his latest book, *Adieu au Proletariat*) but how painful such an ordeal must be — not only to the author but to his utterly confused readers.

That Gorz seems to dislike capitalism is the only certainty with which we can function. For the rest, almost everything that follows the "Introduction" is misty or simply muddled. A few examples should illustrate what I mean:

Item: "It is impossible to derive an ethic from ecology." (pg. 16)
Fact: Perhaps no field these days holds *more* promise of an

---

* Albrecht Wellmer's *Critical Theory of Society* does, in fact, point to the "instrumental dimension" of Marx's writings and subjects it to valuable criticism. But Wellmer's criticism, unfortunately, stops short of an outright rejection of Marxism as a social theory and essentially falls within the orbit of Jürgen Habermas's critique rather than a consistently libertarian one.

ethics than ecology, as Hans Jonas and other searching thinkers have suggested. Gorz, here, simply doesn't know what he is talking about if only because the problem of a nature philosophy is beyond his competence.

Item: We must beware of "centralized institutions and hard technologies (this is the technofascist option, the path along which we are already halfway engaged)" (pg. 17) **Fact:** But only a few pages earlier (pg. 9), Gorz has told us that our "major industries" must be "centrally planned." What are our "major industries" if not "hard technologies" and how can they be "centrally planned" without "centralized institutions"?

Item: "The total domination of nature inevitably entails a domination of people by the techniques of domination" (pg. 20). **Fact:** That Gorz has simply pilfered this sentence with curious modifications from recent American anarchist writings hardly requires discussion. What is interesting is that, even when he uses it, he does so erroneously. Humanity can never achieve the "total domination of nature" if only because it is part of nature — not physically above it or beyond it. For humanity to achieve the "total (no less — M.B.) domination of nature" would be equivalent to lifting oneself up by one's bootstraps — a nice metaphor, perhaps, but a gravitational impossibility. What Gorz apparently means to say (as I have some fifteen years ago) is that the *notion* of dominating nature derives from the domination of human by human — a formulation that reverses the Marxian one that the domination of man by man stems from the need to dominate nature. This is a crucial reformulation that requires considerable discussion. Gorz confuses the *notion* with an illusory reality. What the *notion* has in fact produced is the increasing simplication of nature, the increasing reduction of the organic to the inorganic — a crisis that may well render the planet insupportable for a complex species like human beings.

Item: "All production is also destruction" (pg. 20). **Fact:** "All destruction is also creation" (Mikhail Bakunin). Or for that matter, Hegel.

Item: "Marx demonstrated that, sooner or later, the average rate of profit must decline..." (pg. 22) **Fact:** Utterly false! Marx leaves this question completely open — and, if anything, he speaks of a "tendency," not a certainty. Gorz should at least consult Maurice Dobbs's essays on the subject and the disputes that surround it before he plunges into areas in which he patently has limited knowledge...

Item: "When air, water, and urban (!) land become scarce (pg. 25)... the exhaustion of the most accessible mineral deposits (pg. 25)... the obstacles to growth have become substantive ones (pg. 27)... the increasing scarcity of natural resources (pg. 27)..." etc. *ad nauseum*. In short, Gorz has bought into the entire media myth of a shortage of energy and mineral resources. **Fact**: There are probably some six trillion barrels of oil in the ground today and even the most extravagant estimates of petroleum reserves have proven historically to be underestimations. Actually, not all of this geological largesse is accessible to us, nor is it likely to be historically. What is far more significant for this period and possibly for the next two generations are not the "substantive" limits to capitalism but the structural ones. As Peter Odell, energy consultant to the British government observes: "The so-called 'generally accepted oil shortage' is the outcome of commercially oriented interests rather than a statement of the essential realities of the oil resources of the world." That the "bonanza" oil field like the Texas and Oklahoma ones of the 1920s and the Near Eastern ones of the 1960s are limited may well be true as things now stand, but a mass of material can be adduced to demonstrate that current energy and mineral shortages are the result of oligopolistic market manipulation and controlled petroleum production for price advantages. Indeed, if we were to believe the "official" estimates of various governmental agencies (based almost entirely on oil company reports), we should have exhausted our oil reserves in 1925, 1950, and now, 1980-90. There is no serious evidence that the latest estimates are authentic or based on real facts other than those which the energy industry wants us to believe. For example, the *Oil and Gas Journal* placed the world's "proven reserves" outside of the so-called "socialist world" at 72 billion barrels. Recent evidence now reveals that some 230 billion barrels of oil discovered prior to 1950 somehow failed to appear in the 1950 estimate. This game has gone on repeatedly and seems to find no echo in Gorz's book.

Much the same is true of metals and minerals. Estimates of declining lead, zinc, bauxite, cobalt, manganese, chrome, and similar resources have flooded the press, but much of the data is specious at best and deliberately misleading at worst. Traditional mining operations are largely privately worked and fears of shortages serve the interests of price-fixing operations, not to speak of crassly imperialistic policies. Even some of the most grim predictions of the Brookings Institution's John Titlon are tinged with irony. If the reader finds his predictions "disconcerting," Titlon notes, many important mineral resources are increasing at an even faster rate than they are being depleted and an acceptable substitute can be found for virtually every diminishing mineral in use today. Which is not to say that capitalism can plunder the world forever. But the greatest danger these practices raise is not depletion but simplification and the limits to capitalist expansion are ecological, not geological.

One can go on indefinitely comparing and contrasting Gorz's remarks in one part of the book with contrary ones in another part. The fact is that Gorz simply does not know how to deal with the meaning of the word "scarcity." That "scarcity" is a social problem, not merely a "natural" one, is something he has learned from Marx. But how "natural" it is and how "social" it is confuses him completely — as it has the ecology movement generally. To clearly explore these distinctions and their dialectic would have been the most important service Gorz could have performed in the entire book. Instead, Gorz the Marxist dissolves almost completely at times into the crudest environmentalist. Accordingly, the Club of Rome's notorious report (I refer to the Meadows's version), *The Limits to Growth*, earns Gorz's admiration as a document that "brought grist to the mill of all who reject capitalism because of its logic, premises, and consequences" (pg. 78) Later, Gorz reiterates his concurrence with the report by adding: "Even if the figures in the Meadows report are unreliable, the fundamental truth of its thesis remains unchanged." (pg. 84) Having spent years in the radical ecology movement, I'm not at all certain what "mill" Gorz is talking about or how anti-capitalist the "consequences" of the report may be.

Actually, Gorz would not be Gorz if he did not try to qualify such utterly absurd remarks. So we then learn later that the report is also designed to rescue capitalism. "When the Meadows report looks forward to tripling worldwide industrial production while recommending zero growth in industrial countries, doesn't it imply this neo-imperialist vision of the future?" (pg. 85) — notably, a maximum exploitation of Third World resources. "Americans will become a nation of bankers, busy recirculating their profits levied on the work of others" (pg. 85). That the United States, in fact, is now undergoing a massive, indeed, historic industrial revolution of its own in concert with Western Europe and Japan is an immensely important reality that hardly crosses Gorz's intellectual horizon. The man is still on the level of Lenin's *Imperialism*, a work long-outdated by far-reaching structural changes in the industrially advanced countries of the world.

His Marx, in turn, is a source primarily of the most shallow theories of overaccumulation and classical bourgeois theories of economic crises. Thus the maxim, "Grow or die," finally surfaces well on in the book (page 22) but not to explore its *ecological* implications; rather, Gorz uses it to shore up his emphasis on the "decline in the rate of profit," which he now deals with not as a "tendency" but as a fact. In short, a *social* theory of scarcity is so crudely interlocked with a geological one that it is hard to determine if Gorz has abandoned social theory for economics, economics for biology, or biology for geology. Accordingly, the very man who has told us on the opening page of his "Introduction" that "ecological thinking... has enough converts in the ruling elite to ensure its eventual acceptance by the major institutions of modern capitalism" (pg. 3) has no difficulty in emphasizing (fifteen pages later) that "the ecological perspective is incompatible with the rationality of capitalism" (pg. 18). Gorz literally drops these contradictions all over the place — within his essays, between them, or quite promiscuously, among them.

Gorzutopias and theses abound in one form or another all over the place. In "one of several possible utopias," Gorz presents a scenario of how Gorzutopia (version two) might come about after "the elections, but during the period of transition to the new administration." Exactly who has been elected and by what form of organizational process remains unclear. What we learn is "that a number of factories and enterprises had been taken over by the workers." Is this Paris, 1871? Barcelona, 1936? Budapest, 1956? Paris, again, 1968? These are not idle questions if one wishes, even lightmindedly, to deal with a "period of transition." All we know is that there is "turmoil." Everyone begins to occupy everything—the "young unemployed—who had the previous two years been occupying abandoned plants"; "empty buildings... transformed into communes"; schools, by students and their teachers—and everywhere, "hydroponic gardens" (Gorz, incidentally, couldn't have made a worse choice here for ecological gardening), "facilities for raising fish," installations for "woodworking, metal-working, and other crafts..." We must assume on our own that the CRS has decided to occupy its barracks, the Parisian "flicks" their police headquarters, and the French Army its long-lost forts in Algeria, much to the delight of the ORA.

Suddenly the veil is lifted: the "President of the Republic and Prime Minister" appear on evening television. Mass media scores another triumph! Together, the two men give the French people a heavy dose of Gorzutopia which happily mixes the fancies of Fritz Schumacher and Ivan Illich together with Andre Gorz and Karl Marx. The "*government*," we are told, has "developed a program for an alternative pattern of growth, based on an alternative economy and alternative institutions." Frenchmen and Frenchwomen *will* "work less," "more effectively," and in "new ways." Everyone will, "as a matter of right, be entitled to the satisfaction of his or her needs." "We *must* consume better," the President warns, and "the dominant firms in each sector" will become "the property of society." "We *must* re-integrate culture into the everyday life of all." The Presidential address to the nation runs through such delightfully diverse notions as individual and local autonomy, environmental controls, and a degree of decentralization that will avoid the "dictatorship (not the abolition—M.B.) of the state." (My emphasis throughout—M.B.)

To jazz up the scenario, Groz focuses on the Prime Minister, who rapidly lists "twenty-nine enterprises and corporations" that will be "socialized" by the "National Assembly." Workers will be "*free* to hold general assemblies" that will essentially take over production and work itself will be confined to the afternoon so that the proletariat can be free to make its decisions in the morning—alternating hours, redesigning the goods that befit Gorzutopia, and setting suitable salaries. Somehow "Money itself will no longer confer any rights," declares the Prime Minister—but apparently it will continue to exist, together with prices, markets, and luxuries, which, presumably by governmental edict, will begin to wither away together with the State. But before the State totally disappears, Gorz cannot deny himself one delicious act of coercion: "After completing *compulsory* education, the Prime Minister went on, each individual would be *required* to put in twenty hours of work each week (for which he or she would earn a full salary), in addition to continuing whatever studies he or she desired." (My emphasis — M.B.)

This is no "scenario"; it is a childish "libertarian" Disneyland in which Gorz permits his readers to indulge in social spectacles on a cartoon level. The book itself could already be dismissed as an overdone comic strip were it not for the pits Gorz reaches when he reconnoiters the infamous "population problem." Here, Gorz passes from Marx and Disney to Malthus and Garrett Hardin. "Twelve Billion People?" cries Gorz in alarm — and the reader is enjoined to tremble over the certitude of "famine," "epidemics," "population pressure," resource exhaustion, and "a classic game theory scenario — 'the tragedy of the commons'". Whether Gorz knows that Garrett Hardin's "Tragedy of the Commons" is one of the opening shots in the emergence of ecofascism and the "lifeboat ethic" I do not know. But Hardin's views, like those of Malthus, are trotted out with the same aplomb as those of Marx. Accordingly, if the population growth-rate in not slowed, "there will be 9 billion people in 1995, 40 billion in 2025, and 100 billion in 2075." By this time, Gorz cries, "Catastrophe will be inevitable." Happily, he adds, "the Indian government knows something about this" — and one seriously wonders if Gorz has Indira Gandhi's forced sterilization program in mind when he celebrates "sterilization campaigns" as well as the Gorzian "achievement of a living standard that encourages a spontaneous birth rate," "agrarian reform" and "the emancipation of women." It is noteworthy that feminism, so vital to any libertarian "population" discussion, rates three words in the entire book.

What Gorz does here is simply embarrassing. His population projections, like those of the Population Foundation, deal with human beings as though they were fruit flies. His methodology implies an acceptance of neo-Malthusian demography. Hardin's "Tragedy of the Commons" mentality gains greater creditability and attention than Josue de Castro's views in *The Geopolitics of*

Hunger, which seem more like an after-thought rather than a serious program for analysis and action. The social roots of population growth, not to speak of feminism and Marx's critique of Malthus, are subordinated to hypothetical ratios of proliferation. The "Green Revolution" gets its obligatory wristslap, but Gorz offers only a minimal explanation of the interrelationship between famine and imperialism or, for that matter, hunger and geopolitics. Here, the neo-Malthusian restatement of "original sin" (i.e., the "population problem" begins in everyone's bedroom, not in the world's brokerage houses) acquires an extraordinary degree of eminence. The "crisis" appears more as a crisis of numbers than of social relations in which "technical constraints" like condoms are equally as significant as social factors. What ecology has done for Gorz is to confuse him. Far from enriching his outlook with the need for a nature philosophy, an ethics, the problems of society's interaction with the biotic world, and a radical practice, it has actually cultivated his most philistine intellectual qualities and his inner proclivity for ideological sensationalism. Despite its radical rhetoric, *Ecology as Politics* contains some of the worst, albeit *fashionable*, prejudices of the environmentalist movement, tastelessly decorated with Marxian terminology.

It is time to bring this critical review to an end. I will not follow Gorz through his ritualized discussion of nuclear power and public health. If the reader has scanned Anna Gyorgy's *No Nukes*! and Ivan Ilich's *Medical Nemisis,* she or he requires no additional comments. The book concludes with a series of personal, largely "countercultural" vignettes of a Gorzean journey through California, titled: "The American Revolution Continues." To be frank, in California Gorz might just as well have looked for the world revolution — everything "continues" in one way or another in that part of the world. Needless to say, the vignettes include the prescribed "Jim," who is still active in campus politics; the indispensable "Susie," who hates California smog; the necessary "George," who practices socialism in one neighborhood; the cryptic "Heinz," who has moved to California from Germany. It also contains my personal friends, Lee Swenson and Karl Hess (the latter lives in West Virginia) and there is hardly anything that Gorz can say about them that is harmful.

Perhaps the most interesting remarks in these vignettes however, center around Ralph Nader and Jerry Brown. Nader, Gorz has told his French readers, "believes that people have to organize and take power over their own lives" (pg. 203). Having recently engaged in a brief verbal duel with Nader, I can attest to the fact that this consumer advocate is more oriented toward Establishment politics than popular action. Jerry Brown, in Gorz's sketch, is virtually characterized as a "neo-anarchist" (the term is Gorz's, not mine). Like all "neo-anarchists," no doubt, Jerry's "models are Ho Chi Minh, Ghandi, and Mao. His bedside reading is *Small Is Beautiful*... and he spends a lot of time at the Zen (Buddhist) center." The French reader is further told that "Brown has become immensely popular. He refuses to live in the governor's mansion, he sleeps on a mattress on the floor in a rented apartment, and he makes his staff go on work retreats that can last from 7 A.M. to 2 P.M. Somewhat like Fidel Castro, he shows up where he is least expected... "So on and so forth. Linda Ronstadt receives no mention in this idyllic picture of the "neo-anarchist" Governor of California, so it hardly pays to say more.

That a Marxist, or a publicist trained in *some* kind of Marxism, can believe that *any* Governor of California is a credible figure, however, does warrant some comment. It matters little what Jerry Brown says he is or what he claims he reads. What matters is that a supposedly "leading" French "radical" *believes* it and describes Brown's manufactured persona with an even modest degree of credulity. It now becomes painfully evident that Gorz's absurdities have a rationality of their own. Gorz's reality principle is hopelessly one-dimensional, indeed, surprisingly askew. The book itself is not simply a bizarre mixture of utterly contradictory theories and facts; it is a compelling symptom of the crisis of modern socialism. The double meanings which Gorz gives to "ecological thinking," "decentralization," "autonomy," "the State," and his "utopian" scenarios for a new society become problems not of theoretical analyses but of social diagnoses. What appear as conflicting ideas in the book are not ideological contradictions; they are really cultural traits of an emerging era of intellectual confusion and incoherence as a normal condition of the international Left. If Herb Gintis can praise this book to the skies, if the reviews it receives in the radical press are in any way favourable, it will be because the Left itself has descended to unprecedentedly low depths — together with the *culture* in which it is rooted.

The most disquieting aspect of this theoretical and cultural regression is the inability of Left social critics to distinguish between the differences in the premises and logic of profoundly disparate theories or even bear solemn witness to the internal contradictions that must inevitably cause them to clash with each other. Like those ponderous banks at the turn of the century that combined Greek columns with rococo bas reliefs, leaving the viewer in an architectural limbo, socialist theorists dip freely into disparate and profoundly contradictory traditions to fashion their blurred ideologies. To be out of focus is not merely fashionable today but absolutely necessary if one wishes to resonate with the prevailing culture. Gorz is merely one of the more vulnerable examples of this ideological eclecticism. Perhaps more clearly than most, he is the tombstone to an era when revolutionaries took their ideas seriously; when they criticized their opponents with ruthless logic; when they demanded clarity, coherence, and insight. One may agree or disagree with the Marx who wrote *The Critique of the Gotha Program*; but one cannot help but admire his stunning and unrelenting powers of critique, his willfull demand for consistency, and his meticulous demand for coherence. With Gorz we enter an entirely different era: one where the State legislates anarchy into existence, where Marx must endure the company of Malthus, where centralized production co-exists with decentralized communes, where workers' control is exercised under a planned from above economy, and where not only the State but the market "withers away." Neither Marx nor Bakunin, Engels nor Kropotkin, Lenin nor Malatesta are permitted to speak in their own voices. Gorz tunes them in, out, or up as his journalistic needs require, like a television technician toying with his monitoring panel. Accordingly, fashion becomes a substitute for theory and the latest gimmick a substitute for serious practice.

Books like *Ecology as Politics* are not merely a problem but a challenge. Will ideas become matters of serious concern or mere topics for radical chit-chat? Will revolution be the lived experience that literally provides the substance of life or entertaining and expendable episodes? Will movements be guided by coherent ideas or dissolve into tasteless spectacles? To claim that these questions can be answered today would be mere pretension. But if truth should always be its own end, then the answer too should be clear enough. In any case, it will not be found in "radical" comic books that have been prepared by ideological cartoonists.

September 1980

ACKNOWLEDGEMENTS

I would like to express my appreciation to Dimitri Rousso-poulos and Lucia Kowaluk for the contribution they have made to the preparation and publication of this book. My deep personal friendship and high regard for both of these splendid people should not colour their many years of effort they have given to our shared libertarian ideals. Their own gifts aside, their's is a virtue and dedication of nearly two decades of day-to-day work, of moral probity, and reliability that quietly and unobtrusively turn dreams into reality amidst the clamour and oratorical flourishes of compatriots long gone. For this steadfastness, loyalty to our common ideas, and depth of perception, I thank them earnestly and warmly.

Apart from the "Introduction" and "Conclusion," all the essays in this book have appeared in the periodical literature — although several very important ones are published for the first time in their complete and unedited form. "Toward an Ecological Society" first appeared in *WIN*, "The Open Letter to the Ecology Movement" in *Rain*, the "Myth of City Planning" and "Spontaneity and Organization" in *Liberation*, "Toward a Vision of an Urban Future" in *The Urban Affairs Annual Review*, Vol. 34 (Sage Publications), "The Concept of Ecotechnologies and Ecocommunities" in *Habitat International* (Pergamon Press) "Marxism as Bourgeois Sociology" in *Comment*, and "Self-Management and the New Technology" and an abridged version of "On Neo-Marxism..." called "Beyond Neo-Marxism" in *Telos* (including my review of Andre Groz's book on ecology). To all of these periodicals I would like to express my appreciation for permission to republish the aforementioned works. I owe a special debt of gratitude to Paul Piccone and Paul Breines for their independence of mind in publishing some of my most controversial articles on Marxism in the journal, *Telos*, that has been associated with a neo-Marxian orientation.

THE SUN BETRAYED

A Study
of the Corporate Seizure of
U.S. Solar Energy
Development

by Ray Reece

The Sun Betrayed is a detailed, behind-the-scenes history of the collusion between federal and corporate energy executives against small-scale solar energy development. It traces the evolution of the federal solar program, naming the corporations and government officials who have shaped the program to fit the needs of the corporate elite. It documents the fraud and waste in the program as well as the plight of independent scientists and solar entrepreneurs. Finally, in suggesting a "people's program" of grass-roots solar energy development, the book profiles a number of successful community projets based on innovative, small-scale, liberatory solar technologies.

Solar energy is by its nature the most democratic and humane of the world's energy resources. Properly developed, it could furnish up to 30 percent of our energy requirements by the year 2000; it could also generate a peaceful revolution in the socioeconomic structure of our society.

But the solar promise is being subverted. Since 1971, a technocratic alliance of federal agencies, major corporations, utilities, and elite universities has evolved a solar development strategy aimed at placing control of solar energy in the hands of the same corporate oligarchs who control the rest of the economy.

234 pages
Paperback ISBN: 0-919618-07-3   **$ 7.95**
Hardcover ISBN: 0-919618-08-1   **$16.95**
Contains: Canadian Shared Cataloguing in Publication Data
BLACK ROSE BOOKS No. 151

DURRUTI:
THE PEOPLE ARMED

by Abel Paz
translated by Nancy MacDonald

"... When a column is tired and ready to drop with exhaustion, Durruti goes to talk new courage into the men. When things go bad up Saragossa way, Durruti climbs aboard an aeroplane and drops down in the fields of Aragon to put himself at the head of the Catalonian partisans. Wherever you go it's Durruti and Durruti again, whom you hear spoken of as a wonder-man."

Toronto Daily Star

"This biography of Durruti... captures the complex reality that was the life of (the man) and the Spanish Revolution. Throughout it all Paz reveals the complete personality of the man..."

Industrial Worker

"... Abel Paz has produced a book involving an enormous amount of work — which every libertarian should read and study. Diligent searching of the letters Durruti sent, the speeches he made and the interviews he had with the press... plus the one article he wrote — all this gives us an account of Durruti's thoughts and personality that have not been known before. He was an extraordinary man..."

ZERO new magazine

Forty years of fighting, of exile, of jailings, of living underground, of strikes, and of insurrection, Buenaventura Durruti, the legendary Spanish revolutionary (1896-1936) lived many lives.

Uncompromising anarchist, intransigent revolutionary, he travelled a long road from rebellious young worker to the man who refused all bureaucratic positions, honours, awards, and who at death was mourned by millions of women and men. Durruti believed and lived his belief that revolution and freedom were inseparable.

This book is the story of Durruti and also a history of the Spanish revolution. It is more than theoretical, it is a rich and passionate documentary, of a man and an epoch.

328 pages, illustrated

Paperback ISBN: 0-919618-74-X   **$ 6.95**
Hardcover ISBN: 0-919618-73-1   **$12.95**
Contains: Canadian Shared Cataloguing in Publication Data
BLACK ROSE BOOKS No. F28

LOUISE MICHEL

by Edith Thomas

translated by Penelope Williams

Revolutionary on the barricades of the Paris Commune, tried before the War Council of France, deported to a penal colony, received by enthusiastic crowds upon her return, brillant lecturer throughout Europe, continuously followed by the police, participant in spectacular trials and demonstrations, threatened by assassins, imprisoned time and again, Louise Michel, writer, teacher, poet, feminist, is one of the most extraordinary legends in the literature of freedom.

Edith Thomas has written the first complete biography of this famous anarchist with passion and with a critical balance. The author's research took here through the Historical Archives of the French Prefecture of Police to the International Institute of Social History in Amsterdam.

"...a very complete and very attractive biography of the heroine...

We cannot close this book so richly written without concluding that human beings are more difficult to define and classify than is assumed by history books who line them up against each other."

Le Monde

"Although the Commune remains a controversial phenomenon, one of its best-known figures, Louise Michel, won great sympathy in almost all quarters. She was admired by men as different in their political outlook as Victor Hugo, with whom she maintained a lifelong correspondence,... Henri Rochefort, Clemenceau, and Maurice Barrès, Verlaine himself was inspired to write a *Ballade* for her.

The book's first part, up to the return to France, is well done, especially the account of Louise's adaptation to life in New Caledonia.

...the woman was *sui generis* and matches the legend because of her courage, her limitless generosity, and her singleminded devotion to the cause she made hers..."

American Historical Review

400 pages

Paperback ISBN: 0-919619-07-4   **$ 8.95**
Hardcover ISBN: 0-919619-08-2   **$16.95**

Contains: Canadian Shared Cataloguing in Publication Data
Publication Date — September 1980
BLACK ROSE BOOKS No. J58

THE CITY AND RADICAL SOCIAL CHANGE

edited by
Dimitrios
Roussopoulos

What is the role of the city in determining the evolution of society as a whole? What perspective do people who fight to improve public transportation, housing, public health and related issues have? What are the results of the community-organising movement in cities like Montréal? How have the concepts of participatory democracy, decentralisation, and the creation of neighbourhood councils evolved?

With a focus on Montréal, the book examines through a collection of essays the dynamics of the community-organising movement and its impact on urban politics. The contributors follow the emergence of various municipal political parties including the Front d'Action Politique and the Montréal Citizens Movement (MCM). The major controversies surrounding the MCM are included, after it became the official opposition political party to the Drapeau dominated City Council. The internal developments of the MCM are analyzed, its strategies, its tactics, its overall impact on neighbourhoods as well as the evolution of its programme. Most of the articles are drawn from the journal OUR GENERATION. Additional material on the MCM is drawn from various documents and published reports. An evaluation of the MCM and the municipal elections is included.

280 pages
Paperback ISBN: 0-919618-82-0   **$ 7.95**
Hardcover ISBN: 0-919618-83-9   **$16.95**
Contains: Canadian Shared Cataloguing in Publication Data
BLACK ROSE BOOKS No. H44

THE IRRATIONAL IN POLITICS

by Maurice Brinton

The book gives examples of irrational behaviour — at the level of politics — of classes, groups and individuals. It proceeds to reject certain facile 'interpretations' put forward to explain these phenomena. It probes the various ways in which the soil (the individual psyche) has been rendered fertile (receptive) for an authoritarian, hierarchical and class-dominated culture. It looks at the family as the locus of reproduction of the dominant ideology, and at sexual repression as an important determinant of social conditioning, resulting in the mass production of individuals perpetually craving authority and leadership and forever afraid of walking on their own or of thinking for themselves. Some of the problems of the developing sexual revolution are then discussed. The book concludes by exploring a new dimension in the failure of the Russian Revolution. Throughout, the aim is to help people, acquire additional insight into their own psychic structure. The fundamental desires and aspirations of the ordinary individual, so long distorted and repressed, are in deep harmony with an objective such as the libertarian reconstruction of society.

76 pages
Paperback ISBN: 0-919618-24-3   **$ 2.45**
Hardcover ISBN: 0-919618-50-2   **$10.95**
Contains: Canadian Shared Cataloguing in Publication Data
BLACK ROSE BOOKS No. E16

Printed by
the workers of
Editions Marquis, Montmagny, Québec
for
Black Rose Books Ltd.